Why Kierkegaard Matters

A Festschrift in Honor of Robert L. Perkins

Sylvia and Bob

Why Kierkegaard Matters

A Festschrift in Honor of Robert L. Perkins

Marc A. Jolley
Edmon L. Rowell, Jr.
editors

Mercer University Press
Macon, Georgia
2010

MUP/H811

©2010 Mercer University Press
1400 Coleman Avenue
Macon, Georgia 31207
All rights reserved
First Edition

Books published by Mercer University Press
are printed on acid-free paper that meets the requirements
of American National Standard for Information Sciences —
Permanence of Paper for Printed Library Materials.

Mercer University Press is a member of Green Press initiative
<greenpressinitiative.org>, a nonprofit organization working
to help publishers and printers
increase their use of recycled paper
and decrease their use of fiber derived from endangered forests.
This book is printed on recycled paper.

Library of Congress Cataloging-in-Publication Data

Why Kierkegaard matters : a festschrift in honor of Robert L. Perkins
/ Marc A. Jolley, Edmon L. Rowell, Jr., editors.
    p. cm.
Includes bibliographical references and index.
ISBN 978-0-88146-212-8 (hardcover : alk. paper)
    1. Kierkegaard, Søren, 1813-1855.
    I. Perkins, Robert L., 1930 — .
II. Jolley, Marc Alan, 1959 — . III. Rowell, Edmon L., Jr., 1937 — .
    B4377.W58 2010
    198'.9--dc22

                                        2010037141

Contents

Sigla

AN   "Armed Neutrality." See *Point of View* (PV).

BA   *The Book on Adler*, ed. and trans. Howard V. Hong and Edna H. Hong. Princeton: Princeton University Press, 1995.

C   *The Crisis and a Crisis in the Life of an Actress.* See *Christian Discourses* (CD).

CA   *The Concept of Anxiety*, ed. and trans. Reidar Thomte in collaboration with Albert B. Anderson. Princeton: Princeton University Press, 1980.

CD   *Christian Discourses. The Crisis and a Crisis in the Life of an Actress*, ed. and
C   trans. Howard V. Hong and Edna H. Hong. Princeton: Princeton University Press, 1997.

CI   *The Concept of Irony* together with "Notes on Schelling's Berlin Lectures,"
NSBL   ed. and trans. Howard V. Hong and Edna H. Hong. Princeton: Princeton University Press, 1989.

CUP   *Concluding Unscientific Postscript to "Philosophical Fragments,"* two vols., ed. and trans. Howard V. Hong and Edna H. Hong. Princeton: Princeton University Press, 1992.

COR   *The Corsair Affair*, ed. and trans. Howard V. Hong and Edna H. Hong. Princeton: Princeton University Press, 1982.

EO, 1   *Either/Or*, two vols., ed. and trans. Howard V. Hong and Edna H. Hong.
EO, 2   Princeton: Princeton University Press, 1987.

EPW   *Early Polemical Writings*, ed. and trans. Julia Watkin. Princeton: Princeton
FPOSL   University Press, 1990.

EUD   *Eighteen Upbuilding Discourses*, ed. and trans. Howard H. Hong and Edna H. Hong. Princeton: Princeton University Press, 1990.

FPOSL   *From the Papers of One Still Living.* See EPW.

FSE   *For Self-Examination* and *Judge for Yourself!*, ed. and trans. Howard
JFY   V. Hong and Edna H. Hong. Princeton: Princeton University Press, 1990.

FT   *Fear and Trembling* and *Repetition*, ed. and trans. Howard V. Hong
R   and Edna H. Hong. Princeton: Princeton University Press, 1983.

JC   Johannes Climacus or "De omnibus dubitandum est." See PF.

JFY   *Judge for Yourself!* See FSE.

JP   *Søren Kierkegaard's Journals and Papers*, ed. and trans. Howard V. Hong and Edna H. Hong, assisted by Gregor Malantschuk. Bloomington and London: Indiana University Press, 1, 1967; 2, 1970; 3 and 4, 1975; 5-7, 1978.

LD   *Letters and Documents*, ed. and trans. Hendrik Rosenmeier. Princeton: Princeton University Press, 1978.

NA   Newspaper Articles, 1854–1855. See TM.

NSBL   "Notes on Schelling's Berlin Lectures." See CI.

OMWA   "On My Work as an Author." See PV.

P   *Prefaces* and "Writing Sampler," ed. and trans. Todd W. Nichol.
WS   Princeton: Princeton University Press, 1998.

PC   *Practice in Christianity*, ed and trans. Howard V. Hong and Edna H. Hong. Princeton: Princeton University Press, 1991.

PF   *Philosophical Fragments* and "Johannes Climacus," ed. and

JC   trans. Howard V. Hong and Edna H. Hong. Princeton: Princeton University Press, 1985.

PV   *The Point of View*: 'On My Work as an Author;' 'The Point of View for My

OMWA   Work as an Author"; "Armed Neutrality," ed. and trans. Howard V. Hong

AN   and Edna H. Hong. Princeton: Princeton University Press, 1998.

R   *Repetition.* See FT.

SLW   *Stages on Life's Way*, ed. and trans. Howard V. Hong and Edna H. Hong. Princeton: Princeton University Press, 1988.

SUD   *The Sickness unto Death*, ed. and trans. Howard V. Hong and Edna Hong. Princeton: Princeton University Press, 1980.

TA   *Two Ages: The Age of Revolution and the Present Age. A Literary Review*, ed. and trans. Howard V. Hong and Edna H. Hong. Princeton: Princeton University Press, 1978.

TDIO   *Three Discourses on Imagined Occasions*, ed. and trans. Howard V. Hong and Edna H. Hong. Princeton: Princeton University Press, 1993.

TM   *'The Moment' and Late Writings*, ed. and trans. Howard V. Hong and Edna

NA   H. Hong. Princeton: Princeton University Press, 1998.

UDVS   *Upbuilding Discourses in Various Spirits*, ed. and trans. Howard V. Hong and Edna H. Hong. Princeton: Princeton University Press, 1993.

WA   *Without Authority*, ed. and trans. Howard V. Hong and Edna H. Hong. Princeton: Princeton University Press, 1997.

WL   *Works of Love*, ed. and trans. Howard V. Hong and Edna H. Hong. Princeton: Princeton University Press, 1995.

WS   "Writing Sampler" See P.

Danish editions

SKP   *Søren Kierkegaards Papirer*, 2nd enl. ed., by Niels Thulstrup, with index vols. 14-16 by Niels Jørgen Cappelørn. Copenhagen: Gyldendal, 1968–1978.

SKS   *Søren Kierkegaards Skrifter*, ed. Niels Jørgen Cappelørn, Joakim Garff, Jette Knudsen, Johnny Kondrup, and Alastair McKinnon. Published by Søren Kierkegaard Forskningscenteret. Copenhagen: Gads Forlag, 1997ff.

SKS, K *Kommentar til Søren Kierkegaards Skrifter*, published by Søren Kierkegaard Forskningscenteret. Copenhagen: Gads Forlag, 1997ff.

SKS, J *Søren Kierkegaard Skrifter, Journalerne*, ed. Niels Jørgen Cappelørn, Joakim Garff, Anne Mette, Hansen, Jette Knudsen, Johnny Kondrup, and Alastair McKinnon. Published by Søren Kierkegaard Forskningscenteret. Copenhagen: Gads Forlag, 2000ff.

SKS, KJ *Søren Kierkegaard Skrifter, Kommentarer til Journalerne*, ed. Niels Jørgen Cappelørn, Joakim Garff, Jette Knudsen, Johnny Kondrup, and Alastair McKinnon. Published by Søren Kierkegaard Forskningscenteret. Copenhagen: Gads Forlag, 2000ff.

Preface
Why Kierkegaard Matters to Me

Kierkegaard. . . . The very name makes one shudder. Whether it is an episode of *Jeopardy* or *Family Ties*, or a crossword puzzle, or a book on the shelf of a high school student in *Finding Forrester*, the Grand Dane's name enlightens and intimidates. But the central question is: Does Kierkegaard matter? More importantly: Does he matter to me? To write objectively in answering the question is most un-Kierkegaard-like. To even think one can write objectively about him is to slander his existence and his work.

Personally, the question is reframed to, How does Kierkegaard matter to me? This is easily written about. First, Kierkegaard helps me understand both what a *self* is and how I am a self. The idea of self is very common to explore, but no one can explore it for you. My reading of Kierkegaard always helps me understand my self. No other writer but Henry David Thoreau does this. Second, Kierkegaard has helped me remain a Christian. His devastating attack on the Danish church is an inspiration. True to — at least in this regard — Luther's form, Kierkegaard loved the church so much that he dared not let it get away with a hypocritical and misguided faith.

The Self

At Mercer University I have been teaching in the First Year Seminar for five years. This two semester course is an interdisciplinary course aimed at first-year students and seeks to introduce them to university intellectual life by examining in the fall semester the idea of the "self" and in the spring semester the idea of "engaging the world." When I began, I immediately reached for my Kierkegaard books. Of course, Kierkegaard had many thoughts on the self, but a few struck me as just the kind of things those first-year students needed to hear. After writing about what it means to "exist before God," Kierkegaard goes on to say:

> But to become fantastic in this way, and thus to be in despair, does not mean, although it usually becomes apparent, that a person

cannot go on living fairly well, seem to be a man, be occupied with temporal matters, marry, have children, be honored and esteemed — and it may not be detected that in a deeper sense he lacks a self. Such things do not create much of a stir in the world, for a self is the last thing of all for a person to show signs of having. The greatest hazard of all, losing the self, can occur very quietly in the world, as if it were nothing at all. No other loss can occur so quietly; any other loss — an arm, a leg, five dollars, a wife, etc. — is sure to be noticed.   (SUD 32-33)

A student in one of my classes wrote in her first paper that she was in college to become a doctor because her parents planned for her to do just that. She claimed to be the "Unknown Citizen" that Auden wrote about. In other words, she had no sense of self and no sense of purpose other than that of fulfilling her parents's wishes. She had lost her soul a long time prior to coming to Mercer. Later that semester, I saw signs of her struggling with her identity. While we read no Kierkegaard, I often used quotes or read selections to the class. The quote above I read just before the class wrote their papers on Thoreau's *Walden*. In her paper, that student came very close to finding her self. She admitted that she was on her way to finding out who she was. She cited the Kierkegaard quotation and said she was trying to find her self.

I may have been, but I don't specifically remember being introduced to Kierkegaard in college. I am certain I read nothing by him. I first came across Kierkegaard in seminary. I was in the seminary bookstore and there was a new book on the shelf called *Two Ages*, volume 14 of the International Kierkegaard Commentary.[1] While in seminary I searched for answers to many questions that had plagued me since beginning seminary. Vocation and Church (the two subjects of this essay) were among the most important issues I encountered. I bought that IKC volume and took it home. I had not read Kierkegaard's *Two Ages*, but I kept reading the IKC volume. The one positive result was that I decided I needed to read Kierkegaard. I was convinced that Kierkegaard was worth exploring.

-----

[1]The last thing I then would have thought was that one day I would be employed with the publisher of this commentary series when it reached its conclusion. One of my greatest honors is to have worked with Robert Perkins these past fifteen years on this project.

I began with *Sickness unto Death*. The Penguin edition was afford-able and changed my way of seeing the world. Every now and then I found a idea that spoke to me, but my appetite for this philosopher was now permanent. I had little time to read much Kierkegaard but later I had a great opportunity when I was asked to teach a philoso-phy course at Simmons University Bible College. I put *Fear and Trembling* on my reading list and totally frustrated my students. And yet, our discussions on Kierkegaard were the best of the semester.

For me, however, my understanding (however elementary and misguided) came when I began teaching the First Year Seminar at Mercer. That course forced me to rethink "self" and *my* "self." The first semester I began teaching FYS was the same semester that my book *Safe at Home* was published.[2] My father had died two years earlier and I wrote the memoir in his honor and memory. Much of the book centered on vocation. While I don't talk about Kierkegaard in the book, he overshadows the book. Facing my own mortality, I found myself truly existing before God and I was terrified.[3]

Writing the memoir, reading Kierkegaard, and teaching the class on the self led me to that leap for which Kierkegaard is famous. My journey to that discovery is continuing, but Kierkegaard is my Virgil. He held my hand and told me where and when to turn. He taught me how to look at despair and sin and how to see beyond the dark-ness to find the stars. The self — my self — is me, and I am nothing without my relationship to God. God created me and God completes me.

One other experience was very instrumental. About three years ago I introduced Kierkegaard to my Sunday school class. I did this by discussing Kierkegaard's three "stages on life's way." We were reading a series of lessons that followed the path perfectly from the aesthetic to the ethical to the religious. On the fourth Sunday one classmate said that it seemed to her that the lesson seemed to imply that all three stages were really one and that all three were necessary to understand one's life with God.

---

[2]Marc Jolley, *Safe at Home: A Memoir of God, Baseball, and Family* (Macon GA: Mercer University Press, 2005).
[3]SUD 32.

She got it. A self is a complete whole only when in relationship with God. Away from God one is in despair without knowing it. In God's presence one is in despair and knows it. It's how one responds that makes the difference. Losing one's self may be an easy thing to do and perhaps no one even notices, not even the person who lost it. Finding one's self, however, is difficult, but when it happens the person knows it, and the leap has been made. It happens when one realizes that he or she is that "single individual" that Kierkegaard talks about (PV 10, 11, 18, 37). The rationale of Kierkegaard's writing, *he* says, is for the purpose of becoming a Christian (PV 63ff.). Like Kierkegaard, who did not start living until his father died (PV 82-83), I too faced mortality and focused my life — *and*, I firmly believe, with Kierkegaard's help.

All my work and struggle with vocation and purpose and mortality I found summarized in Kierkegaard's words: "This is how I understand my self in my work as an author: it makes manifest the illusion of Christendom and provides a vision of what it is to become a Christian" (PV 88; cf. 90). Kierkegaard matters because to read Kierkegaard I read my own story and that helps me be that *single individual*.

Kierkegaard helps me understand my self, resulting in a healthy understanding of what it means to be christian. Kierkegaard's attack on the Danish Church is legendary. He called to question church practices and expectations. Being a Christian was not a matter of birth or church membership. Rather it came by, in the words of Kierkegaard,

> What I really lack is to be clear in my mind what I am to do, not what I am to know, except in so far as a certain understanding must precede every action. The thing is to understand myself, to see what God really wishes me to do; the thing is to find a truth that is true for me, to find the idea for which I can live and die.
>
> (JP [1835]; cf. PV 95-97)

To be a Christian, Kierkegaard suggests (in *For Self-Examination*) that we read the Bible as if it is speaking directly to us; that we should imitate Christ; and that we should love others, not objectify them.

In short, Kierkegaard matters because he helped me to find myself before God and that finding myself I needed to decide to live for God or not.

What could possibly matter more?

This Festschrift is a collection of essays by people who are among the best Kierkegaard scholars in the world, in large part because they are also people who believe that Kierkegaard matters. One reason Kierkegaard matters to many is Robert Perkins. Bob has been the editor of the International Kierkegaard Commentary since its birth, the publication of the last volume of which coincides with publication of this Festschrift.

Bob, this book is for you. Each person contributing here and many, many more owe you an unpayable debt for all you have done to promote the study and understanding of Søren Kierkegaard and his "gospel."
Thank you.

Marc A. Jolley, director
Mercer University Press

Acknowledgments

I thank Sylvia Walsh who supported this project from the beginning, and who provided an illuminating foreword.

I thank Edd Rowell — whose own essay also appears herein — for editing this volume and for his tireless work on the International Kierkegaard Commentary for the better part of three decades.

And, I thank the essayists in this volume for their contribution to our understanding of Kierkegaard.

Finally, I wish most of all to thank Robert Perkins who has dedicated much of his career to helping thousands understand why Kierkegaard matters.

maj

MERCER
UNIVERSITY PRESS

Endowed by
TOM WATSON BROWN
and
THE WATSON-BROWN FOUNDATION, INC.

Foreword

This collection of essays honoring Robert L. Perkins celebrates the completion of the International Kierkegaard Commentary (IKC), a twenty-four-volume series of scholarly essays on Kierkegaard's thought and writings edited by Dr. Perkins over a period of twenty-six years. Published by Mercer University Press, this series was initially underwritten by the University of South Alabama, where Dr. Perkins founded the Department of Philosophy and served as its chair for sixteen years. When he returned to Stetson University, his undergraduate alma mater, initially to serve as dean of the College of Arts and Sciences and later as chair of the Department of Philosophy, two presidents of Stetson, Dr. Pope Duncan and Dr. Douglas Lee, both now deceased, continued to provide university support for this vital research project over many years to its completion.

Using as the basis for its commentary the English edition of Kierkegaard's Writings edited and translated by Howard V. Hong and Edna H. Hong and published by Princeton University Press, the IKC has long been a major international venue for publication of scholarly essays on Kierkegaard. Since its inception in 1984, Dr. Perkins, better known as "Bob" to his family, friends, and colleagues, has presided over the selection and publication of a total of 282 essays, a complete list of which appears in the last volume published (fall 2010: IKC 22, on Kierkegaard's *Point of View*). He rightly points with pride and joy to the fact that a number of young Kierkegaard scholars have published their first professional articles in the IKC. It has been a special concern of the editor to nurture their professional development while maintaining rigorous standards for publishing in the IKC.

Although completion of the IKC constitutes the main occasion and rationale for honoring Bob with this festschrift, there are two other major accomplishments of his that must be mentioned here. In addition to conceiving the IKC, Bob was the founder of the Søren Kierkegaard *Newsletter* and the Søren Kierkegaard Society in North America. Unlike the IKC, however, he soon turned these brainchildren over to other colleagues who have continued to nurture and develop them. The Kierkegaard *Newsletter* is now published by the

Hong Kierkegaard Library at St. Olaf College in Northfield, Minnesota, and serves as a major organ of communication among Kierkegaard scholars, pastors, and general readers of Kierkegaard. The Søren Kierkegaard Society now boasts more than a hundred members and holds regular meetings for the presentation and discussion of Kierkegaard scholarship in conjunction with the annual meetings of the American Academy of Religion and the American Philosophical Association.

It is not too much to say, then — although Bob would no doubt object — that just as Kierkegaard is (rightly or wrongly) credited with being the "father of Existentialism," Bob may rightly be called one of the founding fathers and organizers of Kierkegaard scholarship in North America. Just as he adopted two children as his own to raise, he has been a dedicated nurturer in the Kierkegaard community, and for that his colleagues thank him and honor him with this collection of essays.

As his wife, constant companion, and fellow laborer in the Kierkegaardian scholarly vineyard for more than twenty years, I am especially grateful for the love and support he has given me in my own efforts to make a contribution to the understanding of Kierkegaard as a Christian poet and thinker.

Sylvia Walsh

1

To Be the Truth
Is the Only True Explanation of What Truth Is:
Gilleleie and the Twenty-First Century

Wanda Warren Berry

Kierkegaard matters in the twenty-first century because, for those immersed in Western intellectual history,[1] his authorship stimulates a self-conscious decision to test the validity of truth claims by whether they can be lived, without self-deception, by conscious and free subjects. This existential truth criterion is pungently expressed for philosophers by Johannes Climacus in *Concluding Unscientific Postscript* by saying "truth is subjectivity." A parallel expression for Christian theologians is found in *Practice in Christianity* when Anti-Climacus says: "[T]o be the truth is the only true explanation of what truth is . . . truth in the sense in which Christ is the truth is not a sum of statements, not a definition etc., but a life" (PC 205).

The twenty-first century needs to reappropriate Kierkegaard's existential truth criterion as a powerful alternative to cynical relativism as well as to the dangerous religious fundamentalisms that characterize this "present age" (TA). Many of us who came of age in the mid-twentieth century adopted Kierkegaard's religious existentialism as an alternative to the arid scientism of logical positivism as well as the despairing cynicism of "the death of God" movement. Those of a philosophical bent then found it liberating to claim a right to "truth-talk" as well as "God-Talk" in terms of self-consciously existential criteria. Now, early in the twentieth-first century, strident voices are resurrecting purportedly scientific arguments about the foolishness of "God-talk."[2] Mirroring the 1960s,

---

[1]While Kierkegaard has been influential in various parts of the world, I assume that traditions other than the Western European have produced their own powerful maieutics for authentic existence.

[2]See, e.g., Christopher Hitchens, *God Is Not Great: How Religion Poisons Everything* (New York: Twelve, 2007); Richard Dawkins, *The God Delusion* (New

many religious responses again are grounded only in either a disengaged relativism or an antiscientific fundamentalism.[3]

At the outset, this essay must acknowledge that the twenty-first century has opened with numerous deconstructionist/postmodern denials of any unifying existential thread in Kierkegaard's works.[4] Michael Strawser, for example, says that one cannot find "Kierkegaard, that historical person with certain views" or "the ultimate view of reading of Kierkegaard's writings."[5] Such postmodern challenges have caused a rereading of Kierkegaard with new questions in mind, even by those who always recognized that Kierkegaard was "a kind of poet"[6] who called for attention to his imagery, ironic indirection, and multivalency.[7] This rereading has led some to reidentify Kierkegaard with the existentialists. For example, while George Pattison says the existentialists share a "rejection, with varying degrees of hostility, of the ambition of formulating a unitary worldview,"[8] he also identifies Kierkegaard

---

York: Houghton Mifflin, 2006).

[3]A discussion of recent fundamentalist as well as scientific arguments that is deeply informed by Reinhold Niebuhr's mid-twentieth century calls for existential commitment and social justice can be found in Chris Hedges, *I Don't Believe in Atheists* (New York: Free Press, 2008).

[4]See collections of articles that urge recognition of a "new Kierkegaard," e.g., Jonathan Rée & Jane Chamberlain, eds., *Kierkegaard: A Critical Reader* (Oxford: Blackwell, 1998); Elsebet Jegstrup, ed., *The New Kierkegaard* (Bloomington and Indianapolis, Indiana University Press, 2004). Also see Roger Poole, "The unknown Kierkegaard: Twentieth-century receptions," *The Cambridge Companion to Kierkegaard*, ed. Alastair Hannay and Gordon D. Marino (Cambridge: Cambridge University Press, 1998) 48-75.

[5]Strawser, *BOTH/AND: Reading Kierkegaard from Irony to Edification* (New York: Fordham University Press, 1997).

[6]Louis Mackey, *Kierkegaard: A Kind of Poet* (Philadelphia: University of Pennsylvania Press, 1971).

[7]My own rereadings have emphasized Kierkegaard's imagery and pseudonymous strategies in order to enter into dialogue with him about contemporary perspectives on sexual identity. See, e.g., those for which Robert Perkins was a demanding yet supportive editor in the International Kierkegaard Commentary, vols. 3. 4, 10, and 20.

[8]George Pattison, *Anxious Angels: A Retrospective View of Religious Existentialism* (New York St. Martin's Press, 1999) 2.

with the existentialists' rejection of "theorizing that cannot be reduplicated in life."[9] He says:

> "Subjectivity," as recommended by Kierkegaard, is not simply a substitute for "objectivity." Instead it points to a prioritizing of the "how" over the "what" of truth, something that problematizes various models of subjectivity no less than it challenges an empiricist approach to religious belief.[10]

Just as Kant had refused to acquiesce in the claim that "truth-talk" belongs only to the empirically and logically verifiable and spoke of the "truth" of freedom as a necessary presupposition of practical reason, so Kierkegaard and the other existentialists judge authenticity by that which can be lived, rather than only objectively observed or rationally analyzed. Even Michael Strawser, has recognized that

> Kierkegaard stands for a turning point of sorts from a type of systematic philosophy that, by means of a conspicuous focus on objectivity, attempts to place itself on the secure path of science, to a "philosophy" — already viewed with a difference — that focuses its attention on subjectivity and openly acknowledges itself as fragmentary and provisional.[11]

This essay will work first with Kierkegaard's journals, using the Hong and Hong edition,[12] in order to argue that self-conscious choice of an existential truth criterion initiated Kierkegaard's own development as a thinker and provided continuity to his thought. Then it will indicate how this criterion plays out elsewhere in the authorship. Finally, it will indicate that such a criterion can serve well those in the twenty-first century who seek to join Kierkegaard in opposing

---

[9]Pattison, *Anxious Angels*, 258.

[10]Pattison, *Anxious Angels*, 269.

[11]Strawser, *Both/And*, 97. Strawser, of course, does not talk of the turning point he notes as a turn to "the existential." Instead he identifies Kierkegaard's recognition of the "fragmentary and provisional" with postmodernism. In contrast, I hold that Kierkegaard "openly acknowledges" that existential truth claims express particularity and commitment at the same time as they resist relativism.

[12]*Søren Kierkegaard's Journals and Papers*, vols. 1-7, ed. and trans., Howard V. Hong and Edna H. Hong (Bloomington and London: Indiana University Press, 1967–1978).

conformism and cynical relativism as well as religious fundamentalism.

I. Evidence of an Existential Orientation in the Journals[13]

A. Gilleleie, 1 August 1835.

In order to respond to current denials of Kierkegaard's existential-ism,[14] I first will provide a close exegesis of the familiar youthful entry written while on vacation in Gilleleie (JP 5:5100).[15] The next step will be to note its resonance in some later entries in the Journals. Written when Kierkegaard was just twenty-two years old, this vacation-time entry often is dismissed as fictional autobiography. Whether fictional or not, close exegesis of its interwoven concerns shows the birth of what came to be known as religious existential-ism.

First, the Gilleleie entry calls for a self-conscious orientation that tests one's direction not by external factors or objective knowledge but by that which can *"come alive"* in a *"completely human life"* as opposed to a life of "mere knowledge." Repeatedly, the entry contrasts "so-called objective truth" with that which has a "deeper meaning *for me and my life*." The "objective" is contrasted with "something bound up with the deepest roots of my existence [*Existents*]" (35). Nevertheless, that this is not obscurantist is clear when the young Kierkegaard says "I still accept an *"imperative of knowledge,"* but such an imperative must not obscure the test that is "most important of all," the truth that can be lived.

Second, paralleling this opposition to the restriction of truth-talk to the empirical is a concern to orient the self toward "the inward activity of man" as opposed to "a mass of data." If the goal is to

---

[13]An earlier version of this paper with additional analysis of the *Journals* was presented at the Fifth International Kierkegaard Conference at St. Olaf College in July 2005. The conference focused on Kierkegaard's *Journals*.

[14]See, e.g., Rée and Chamberlain, *Kierkegaard*, 2, where the idea that Kierkegaard was "the unwitting forerunner of a philosophical 'movement' called Existentialism is called "romantic and sentimental."

[15]Page references to JP 5:5100 in the Hong and Hong edition will be inserted in parentheses in the text. See also that the Gilleleie entry is included in *The Essential Kierkegaard*, ed. Howard V. Hong and Edna H. Hong (Princeton: Princeton U. Press, 2000) 7-12.

know *"what I must do"* rather than only "what I must know," one must "know oneself with inward understanding"; an understanding of one's "life course" will follow from "knowing oneself" rather than from deciding "the externals" (36).

Third, from Gilleleie we learn that this inwardness is humanity's "God-side" (36). Throughout this entry, the search for a life orientation is framed religiously. From the first identification of the search for "a purpose" with "what it is that God wills that *I* shall do" (34) to the identification of the "roots of my existence" as that through which one is "grafted in the divine," the Gilleleie entry frames the self religiously. The theological sophistication that underlies this religiousness is indicated through metaphors, rather than directly. It is not far-fetched to hear resonances with contemporary arguments for panentheism in the talk of the "roots" of existence "grafting" one to the divine. Later in the entry, the wrongness of the turn toward externals is compared to a "cosmic body" (a planet?) forming itself in terms of its surface rather than in terms of the harmony of forces in terms of which it moves. The God-relationship here is compared to such a body allowing "the harmony of centrifugal and centripetal forces" to "realize its existence [*Existents*] and letting the rest come of itself" (36).

A linked *fourth* theme that recurs in the Gilleleie entry and that is identified with existentialism is what it may seem trite to call 'the quest for ultimate meaning.' In the second paragraph, the "truth which is truth *for me*" is linked with *"the idea for which I am willing to live and die."* (34). Perhaps it is best to allow this theme at first to stand separately as a call for infinite passion, rather than too quickly to identify it with the God-relationship.

A *fifth* existentialist theme is found at the end of the Gilleleie entry (39) where Kierkegaard identifies "the spiritual world" with the realm of "work," with human striving (see also 35), with "struggling up a hill." He says, "[I]in the spiritual world one must first work forward for some time before the sun really shines for us" (39). While we do not have in this early entry explicit talk of freedom, Kierkegaard here pictures the task as a conscious effort to "be able to call myself 'I' in a profounder sense" (39). Thus being "grafted into the divine," harmonizing with ultimate forces, nevertheless is conjoined with picturing the relationship to God as realized through freedom and action. Agency also is invoked by the entry's emphasis on "intense" conviction (37) and the kind of self-understanding that avoids "surrendering one's own 'I' " (38). The young Kierkegaard identifies the "individuality" of "interior understanding" of oneself with worshipping "the unknown God" (38).

Such an interweaving of existentialist themes in the Gilleleie journal entry continues when Kierkegaard, after judging as inadequate the aesthetic search for meaning through "the boundless sea of pleasure as well as in the depths of knowledge," attributes "peace and meaning" to true self-knowledge (37). That this is not immature naïveté is shown when this is said to liberate one from "that irksome, sinister traveling companion — the irony of life." He also offers brief cautions to ethical commitment as he talks of being "tumbled about" outside "the tradewinds of virtue" and of the vulnerable "resolve to go ahead along the right path" to "the abyss of despair" (37). The fatalistic threat to meaning is invoked with the message that, "After all, things cannot be otherwise." But this is countered by the self-knowledge that enables the swimmer "to keep afloat in a storm" because he knows "he is actually lighter than water" (37).

This brief use of the swimming metaphor illustrates being "intensely convinced and . . . experienced" of a *fact*: that of being lighter than water. Thus the "inward point of poise" that enables "independent existence" (38) is not based on an obscurantist denial of known facts. In addition, the young Kierkegaard describes avoiding that which would be "too powerful" for the emerging equilibrium of the self. We see here that existential truth seeking is based on sorting out what can and what cannot be self-consciously appropriated by the existing self.

As to an attitude toward the social self in this early entry, Kierkegaard clearly has chosen not to let his "life's compass" be overly influenced by "companions" who do not embrace humanity's "spiritual and deeper currents" (38). His later critique of conformism is here expressed autobiographically but does allow for "a few exceptional" companions.

In conclusion, JP 5:5100 suggests that Kierkegaard at age twenty-two had chosen a philosophical orientation appropriately called "religious existentialism." Central to this orientation is a decision to seek the truth that can be lived rather than only thought or observed. This criterion is surfaced primarily in terms of refusing to allow "truth" to be reduced to the objectively verifiable. It is worked out through affirmation of the self-conscious and free agency of the person who relates the self to the ultimate ground of existence.

B. Existential Themes
in *Søren Kierkegaard's Journals and Papers*

Since my approach is at such variance from some current interpreters of Kierkegaard, I need at least briefly to indicate evidence from elsewhere in the *Journals* that Gilleleie was not an aberration. This can be facilitated by using some entries organized in the Hong and Hong edition under "Exist, Existence, Existential," "Truth," and "God."

Gregor Malantschuk, editorial assistant to the Hong and Hong edition of the Journals, introduces the reader to the two key words involved in this section and he summarizes their meaning, indicating normal usage as: "*existere* (to exist as a striving person) and *være til* (to be there in time and space)" (JP 1:535).[16] With this in mind, it is significant that twelve years after the Gilleleie passage, we find:

> If a couple thousand years are not suddenly sliced away for men and this bridge demolished in order to teach men to begin with the problems of actual life and existence [*Tilværelse*], everything is unhinged. We confuse the existential [*existentielle*] problem itself with its reflex in the consciousness of all the generations of the learned. The main issue in regard to every existential [*existentielt*] problem is its significance to me; after than I can see whether or not I am fit to discuss it learnedly.
>
> (JP 1:1040)

A number of entries collected in this section call for such a recognition of the distinction between existence and thought. Speculation is contrasted with "historical existence [*Existents*]" (JP

---

[16]This topical section is most helpful when these two key words are indicated in brackets, making it clear why the entry was included here. Out of the 48 entries in the section, I found at least 12 for which I could recognize no clear connection to the title of the section (JP 1:1020-23, 1031, 1036-37, 1041, 1044, 1050, 1053, 1055). For others, the connection seems to be uses of terms translated "life" (*liv, livet*) or "actuality" (*Virkeligheden, Virkelighedens*) (JP 1:1047, 1026-27, 1029, 1032-33, 1048-49, 1051, 1054). Some entries seemed to be focused on a topic unrelated to the current argument, though they use cognates of the key words (JP 1:1026 and 1027, 1029, 1032-33).

1:1028). Abstract thought is contrasted with concrete existence (JP 1:1039, 1042-43). One hears the familiar Kierkegaardian complaint about "how infinitely remote most men's thinking usually is from their existence" (JP 1:1043) and hears that

> ordinarily philosophers . . . as most men, in daily affairs basically exist [*existere*] in categories entirely different from those in which they speculate, and they console themselves with something entirely different from what they solemnly discuss. Out of this come the untruthfulness and confusion prevalent in science and scholarship.   JP 1:1042

Several entries from 1850 contrast the existential with the scientific, emphasizing the existential as the concrete "actuality" that "cannot be conceptualized" (JP 1:1058 and 1059). "Thought actuality" or "possibility" is contrasted with "ideal actuality." History is spoken of as "traversed actuality" and contrasted with existential actuality wherein persons aim to realize "[*realiseret*] existentially [*existentielt*] the tasks before them in actuality" (JP 1:1059). The scientific is subordinated in value to the existential. At the same time, making "science and scholarship" unconditional is identified with the erasure of the religious (JP 1:1059, p. 462).

In addition, in a different philosophic vein than Gilleleie, the meaning of "existence" sometimes is developed through the contrast with "essence." Briefly exploring the Kantian and Leibnizian ways with the "concept of existence," Kierkegaard moves toward his emphasis that "existence corresponds to the individual" and is not "absorbed in the concept." "For a particular animal, a particular plant, a particular human being, existence (to be — or not to be) is very crucial: a particular human being is certainly no concept-existence" (JP 1:057).

Perhaps the best indication of the religious framing of Kierkegaard's existentialism in this section is found in JP 1:1056 where he says "the essential sermon is one's own existence [*Existents*]." Other entries from the same period (ca. 1850) contrast Christian existence with doctrine (JP 1:1061) and preaching and eloquent speechifying (JP 1:1062 and 1063). Listening to sermons for two weeks "without changing one's way of life" is contrasted with the earnestness of actually fasting for one day.

Here we see Kierkegaard's main point in emphasizing "existence" and "the existential." Existing is identified with "an exercising," with "an existential [*existential*] transformation" that requires "the *internal*, the inward, 'the single individual'" (JP 1:1060). This striving "in daily existing [*Existeren*]" (JP 1:1063) is like being "contemporary with oneself" (JP 1:1050) and is said to involve "transparency in repose . . . that is "possible only in the God-relationship." A characteristic theme is found: "When an existence [*Existens*] is genuinely considered *under the aspect of the eternal, the result is,* eo ipso, *isolation*" (JP 1:1034). Reflecting on the introduction to the *Concluding Unscientific Postscript*, Kierkegaard emphasizes that the only teacher of "the art of existing *at existere*" is "existence itself."

> With respect to existing, there is only the learner, for anyone who
> fancies that he is in this respect finished, that he can teach others
> and on top of that himself forgets to exist and to learn, is a fool. In
> relation to existing there is for all existing persons one schoolmas-
> ter — existence itself.   (JP 1: 1038)

Nevertheless, the passages that emphasize *Tilværelsens* rather than *Existens* manifest a tone that contrasts with those that call for existential striving. These clearly invoke human finitude more than human striving (JP 1:1019, 1035, 1046), speaking of the "conditions of existence" (JP 1:1046). One entry from 1854 employs importantly the category of truth and says, "existence is ordered in such a way that truly to relate oneself to truth is impossible without suffering" (JP 1:1066). From 1848 an entry identifies *Tilværelse* with "temporal existence," speaks of "earthly existence" as suffering, and disparages the idea of progress. Such emphases increase in the later entries included in this section. However, this may be an insignificant change, since one does not find a comparable change of emphasis away from existential themes in the later entries included in the section on "Subjectivity/Objectivity" (JP 4:345-65), a section that would provide considerable support for my thesis if space allowed its analysis. The entry titled "Christianity" under "Subjectivity/Objectivity" (from 1854; Kierkegaard died in 1855) might as well have been included in either "Exist, Existence, Existential" or "Truth." It begins:

> Christianity relates to existence. The expression, "Truth is naked"
> may also be interpreted in this way, for truly relating to truth

means that all the inner and the outer garments of illusion have to be discarded, and you are brought into touch with truth so that this truth itself becomes your very own existential truth.   (JP 4:4572)

Among the remarkable aspects of the section titled "Truth" in the *Søren Kierkegaard's Journals and Papers* is the lengthy introduction that Malantschuk provides for the notes (JP 4, pp. 749-50). Starting with a summary of Johannes Climacus's analysis of empirical and logical definitions of truth in order to contrast his use of "truth is subjectivity," this note goes on to say that "Climacus's and Kierkegaard's concept of truth is completely oriented to existence." Of the six criteria for such truth surfaced by Malantschuk through Johannes Climacus's exposition of "an ethical-religious understanding of human existence" (p. 749), only the specifically Christian reference to the actualization of truth in Christ was not forecast in the Gilleleie entry.[17]

Malantschuk's introduction to the notes concludes by recalling the last line of *Either/Or*: "Only the truth that builds up is truth for you" and says, "Kierkegaard's original concept of truth is not only the basis for all his pseudonymous authorship but to an exceptional degree is the basis for all his upbuilding literature" (JP 4, p. 750). Although it is the case that the criterion of the upbuilding is ironically expressed in JP 4:4847, where the conclusion of *Either/Or* also is invoked, the entries collected under the topic of truth usually express the existential truth criterion quite indirectly and not at all in the vein of Johannes Climacus's philosophy, to which Malantschuk draws so much attention. Instead, a surprising number of entries in this section manifest existential themes only through opposing the idea of the rule of the majority and ironically criticizing

---

[17]Malantschuk says that "Truth Is Subjectivity" contains these elements: "(1) Truth must always stand in relation to the person, to subjectivity. (2) This truth can only be something eternal. . . . This means that subjectivity must never be confused with subjectivism, in which one arbitrarily decides what is truth. . . . (3) This eternal truth . . . must be actualized by the person. . . . (4)The only example of the actualization of this truth is provided by him who said: 'I am the way, the truth, and the life.' . . . (5) But it is up to each and every person to try to actualize the ethical-religious truth in his life. . . . (6) In sum, 'the final result of this effort is that one fails to reach his goal and thereby becomes guilty. . . . By forgiveness a person can once again come into a positive relation to the truth.' " JP 4:749-50.

the idea that the truth will be known through the ballot box.[18] The constructive point here is to emphasize that

> the only way there can be any possibility of coming to the truth is
> . . . to become single individuals—joining together is nothing but
> untruth. To become a single individual, to continue as a single
> individual, is the way to the truth.   (JP 4:4887)[19]

That the opposition to the majority and the crowd intends to oppose relativism rather than sociality is clearest in the one entry in this section that refers to "the unconditioned."

> The exact opposite of the truth, unconditioned truth, the uncondi-
> tioned, is everything that is called: to a certain degree.
>   The unconditioned does not consist of an approximation, but
> it is a point of repulsion. That which lies nearest to the truth is not,
> if you please, closest to the truth—no, this is the most dangerous
> delusion of all, the most dangerous simply because it lies so near to
> the truth without being the truth.   (JP 4:4884, p. 503)

In the entries collected under "Truth" the test of truth again and again is linked with encountering opposition (JP 4:4855) and suffering (JP 4:4857, 4867, 4868, 4881). At one point this connection between suffering and truth is explained in terms of the fact that suffering reveals "inwardness": "That the distinctive mark is opposition is really the expression for the inwardness of the conviction; indeed, it is hoping against hope, believing against the understanding etc" (JP 4:4855). This "existential" theme is autobiographically framed in some contrast with Christianity in the entry entitled "Concerned Truth" (JP 4:4862). The Christian concern "which, eternally certain of being the truth" is concerned to communicate that truth to others is contrasted with the person who "struggles to find the truth for himself." As late as 1849 Kierkegaard says:

> This is the case with my striving, which in great part is also purely
> intellectual but has not been able to concern itself with communica-
> tion to others because I myself was striving and readily perceived
> what is only all too true—that getting a few others along simply

---

[18]JP 4:4850, 4852, 4866, 4873-76, 4880.
[19]See also JP 4:4864 and 4885.

means delay. To want to have the others along in order to find the truth betrays a muddlehead. In Christianity the relationship is altogether different: out of concern for the others to be willing to endure the suffering and torment of communicating the truth to them.

(JP 4:4862)

What does such a passage add to the themes of religious existentialism surfaced at Gilleleie? It shares existentialism's emphasis on individual striving to find the truth that can be lived. It calls "muddleheaded" the expectation that truth can be discovered in any joint effort that substitutes for personal struggle. It adds the identification of Christianity with "concern for others" and with willingness to suffer in order to communicate to them the truth of which it is "eternally certain."

Although there is little explicit talk in the section of *Journal* entries listed under "Truth" that is comparable to Johannes Climacus's "truth is subjectivity," there is clear emphasis that *"An objective uncertainty, held fast through appropriation with the most passionate inwardness, is the truth*, the highest truth there is for an *existing person*" (CUP 1:203). The subordination to the ultimate called "divine" is established by commitment, by faith, rather than by an objectively grasped revelation: "To commit oneself in such a way that one sinks under the truth, happy only to help the truth get ahead . . . " (JP 4:4871).

There is not space here for thorough analysis of this long section of *Journal* entries collected under "God." We can note only a few entries that support the above analysis of the treatments of "truth" and "existence."

Immanently (in the imaginative medium of abstraction) God does not exist or is not present [*er ikke "til"*] — only for the existing person [*Existerende*] is God present, i.e., he can be present (*være "til"*) in faith. A providence, an atonement, etc. exist or are present only for an existing person. . . . Faith, therefore, is the anticipation of the eternal which holds the elements together, the discontinuities of existence [*Existentsens*]. If an existing person does not have faith, then [for him] God neither is nor is God present, although understood eternally God nevertheless eternally is.

(JP 2:1347)

If one frames this entry with others that speak of the God-relationship as a "chosen" relationship to "everything" (JP 2:1356), it becomes clear how Kierkegaard can say that "God . . . eternally is" at the same time as he says God is present "for the existing person" only in faith. Although in some entries (e.g., JP 2:1449) we hear language that suggests a metaphysical foundation ["the uncondi-tioned, being-in-and-for-itself"], we learn very quickly that the issue for Kierkegaard is not speculation about God's "objective being." Instead the point is that the "majesty" of God is experienced in faith as an "unconditioned requirement" (JP 2:1449). Entries from this period (ca. 1854) are particularly concerned that God not be inter-preted as having purposes or causes in a human sense (see also JP 2:1447). God's majestic "enormous proportions" mean that God "is infinitely interested" but, at the same time, "refrains completely from intervening" except "in Christ" (JP 2:1450).

As in the sections on "Truth" and on "Exist, Existence, Existen-tial," the existential truth criterion is very clear when one encounters the familiar usage of the *how* and the *what*, e.g., "for God himself is this: *how* one involves himself" with God. As in the following, sometimes this is accompanied with the concern for an absolute or ultimate relationship.

> As far as physical and external objects are concerned, the object is something else than the mode; there are many modes; someone perhaps stumbles upon a lucky way, etc. In respect to God, the *how* is *what*. He who does not involve himself with God in the mode of absolute devotion does not become with God. In relationship to God one can not involve himself to a certain degree, for God is precisely the contradiction to all that which is to a certain degree.
>
> (JP 2:1405)

Existential themes are clear when the Gilleleie emphasis on the search for an ultimate purpose is transformed in terms of a "strenu-ous" relationship to the Absolute (see JP 2:1409) who transcends all human purposes but, nevertheless, requires that one live a

> daily fear and trembling, every day, every moment of the day, the possibility of being thrown into decisions of prime importance — or, more correctly, that one is in the position, because every spiritual existence is out in the depths of "70,000 fathoms."
>
> (JP 2:1402)

It seems, then, that entries collected under the topic "God" share the existential truth criterion with the Gilleleie passage; but they develop in terms of Kierkegaard's strongly theistic faith, rather than the less-personal metaphors for our relationship to ultimacy explored at Gilleleie. If at times these entries seem unreflective about the meaning of "God," it is best to see this as revealing that, in the journals, Kierkegaard tends to speak confessionally, i.e., in terms of his commitment to Christian faith, rather than philosophically. This does not deny his existentialism, since he always is clear that faith is established by a decision and that becoming a Christian requires active appropriation or faith by the existing self.

II. The Existential Truth Criterion and the Published Works

I believe the analysis of additional relevant topical sections would strengthen my conclusion that the existential truth criterion provides a thread of continuity in *Søren Kierkegaard's Journals and Papers*. Although there seems to be a decreased emphasis on existential themes in the later entries in some topical sections, the fact that this criterion is clearly present in other late entries combines with evidence in late published works to support my thesis that it provides philosophical continuity.

There is not time or space here to argue my conviction that "at each stage of the authorship, the existential truth criterion was formulated in terms of the issues specific to a particular 'stage on life's way,' 'existence sphere,' or pseudonym."[20] We have seen some evidence of this above, for example, in the criterion of "the up-building" at the end of *Either/Or*. And we have called to mind Johannes Climacus's: "*An objective uncertainty, held fast through appropriation with the most passionate inwardness, is the truth*, the highest truth there is for an *existing* person" (CUP 1:203). We will only add here brief indications of how the existential truth criterion is expressed in certain published Christian works, since continuity

---

[20]I assert this in my "Practicing Liberation: Feminist and Womanist Dialogues with Kierkegaard's *Practice in Christianity*," *Practice in Christianity*, IKC 20, ed. Robert L. Perkins (Macon GA: Mercer University Press, 2004) 303-41.

in this orientation is most likely to be questioned in those parts of the authorship.[21]

First, as a Christian psychologist, Anti-Climacus in the preface to *The Sickness unto Death* calls for an approach like that of a physician at a sickbed who seeks the "upbuilding" and "concerned" rather than "indifferent" "scienticity and scholarship." He goes on to say: "All Christian knowing, however rigorous its form, ought to be concerned, but this concern is precisely the upbuilding. Concern constitutes the relation to life" (SUD 5). When he speaks theologically in part II we hear that

> God is not some externality in the sense that a policeman is. The point that must be observed is that the self has a conception of God and yet does not will as he wills. . . . Not until a self as this specific single individual is conscious of existing before God, not until then is it the infinite self. . . . (SUD 80)

Indeed, in an upbuilding discourse we hear Kierkegaard say "God is only in the internal" (TDIO 64). The point such passages stress is that both the ethical-religious and the Christian are matters of "inwardness before God" (WL 137-38) in which infinite concern appropriates the God-relationship without "objective certainty."

Next we can call into evidence the fact that when Anti-Climacus turns to Christological reflection in *Practice in Christianity*, the existential truth criterion is expressed as the challenge to "contemporaneity with Christ." Criticizing Christendom's trust in "the eighteen hundred years of Christian history and doctrine, rather than in the actual relationship to Christ," Anti-Climacus asks that existential validity be tested by whether life is lived in the presence of Christ, imitating him as one's prototype of what it means "to be the truth."[22]

In addition, it is interesting that the addendum that introduces *The Moment,* identifies Kierkegaard's aim at this late stage with challenging readers into a sense of the "Either/Or" of existential decision, and expresses "an indescribable horror for both-and" (TM

---

[21]Sylvia Walsh's recent work has contributed thorough theological analyses of the Christian works that offset such questioning. See, e.g., her *Kierkegaard: Thinking Christianly in an Existential Mode* (Oxford: Oxford University Press, 2009).

[22]Wanda Warren Berry, "Practicing Liberation . . . ", 315.

101). In the notes to the Princeton edition of *The Moment* the Hongs present Kierkegaard's metaphorical usage of *øieblikket* as signifying "the moment of decision and newness when time and eternity meet" (TM 630n.1). Such interpretations of "the moment" witness that, even in "Religiousness B," Kierkegaard's emphasis is upon the truth that is chosen and to which one is committed, rather than upon foundationalist, objective claims to religious validity or superiority.

Perhaps most important, we should note that *Works of Love* from its title through to its conclusion is framed existentially. The emphasis upon "works," upon the appropriation in one's concrete actions of the love command rejects an ethic of rational principles as well as of sentimental or romantic love that is felt rather than enacted. This volume develops Christian ethics in consistency with Gilleleie's call for "*what I must do*" as opposed to what I must know. In the conclusion, *Works of Love* expresses the existential truth criterion as "redoubling" and the discussion of "the Christian like-for-like" makes clear that in Religiousness B subjective appropriation is the criterion for truth and yields an existential theology.

Let us suppose that someone asked Christianity, "is it certain, then, that I have faith?" Christianity would answer:

> "Be it done for you as you believe." . . . Christianity guarantees you that, but whether you, precisely *you,* have faith certainly does not belong to Christianity's doctrine and proclamation. . . . It is eternally certain that it will be done for you as you believe; but the certitude of faith, or the certitude that you, yes, you, have faith, you must at every moment gain with God's help, that is, not in any external manner.   (WL 378-79)

> God is actually himself this pure like for like, the pure rendition of how you yourself are . . . God's relation to a human being is at every moment to infinitize what is in that human being at every moment.   (WL 384)

These reminders of the existential truth criterion in *Works of Love* are important because this text more clearly than most provides a corrective to any tendency to see the existential truth criterion as promoting a hopelessly privatistic and anticommunal orientation. In this text we hear, "to love human beings is still the only thing worth living for; without this you really do not live" (WL 344). While the twenty-first century needs Kierkegaard's emphasis on individual responsibility as the "Single One" before God, it also needs an eco-logical awareness that the truth that can be lived will need to recognize profound interdependence as well as the value of community.[23]

III. Why This Matters:
Existentialism versus Fundamentalisms

Perhaps these sketchy references to later works suffice to indicate how I would argue for the continuance of the existential truth criterion in the published authorship. Assuming that the preceding analyses of some sections of *Søren Kierkegaard's Journals and Papers* also justify seeing considerable continuity in this respect, the next step might be to ask why this is significant. The briefest answer to this question might be, "because it is upbuilding." Self-conscious appropriation of the existential truth criterion can have for the twenty-first century the same constructive theological and ethical effect that it had for the twentieth. In addition, recognizing Kierke-gaard as a resource for religious existentialism can bring this liberatory effect into the mainstream of a religious tradition that presently is endangered by literalistic and fundamentalist interpreta-tions.

I have argued elsewhere for the liberating effect of embracing the existential truth criterion for contemporary theology, especially for feminist liberation theology and feminist theory.[24] Here I want to suggest existentialism as a resource for a religious reorientation that provides an alternative to the strong appeal of religious fundamentalisms in our "present age." Diane Eck joins others in pointing out how such movements "may be seen as a widespread

---

[23]For exposition of the import of Kierkegaard's emphasis on "The Single One," one cannot do better than Robert Perkins analysis of Martin Buber's mistaken interpretation. Robert L. Perkins, "Buber and Kierkegaard: A Philosophic Encoun-ter," *Martin Buber: A Centenary Volume*, ed. Haim Gordon and Jochanan Bloch (Israel: Ben Gurion University of the Negev, 1984) 275-303.

[24]Wanda Warren Berry, "Kierkegaard and Feminism: Apologetic, Repetition, and Dialogue," in Martin J. Matustik and Merold Westphal, eds. *Kierkegaard in Post/Modernity* (Bloomington and Indianapolis: Indiana: Indiana University Press, 1995) 110-24. Also Wanda Warren Berry, "Religious Existentialism and Feminist Liberation Theology," presented to the Theology and Religious Reflection Section of the American Academy of Religion, Kansas City MO, November 1991.

revolt against the relativism and secularism of modernity," going on to remind us that fundamentalists tend to reject "the evolutionary claims of science," modern study of scripture, society, and religion — and that they feel threatened by the plurality and choice characteristic of our age.[25]

By way of contrast, self-conscious appropriation of religious existentialism can oppose relativism and secularism without at the same time encouraging an obscurantist rejection of scientific and intellectual inquiry. We remember that, even at Gilleleie, Kierkegaard said "I still accept an "*imperative of knowledge*" at the same time as he insisted that "mere knowledge' could not yield "deeper meaning." In the journals we have seen that existential truth is not defined as a rejection of the empirically verifiable. Rather, it is defined by a refusal to recognize objective knowledge as the only legitimate claim to truth. It is clear in *Concluding Unscientific Postscript* that science and objective knowledge are not rejected in themselves. Instead they are cautioned not to usurp the ethical (existential) as the highest task (CUP 1:151-52).[26] The model for the relationship between science and religion that is suggested is that of the relationship between a source of objective information and a conscientious decision about the meaning and value of that information. Religious existentialism can hold theology responsible to the results of scientific objectivity at the same time as it calls such objectivity to the task of ethical evaluation and existential commitment.

Existential authenticity asks for that which can be appropriated without self-deception by conscious and free persons. As religious, it relates the self to the ultimate in terms of passionate concern rather than in terms of what is claimed to be objectively demonstrable revelation. This provides an alternative to the relativism associated

---

[25]Diana L. Eck, *Encountering God: A Spiritual Journey from Bozeman to Banaras* (Boston: Beacon Press, 1993) 175.

[26]Without referring to Kierkegaard, Chris Hedges argues that the new atheists do this; he says their hubris leads them beyond what science can justify so that they do what Johnannes Climacus described as "usurping the sphere of the existential." Hedges sees the new atheists as another kind of fundamentalism that claims absolute truth and fails to acknowledge human realities and limitations. See *I Don't Believe in Atheists*, 32.

with postmodernism as well as to the absolutism of fundamental-isms. Relativism can defuse both religious concern and ethical passion. But absolute claims to the truth of doctrines presented as valid independently of commitment flies in the face of modern knowledge and sets up imperialistic relationships to others. Kierke-gaard's religious existentialism encourages the existing self to see itself before an Ultimate Truth/God that it cannot know or define, but which it can worship and to which it is responsible. By encourag-ing infinite concern and passionate commitment, religious existen-tialism transcends the nihilism and relativism that motivates many to turn to fundamentalisms. At the same time, existentialism's emphasis on human freedom facilitates hope to change the world, avoiding the fatalistic determinism sometimes associated with postmodernism.

Kierkegaard's existentialism can address the biblical literalism through which fundamentalists interpret Christianity. Kierkegaard says "All human speech, even the divine speech of Holy Scripture, about the spiritual is essentially metaphorical" (WL 209). He also recognizes that scripture gains its authority by virtue of one's commitment to a particular religious tradition, rather than through a claim to objective historical validity that can be known apart from faith.[27]

Religious existentialism aims to engage the existing individual in terms of ultimate concern, i.e., in terms of commitments the validity of which can never be objectively demonstrated. Its emphasis on concrete existence enables one to embrace difference at the same time as one is empowered by the choice of one's own particular life, communities, and/or traditions. Rather than being based on religious claims to objective, literalistic absolute truth, religious existentialism encourages seeing oneself in humility before a transcendent truth before which one is responsible.

---

[27]I argue this with regard to *Practice in Christianity* in "Practicing Liberation," 306-308.

Works Cited

JP   *Søren Kierkegaard's Journals and Papers*. Seven volumes. Translated
         and edited by Howard B. Hong and Edna H. Hong, with Gregor
         Malantschuk. Bloomington and London: Indiana University Press,
         1967–1978.
KW   Kierkegaard's Writings. Edited and translated by Howard V. Hong
         and Edna H. Hong. Princeton NJ: Princeton University Press.
CUP   Concluding Unscientific Postscript to "Philosophical Fragments."
         KW 12. 1992.
PC   *Practice in Christianity*. KW 20. 1991.
SUD   *The Sickness unto Death*. KW 19. 1980.
TA   *Two Ages*. KW 14. 1978.
TDIO   *Three Discourses on Imagined Occasions*. KW 10. 1995.
TM   *The Moment and Late Writings*. KW 23. 1998.
WL   *Works of Love*. KW 16. 1995.

Berry, Wanda Warren, "Practicing Liberation: Feminist and Womanist
      Dialogues with Kierkegaard's *Practice in Christianity*," *International
      Kierkegaard Commentary: Practice in Christianity*, IKC 20, ed. Robert L.
      Perkins (Macon, GA: Mercer University Press, 2004) 303-341.
"Kierkegaard and Feminism: Apologetic, Repetition, and Dialogue," Martin
      J. Matustik and Merold Westphal, eds. *Kierkegaard in Post/Modernity*
      (Bloomington & Indianapolis: Indiana: Indiana University Press, 1995),
      110-24.
Dawkins, Richard , *The God Delusion* (New York: Houghton Mifflin, 2006).
Eck, Diana L., *Encountering God: A Spiritual Journey from Bozeman to Banaras*
      Boston: Beacon Press, 1993).
Hedges, Chris, *I Don't Believe in Atheists* (New York: Free Press, 2008)
Hitchens, Christopher, *God Is Not Great: How Religion Poisons Everything*
      (New York: Twelve, 2007)
Jegstrup, Elsebet, ed., *The New Kierkegaard* (Bloomington & Indianapolis,
      Indiana University Press, 2004).
Mackey, Louis, *Kierkegaard: A Kind of Poet* (Philadelphia: University of
      Pennsylvania Press, 1971).
Pattison, George, *Anxious Angels: A Retrospective View of Religious Existential-
      ism* (New York, NY: St. Martin's Press, Inc., 1999).
Robert L. Perkins, "Buber and Kierkegaard: A Philosophic Encounter,"
      Martin Buber: A Centenary Volume, eds. Haim Gordon and Jochanan
      Bloch (Israel: Ben Gurion University of the Negev, 1984) 275-303.
Poole, Roger, "The unknown Kierkegaard: Twentieth-century receptions,"
      in *The Cambridge Companion to Kierkegaard*, eds. Alastair Hannay and

Gordon D. Marino (Cambridge: Cambridge University Press, 1998) 48-75.

Rée, Jonathan & Chamberlain, Jane, eds., *Kierkegaard: A Critical Reader* (Oxford: Blackwell, 1998)

Strawser, Michael, *Both/And: Reading Kierkegaard from Irony to Edification* (New York: Fordham University Press, 1997).

Walsh, Sylvia, *Kierkegaard: Thinking Christianly in An Existential Mode* (Oxford: Oxford University Press, 2009).

2

Kierkegaard's Call for Honesty

Andrew J. Burgess

"What do I want?" Søren Kierkegaard asks in 1855, in the heat of his attack on the hypocrisy of the established Danish church. His answer: "Very simply: I want honesty" (TM 46). Honesty is a virtue he lauds, when it is present, and demands, when it is not. It is also a value on which people, by and large, agree. Still, there is something disquieting about the approach Kierkegaard takes in calling for honesty. Time and time again I come across students, colleagues, or others, who have picked up and read a Kierkegaard book somehow, and then they found it kept disturbing them and would not let them go on as before. They might miss the book's philosophical subtleties, care little for its literary merits, or see no point in its religious orientation; but they still feel its ruthless honesty. It hits a nerve. Kierkegaard gets under their skin, and he gets under mine too.

Since Kierkegaard's concept of honesty can be tough to pin down, I propose to start first with the short essay within which Kierkegaard poses this question, before I widen the focus to include other writings. Why does he pinpoint honesty here as the decisive failing of the Danish state church? What does the term "honest" mean in this context? How could Kierkegaard avoid falling into the same dishonesty as that which he attacks? These are good questions with which to begin, in a search for the source of the uneasiness I feel upon opening a book of Kierkegaard and applying it to myself, and which, I suspect, other readers may feel as well, if they approach his texts with the seriousness their message deserves.

"I am human honesty"

Leading up to to this statement, Kierkegaard says

> I am not, as some well-intentioned people — I cannot pay attention to the opinions of me held in bitterness and rage and impotence and blather — have wanted to represent me, I am not a Christian stringency in contrast to a Christian leniency.

> Certainly not, I am neither leniency nor stringency—I am human honesty.   (TM 46)

This quotation fits well, not only into the 1854–1855 attack, but also into his writings during 1850, the year when Kierkegaard lays the foundations for the attack by publishing *Practice in Christianity*. That book leaves the reader with some ambiguity. While its overall thrust pushes hard toward rigor, it also includes a "Moral" that allows the reader to follow the lenient path—if, but only if, "he before God shall honestly humble himself under the requirement of ideality" (PC 67). The ethical requirement is for the utmost rigor, infinite rigor, in fact, but as in all traditional Lutheran theology that requirement can still be satisfied by God's grace.

When Kierkegaard finally mounts his attack in 1854–1855, he plays down that ambiguity, because he is addressing not the penitent Christian but a self-satisfied clerical establishment. The essay "What Do I Want?" (March 1855) makes this plain.[1] Far from wanting to diminish the importance of the concept of grace, he is concerned about its misuse. One thing grace should not be used for, he writes, is to "suppress or to diminish the requirement. In that case 'grace' turns all Christianity upside down" (TM 47). For example, the Christian requirement is for poverty. He does not object here to the clergy members' rejection of that requirement (although in another context he might do so), but to the dishonest way they "suppress" and "diminish" that requirement.

Already by this time in the attack the atmosphere in Copenhagen is charged with hostility. From every side Kierkegaard's detractors are questioning both his critique and his right to advance it. He is impossibly strict, they say. Who can possibly meet such standards? Can he himself do it? His response is sharp. He does not set himself up as a model. He does not even claim to be honest. Far from it. He merely announces that he has taken up honesty's cause: "I am human honesty."

---

[1] The essay is the twelfth in a series of twenty-one essays published in the journal *Fatherland*. The series started in February 1854 and concluded in May 1855 and it laid the groundwork for Kierkegaard's own ten-part series, called *The Moment*.

Kierkegaard therefore highlights his claim through two "most extreme" (as he calls them) hypothetical statements.

> If this, then, is what the generation or the contemporaries want, if they want straightforwardly [*ærlig*], honestly [*redelig*], candidly [*uforbeholdent*], openly [*aabent*], directly [*ligefrem*] to rebel against Christianity and say to God "We cannot, we will not submit to this power"—but, please note, this is to be done straightforwardly, honestly, candidly, openly, directly—well, then strange as it might seem, I go along with it, because I want honesty.   (TM 48)

He does not here oppose an "honest rebellion against Christianity," as long as it is really honest. Then he goes further, with his second hypothetical:

> [I]f one straightforwardly, sincerely, candidly, makes full confession to God with regard to the actual situation . . . that . . . we finally have managed to get it [Christianity] to be the very opposite of what it is in the New Testament—and that we now wish, if it can be done, that this might be Christianity—if this is what one wants, then I go along with it.   (TM 48-49)

How can he say this? Because, even if all other goods he values should be abandoned, he wants honesty.

This is explosive stuff. It speaks directly to everyone. No one has to have a theological education to understand what Kierkegaard calls the "requirement" of poverty. All someone has to do is to recall how the disciples and the apostles in the New Testament actually carried out their mission—hungry, harried from place to place, in constant danger of imprisonment or death—and then to compare this picture with the expectations of many clergy today. Nor does it require much philosophy to parse Kierkegaard's concept of honesty in this essay, since the above list, with a half dozen or so overlapping words for honesty, includes virtually any aspect one might want to include within that concept. Any of these words could be used as the key term in his line of reasoning without much changing the force of the argument.

The result is that Kierkegaard's works can be uncomfortable reading, more than those of all but a few other thinkers. Such people can be disconcerting, even frightening. The twentieth-century Christian theologian Karl Barth tells how, on being invited to Copenhagen to receive a prestigious humanities prize, he almost turned the offer down.[2] He was afraid, he says ironically, that as he wandered the crooked streets of that city he might meet a little, spindly man, who would greet him warmly and exclaim: Karl, Karl! What brings you to Copenhagen? Then, when Barth admitted he was there to receive a prize, he was sure Kierkegaard would ask: A prize for Christian theology? Do you mean the prize of persecution? of poverty? or perhaps even of martyrdom? And Barth did not know how he could answer. Any theologian who sets out to meet Kierkegaard's standards for honesty will walk a hard and lonely path.

Honest—and Dishonest—Philosophers

While Kierkegaard is notorious for puncturing the egos of theologians, he is no easier on philosophers. Hegel and Hegel's disciples in particular meet his unsparing scorn. On the other hand, high up on the list of adjectives Kierkegaard uses when he speaks positively about some philosopher is the word "honest." Even if he disagrees with that philosopher's position, when Kierkegaard applies the word "honest" the reader knows that, despite everything, this is someone he wants by his side.

Immanuel Kant is a case in point. In an out-of-the-way fragment from his notebooks, where he is discussing how Kant disparages the practice of offering prayers for daily bread, Kierkegaard writes: "Let us rather say it straightforwardly with honest Kant, who declares the relationship with God to be a kind of weakness, a hallucination. To be involved with something unseen is this, too" (JP 2:2236).[3] Of course, this is not Kierkegaard's own attitude toward such prayer. Not at all. A large part of his upbuilding literature, for example, is as much a dialogue with God as it is with his readers. Even where passages are not explicit prayers, a reader senses that petitions are being directed toward God. Most of one chapter in a major pseudonymous work, *Practice in Christianity*, is such a prayer (PC 260-62).

------

[2]Karl Barth, "A Thank You and a Bow: Kierkegaard's Reveille,' *Canadian Journal of Theology* 11/1 (1965): 3-7.

[3]The reference is to a passage in Kant's famous essay "Religion within the Boundaries of Mere Reason," in *Practical Philosophy*, trans. and ed. Allen W. Wood, Cambridge Edition of the Works of Immanuel Kant (Cambridge UK: Cambridge University Press, 1996) 210-11.

Yet Kierkegaard writes in his notebook *"honest* Kant." Why? It is true that, for Kierkegaard, as for William James, psychological weaknesses may open the door to spiritual strengths. Although fear, trembling, anxiety, and even despair, are negative sides of every human life, Kierkegaard argues they offer something eternally positive too. But Kierkegaard does not suppose that this is Kant's view, since he recognizes that Kant believes prayers for daily bread to be mere hallucinations. Why, then, does Kierkegaard so admire Kant here? Probably because Kant announces his conclusion publicly, even though doing so might make him unpopular with the Prussian rulers and the general public. Kant is justly famous for taking the hard line on verbal honesty, especially in the essay "On a Supposed Human Right to Lie from Philanthropy," in which he insists that no one has a right to tell a lie under any circumstances.[4] Here in "Religion within the Boundaries . . . " Kierkegaard finds Kant taking an equally hard line, not merely upholding the universal principle that everyone should tell the truth, but courageously putting his own career on the line for what he believes. Honest Kant!

Johann Gottlieb Fichte is someone Kierkegaard evaluates in much the same way as he does Fichte's mentor, Kant. In his dissertation, *The Concept of Irony* (1841), Kierkegaard presents Fichte as someone who paves the way for Friedrich Schlegel's and Ludwig Tieck's "extreme subjectivity," and Kierkegaard rejects the way these two Romantic ironists imagine they have "the absolute power to do everything" (CI, 275).[5] Later, in *Stages on Life's Way* (1845), however, one of Kierkegaard's main pseudonyms, Frater Taciturnus, portrays Fichte in a much more positive light than that. Just as Kierkegaard had done in disagreeing with Kant, Taciturnus does the same with Fichte. Although convinced that Fichte is mistaken, Taciturnus still finds it "inexplicable" that such an "energetic and, in the noble Greek sense, honest philosopher" should take this position (SLW, 476). And what is this "noble Greek sense" of "honest" philosophizing? The answer is obvious. Taciturnus is identifying Fichte's

---

[4]*Practical Philosophy*, trans. and ed. Allen W. Wood, Cambridge Edition of the Works of Immanuel Kant (Cambridge UK: Cambridge University Press, 1996) 611-15.

[5]In this respect these two Romantics resemble the aesthete, Mr. A, in the first volume of *Either/Or*.

honesty above all with that of Socrates, the greatest philosopher he knows, a man who taught simply by the way he lived.

In the preface to *Fear and Trembling*, René Descartes, too, turns out to be a model of honesty. The preface begins by noting ironically that some (presumably Danish Hegelian) philosophers claim to have already doubted everything, and now they propose to go on even further. How these philosophers could have managed such an amazing, apparently contradictory, feat as going beyond universal doubt they do not explain. Instead, they appeal to Descartes; but his example is far from supporting their case. "Descartes, a venerable, humble, honest thinker, whose writings no one can read without being profoundly affected — he did what he said and said what he did. Alas! Alas! Alas! That is a great rarity in our day!" he says in the preface to *Fear and Trembling* (FT 5). With great fanfare the reigning philosophers in Denmark have announced that their culture is getting closer and closer to achieving the standpoint of universal reason, through which it will be able to go beyond faith. As this preface describes Descartes, however, he makes no such grandiose pretensions. He does not claim to doubt everything. For example," he did not doubt with respect to faith" (FT 5), but quietly and modestly "let it be known that his method had significance only for him and was partly the result of his earlier warped knowledge" (FT 6). Accordingly, the preface maintains that Descartes's honesty brought him what some Hegelians sorely lacked: humility.

The examples of Kant's courage, Fichte's Greek nobility, and Descartes's humility, all express some part of a basic insight in Kierkegaard's thinking, and at various places in his authorship Kierkegaard has different ways of expressing this insight. In *Concluding Unscientific Postscript*, for example, Kierkegaard's pseudonym Johannes Climacus covers some of the same conceptual ground with the phrase "subjective truth." A problem with that expression, however, is that it only makes sense to those who are adept in Hegelian terminology. For myself I prefer something simpler than that, some word people are more likely to understand. Why not just call it "honesty"?

Meeting Kierkegaard's standards for honesty would pose a stiff challenge for philosophers of any age. In ancient Greece Socrates, like Kierkegaard centuries later, walked about the streets of his native city asking straightforward questions that exposed the intellectual pretensions of religious and academic authorities alike. That great twentieth-century admirer of Kierkegaard,[6] Ludwig Wittgenstein, is another example of such honest philosophizing. Wittgenstein despised glib answers, and he was tormented by an ideal of philosophical integrity so high that it seemed as if neither he nor anyone else could satisfy it.

Confessional Philosophizing

Still, the honesty and dishonesty with which Kierkegaard is most concerned is not just that of the theologians or philosophers, in their professional capacities, but that of all his readers, including the theologians and philosophers, as individuals. The "human honesty" he demands from the theologians, in the essay "What Do I Want?" he demands from everyone else, too, including himself. For people as individuals, moreover, he also wants another kind of honesty as well, what he calls an honesty "before God"; but, because this latter type of honesty is not as likely as the other type to be the cutting edge of an attack, it is easier to overlook.

All of Kierkegaard's authorship, including both the published and unpublished elements, exhibits a deep commitment to what he calls "human honesty." In one popular sense of the term, Kierkegaard's writing is "confessional" from start to finish. That is to say, if the term "confessional" is taken to mean that a person is rigorously honest with oneself in one's writings, setting the moral standard as high as possible, and sparing no pains to scrutinize every action to see whether it measures up, then not only his published works but also his journals are about as "confessional" as can be. Page after page in his journals chronicle his misgivings about what he had thought or did, or what he might yet think or do. Has he really been willing to give up his authorship and spend his remaining life in a country parish? Is he ready, if called upon, to become a martyr for the truth? Has he been fair to Regine? Is he

---

[6]Wittgenstein read *Concluding Unscientific Postscript*, but he described it as too "deep" for him. In a letter to Norman Malcolm, Wittgenstein wrote: "I've never read 'The Works of Love.' Kierkegaard is far too deep for me, anyhow. He bewilders me without working the good effects which he would in deeper souls." Norman Malcolm, *Wittgenstein: A Memoir* (Oxford UK: Oxford University Press, 1958) 71, 75.

willing to lead a life of voluntary poverty? And is he willing to lead a life voluntarily that, while not starting in poverty, takes on a mission that will inevitably leave him there? Looking forward, such ethical decisions confront him with alternative futures, with no certainty that a particular option will be the right choice. But looking backward turns out to be no better, perhaps even worse, since it brings no certainty either and leaves him with regret besides. Instead of providing security and rest, recollecting his earlier decisions discloses to him only a bewildering set of alternative pasts, no one of which is obviously what he should have chosen.

His pseudonymous writings project reveals much the same picture, but onto a more public screen than do the journals, which remained unpublished during his lifetime. Each of the works *Fear and Trembling, Repetition*, and *Stages on Life's Way*, for example, casts some light on his engagement with Regine, in one way or another; but none of the interpretations is definitive. The distraught Constantin Constantius in *Repetition*, the merman in *Fear and Trembling*, and the weepy, self-pitying Quidem in the "Guilty?/Not Guilty?" essay from *Stages on Life's Way* may all reflect aspects of Kierkegaard's psyche, but how, and to what extent, they hit the mark, even he does not seem sure. Despite the self-scrutiny of his motivations, often the best answer he can give is that he (honestly?) does not know what they were. Such protestations of ignorance have a surprisingly contemporary sound today. For a century that understands human motivation to be largely, perhaps entirely, subconscious, and that expects to find self-deception at every turn, Kierkegaard's penchant for radical self-analysis fits right in.

Most of his writings, however, Kierkegaard might not call "confessional, since, like Augustine, he would be inclined to reserve that category for confession that is offered to God in prayer. Like Augustine, too, he recognizes some value in recording a confession for others to read, since those readers who are honest with themselves might learn from his anxieties and even from his doubts of God's grace. Yet Kierkegaard does not understand his writings to be confessional for anyone else but himself. Confession is between the individual and God. Trying to peek in on someone else's private confession to God would be spiritual voyeurism of the worst order.

In his writings Kierkegaard devotes considerable attention to this kind of honesty in which someone bares one's soul "before God" in confession. The Danish term for the concept is *Oprigtighed*, and, when the Hong and Hong translations do not translate it with the English term "honesty," they frequently render it as "sincerely." The essay "What Do I Want?" just takes up the concept on honesty "before God" [*Oprigtighed*] in passing, along with its discussion of honesty as "human honesty" [*Redelighed*], that is, in relations between people. The two concepts come up in the essay when he discusses two possible, "most extreme," hypothetical cases of rebellion against God. "Human honesty" is the term employed in the first case, and honesty "before God" in the second. The Danish word *redeligt*, translated here with the English word "honestly," is the main term for honesty he uses in this essay. Mainly it connotes verbal truthfulness; although for Kierkegaard it very often has a wider meaning as well, such as doing the truth as well as saying it. For the second "most extreme" hypothetical case, however, he shifts the context to something like the rite of the confessional, and he therefore introduces a new term for "honesty" that is especially appropriate for the new context. He writes:

> If this is what one wants: straightforwardly, openly, sincerely [*oprigt*] as is seemly when a person speaks with his God, as everyone acts who respects himself and does not despise himself so deeply that he will be dishonest before God—thus, if one straightforwardly, sincerely [*oprigt*], candidly makes full confession to God with respect to the actual situation with us human beings . . . I go along with it.   (TM 48)[7]

What is important here is that Kierkegaard has switched his term for "honestly," from the term for honesty between human beings [*redeligt*]—to a new term, for honesty before God, "sincerely" [*oprigt*]. The latter term he explains with a pair of phrases: "as is seemly when a person speaks with his God, as everyone who respects himself and does not despise himself so deeply that he will be dishonest [*uoprigt*] before God." The context for the new term is

---

[7]Translation modified. In accordance with the original Danish text, the comma has been omitted here after the word "sincerely." This change makes clear that the phrase "as is seemly when a person speaks with his God" modifies the term "sincerely" and not, or at least, not as directly, the other two terms as well.

the confessional. As he writes, such honesty happens when someone "makes full confession before God."

The phrases "dishonest [*uoprigt*] before God" and "speaks with his God" are decisive. The reason is not just theological but logical. In interactions between human beings, dishonesty involves some sort of deception, and these are the situations to which the other terms on Kierkegaard's "honesty" list may apply. Before God, however, such deception is excluded, since God knows everything, including whatever motivations the speaker might have for trying to lie. Accordingly the situation in the confessional requires a separate terminology, both for "honesty," in the sense of a special openness to God's truth, and for "dishonesty," which in this situation might be an attempted, but unsuccessful, effort to deceive God.

Yet how inevitable such dishonesty seems to be, on the account that Kierkegaard provides. One of the passages in which he discusses such honesty "before God" is, appropriately enough, in the occasional discourse entitled "On the Occasion of a Confession" (1845). He writes there:

> There is a quality that is highly praised but not easily acquired: it is honesty [*Oprigtighed*]. I am not talking about that charming honesty of children, which is certainly also to be found in some adults . . . Such a discourse belongs only where fortune separates people, not where the God-relationship recognizes equality. No, honesty [*Oprigtighed*] is a duty, and everyone is supposed to have it.
> (TDIO 32-33)

The distinction he draws here, between the charming, but childish kind of honesty, in which "fortune separates people," on the one hand, and the honesty bound by duty, on the other, is the familiar Kierkegaardian distinction between the aesthetic and the ethical-religious. After pointing out the problems people have in dealing with the guilt that they feel over past sins, Kierkegaard then goes on:

> And God can certainly require honesty [*Oprigtighed*] of a person. How much more difficult that becomes! A person can actually strive in all honesty [*Oprigtighed*] to become more and more transparent to himself, but would he dare to present this clarity to a knower of hearts as something positively trustworthy between himself and him? Far from it! Even the person who inwardly strives honestly [*redeligt*], even that person, and perhaps he most of

all, will always have an outstanding account that he is not confident of being able to settle. . . .   (TDIO 33-34)

Here again is the conceptual tie, which the essay "What Do I Want?"
also recognizes, between transparent openness and honesty "before
God." Yet, as Kierkegaard understands the matter, it must be
difficult to attain such transparency before God. He continues some
lines later: "Thus honesty [Oprigtighed] is difficult. It is easier to hide
in the crowd and drown one's guilt in that of the human race, easier
to hide from oneself than to become open in honesty before God"
(TDIO 34). Why, then, would anyone want to take on such a task?

The Joy of Reading Kierkegaard

Accordingly the person who goes through Kierkegaard's works
seems to be thus faced with a double duty. First, one faces the
challenge of just being honest with oneself and the other people
around. For anyone with moral sensitivity that is a hard enough
challenge, while for someone such as Wittgenstein it can be overwhelming. But then to that task is added another, infinitely more
difficult: letting one's life become fully transparent to God. Who
could bear such a load? No wonder Kierkegaard's works get a
reputation for fostering fear, anxiety, and even despair.

As Kierkegaard writes, however, there is no such double burden.
He is neither leniency nor stringency, but simply "human honesty";
and, in the sense in which he understands "human honesty," such
honesty is the way in which the real difficulty, becoming transparent
to God, is to be overcome. In a notebook entry from that period,
Kierkegaard expands on this point.

> It is my conviction that rigorous as Christianity is (and I have never
> understood Christianity in any other way) it is also gentle. It is not
> given to everyone nor is it unconditionally required of everyone
> that he must live, in the strictest sense of the word, in poverty and
> abasement. But he must be honest, he must admit candidly that
> such a life is too high for him and then rejoice as a child in the more
> lenient conditions, since ultimately grace is sufficient for all.
>   (JP 1:174)

Human honesty is thereby the way in which a person opens oneself up to God by acknowledging one's incapacity to go it alone. With that assurance, a person can rejoice like a child.

The path lies not through fear, trembling, or despair, but through honesty. As the conclusion of the first part of *Practice in Christianity* puts it, in its run-up to Kierkegaard's final attack:

> Whether one will succeed in becoming essentially Christian, no one can tell him. But anxiety and fear and despair are no help, either. Honesty [*Oprigtighed*] before God is the first and the last, honestly to confess to oneself where one is, in honesty before God continually keeping the task in sight. (PC 66)

3

Why Kierkegaard Still Matters:
"The Gleam of an Indication" —
Adventures of the Text

David Cain

"The gleam of an indication" (PV, 7; SKS, 13, 14; "*Antydnings Glimten*"[1]) is a phrase occurring in "The Accounting" section of *On My Work as an Author* by S. Kierkegaard, published 7 August 1851. Kierkegaard stays with the gleam theme. His context is the shape of the authorship, with a gleam of the religious in the midst of the pseudonymous-aesthetic-maieutic ("*Two Upbuilding Discourses* [1843] is in fact concurrent [*samtidige*, at the same time, contemporary, simultaneous] with *Either/Or*" [PV, 8]) and a gleam of the aesthetic (*The Crisis and a Crisis in the Life of an Actress*) in the midst of the religious. The phrase is apt for characterizing the nature of the authorship generally and for any attempt to address "Why Kierkegaard Still Matters." So here is "the gleam of an indication."

Goad, provocation,[2] spur, prod, instigation, incitement, excitation: such words tell of a track indicating why Kierkegaard still matters. Kierkegaard's authorship is an embarrassment of embarrassments of riches. "How do I love thee? Let me count the ways" (Elizabeth Barrett Browning, *Sonnets from the Portuguese* [1850]). But no; for this daisy will soon run out of petals. Besides, daisy petals give us "She loves me; she loves me not." Many readers of Kierkegaard might say, "I love him; I love him not." Much in Kierkegaard is not to love. Individual readers will have their own lists. But let us return to the love list and counting the ways — or paths.

Surely in the top ten most-famous moments in Kierkegaard's authorship is the moment when William Afham writes: "In Gribs-Skov there is a place called the Nook of the Eight Paths [*Otteveiskrogen*];

---

[1]Or "the hint's glint," "the suggestion's flash," "the intimation's gleam."

[2]See Charles E. Moore, ed., *Provocations: Spiritual Writings of Kierkegaard* (Farmington PA: Plough Publishing House, 1999).

only the one who seeks worthily finds it, for no map indicates it" (SLW, 16).[3] The adverbial emphasis is the all-important how. Let the map be the what. Elemental in Kierkegaard's authorship is an eye out for what/how relationships. These what/how relationships are mobile, on the move: what one says and how one says it; what one does and how one does it; what one says and how one lives, that is, what one says with one's words and what one says with one's life, which latter what is again a how. The authorship both enacts what/how sensitivity and exposes what/how obliviousness. If love makes the world go round, so, too, do ironic what/how gaps.

William Afham continues: "Indeed, the name itself seems to contain a contradiction, for how can the meeting of eight paths create a nook, how can the beaten and frequented be reconciled with the out-of-the-way and the hidden?" Yet in good dialectical fashion, Afham can do it: "the contradiction in the name only makes the place more solitary, just as contradiction always makes for solitariness" (SLW, 16):

> Thus I have frequently visited my sequestered nook. I knew it before, long before; by now I have learned not to need nighttime in order to find stillness, for here it is always still, always beautiful, but it seems most beautiful to me now when the autumn sun is having its midafternoon repast and the sky becomes a languorous blue when creation takes a deep breath after the heat, when the cooling starts and the meadow grass shivers voluptuously as the forest waves, when the sun is thinking of eventide and sinking into the ocean at eventide, when the earth is getting ready for rest and is thinking of giving thanks, when just before taking leave they have an understanding with one another in that tender melting together that darkens the forest and makes the meadow greener.
>
> (SLW, 17)

Here, at the Nook of Eight Paths, is one reason why Kierkegaard still matters—or two reasons, closely linked: beauty and mood (*stemning*). But the Nook of Eight Paths does not limit us to one or two reasons. When I was a child and heard those fairy stories about the granting of three wishes, I knew precisely what I would wish for

---

[3]See David Cain, *An Evocation of / En Fremkaldelse af Kierkegaard* (København: C. A. Reitzel, 1997) 77-80. I have sought to seek *værdeligen*.

first of all: lots more wishes! So the Nook becomes an image of eight or endless paths and ways why Kierkegaard still matters. The remarkable and admirable diversity of approaches to, investments in, and explorations of his texts today attests to the waxing of this mattering. Surely Kierkegaard would have been pleased, but pleasure would not have put off polemics. Johannes Climacus proclaims in the preface of his *Philosophical Fragments*:

> Heaven preserve me and my pamphlet from the meddling of such an uproarious, bustling oaf [someone adrift in "world-historical importance," "era," "epoch," and, of course, "the system"] lest he tear me out of my carefree contentedness as the author of a pamphlet, prevent a kind and well-disposed reader from unabashedly looking to see if there is anything in the pamphlet he can use. (PF, 6-7)

Fruitful users of this pamphlet and of this authorship are legion. With Kierkegaard, one can get on anywhere and off anywhere. This is happening. Where do the eight paths of the Nook lead? They lead to the adventures of the text.

The adventures of the text: where is the text going? This question asks after the text's adventures. The adventures of the text are also our adventures with the text. Where does the text take us? This question asks where we go with it. And how do we go? For the how of going so often is decisive for the where of arriving. At this juncture, Kierkegaard says well why he still matters: "I am a poet, but a very special kind, for I am by nature dialectical, and as a rule dialectic is precisely what is alien to the poet" (PV, 162). As a "poet-dialectician" (PV, 133), he keeps concepts vivid and clear, dramatically gripping and intellectually rigorous in an imagistic extravaganza of authorship, a dance and dazzle of conceptual choreography, word orchestration. Kierkegaard clarifies the landscape of intellectual deliberation. His sharpened concepts consolidate the thinker. He invites a more capable existence.[4]

---

[4]See PV, 17: "What I have wanted has been to contribute, with the aid of confessions, to bringing, if possible, into these incomplete lives as we lead them a little more truth (in the direction of being persons of ethical and ethical-religious character, of renouncing worldly sagacity, of being willing to suffer for the truth, etc.), which indeed is always something and in any case is the first condition for beginning to exist more capably." (This is from the appendix to *On My Work as an Author*.)

One powerful instance of this occurs in a section of Johannes Climacus's *Concluding Unscientific Postscript*, to which we will be turning shortly. Kierkegaard's how of going is often delightful. Why Kierkegaard still matters? Fun still matters, and Kierkegaard can be fun. Johannes de Silentio refers to "an age when an author who desires readers must be careful to write in such a way that his book can be conveniently skimmed during the after-dinner nap" (FT 7-8). Then we have Climacus's "estheticizing hobnobbing with our Lord" (CUP 488).[5] And from Frater Taciturnus near the end of *Stages on Life's Way*: "My dear reader—but to whom am I speaking? Perhaps no one at all is left" (SLW, 485).

Kierkegaard still matters because time cannot outrun the real, because we can still embrace works written BC (Before Computers), because of his use of his inequality of genius to secure fundamental ethical-religious equality among human beings. Climacus declares, "But to comprehend equality most earnestly just when one is most earnestly aware of what differentiates—that is the noble piety of the simple wise person" (CUP 228). And that is Kierkegaard. Two of the great passages in the authorship are these:

> Faith is a marvel, and yet no human being is excluded from it; for that which unites all human life is passion, and faith is a passion.
> (Johannes de Silentio, FT 67)

> Whatever one generation learns from another, no generation learns the essentially human from a previous one. In this respect, each generation begins primitively, has no task other than what each previous generation had, nor does it advance further, insofar as the previous generations did not betray the task and deceive themselves. The essentially human is passion, in which one generation perfectly understands another and understands itself. For example, no generation has learned to love from another, no generation is able to begin at any other point than at the beginning . . .
>
> But the highest passion in a person is faith, and here no generation begins at any other point than where the previous one did.

---

[5]I confess an affection for the Swenson-Lowrie translation: "aestheticising clinking the glasses with Providence." Søren Kierkegaard, *Concluding Unscientific Postscript*, trans. David F. Swenson and Walter Lowrie (Princeton NJ: Princeton University Press, 1941) 436n. Climacus writes, "*æsthetiserende Klinken med Vorherre*" (SKS, 7, 442n.1).

(Johannes de Silentio, FT 121-22)

Kierkegaard loves to depict and dramatize ideas and perspectives through conversations in the first person. Climacus has "the simple wise person" speaking with "a simple person":

> My advantage, when regarded as the fruit of study, is something both to laugh at and to weep over. Yet you are never to scorn this study, just as I myself do not regret it, since on the contrary it pleases me most when I smile at it, and just then enthusiastically resume the effort of thinking.   (CUP 228)

This is autobiography—Kierkegaard speaking from the heart.

Does "matters" matter? Kierkegaard still matters because he is capable of instigating such questions.

Paul L. Holmer writes of Kierkegaard's "intellectual modesty."[6] Kierkegaard begins a newspaper article, "What Do I Want?" (*Fædrelandet* 77, 31 March 1855): "Very simply—I want honesty" (NA, 46). Modesty is honesty. Kierkegaard's context is the gap between the Christianity of the New Testament and "the mitigation that is the current Christianity here in this country" (NA, 46). But let us broaden the context to the authorship: I want honesty. Honesty is a major reason why Kierkegaard still matters. Happily, that mattering is not standing still. As indicated, the surprising freshness and richness of his writing is still not standing still.

But we are out on many paths from that Nook. Time to settle down to one. Honesty is evidenced when Kierkegaard declares, "Nothing is more foreign to my soul and nothing is more foreign to my nature (the dialectical), nothing more impossible, than fanaticism and fury" (PV, 132; this is from *Armed Neutrality: Or My Position as a Christian Author in Christendom*). "Thus in one way or the other I would be a hindrance to setting fanaticism in motion" (PV, 133). One important way Kierkegaard still matters, one path through and out of that pregnant Nook, is the path of Kierkegaard's honest hindrance to fanaticism.

* * *

[6]Paul L. Holmer, "Kierkegaard and Logic," *Kierkegaardiana II*, Søren Kierkegaard Selskabet ved Niels Thulstrup, ed. (København: Munksgaard, 1957) 42.

Kierkegaard's hindrance to fanaticism—and what still matters more today or any day?—may be found throughout the authorship and is effectively developed in what might be considered the heart of the authorship: Climacus's *Postscript*, section II, chapter II, "Subjective Truth, Inwardness; Truth Is Subjectivity." Climacus is able to emphasize the risk of faith without weakening the possibility of "holding fast" to faith. I put this forward as an important reason why Kierkegaard still matters and will note certain stylistic factors and felicities along the way.

So much of Kierkegaard is manifest in these pages—the dialectical dexterity, the poetic passion and poignancy, the serious playfulness—the wedding of jest (*spøg*) and earnestness (*alvor*), and the just plain playfulness. Merold Westphal catches nicely the dramatic shifts in style when he identifies "satire," "parable," "definition," and "portrait"[7] in renditions of "truth is subjectivity." If one finds Kierkegaard—or Climacus—impenetrable, turn the page. The satire is "Boom! The earth is round" (CUP 195). A patient escapes from a madhouse and wants to prove his sanity. He has the right what but the wrong how. The parable is about the contrast between praying falsely to the true God (right what, wrong how) and praying truly to an idol (wrong what, right how) (CUP 201). The definition is of truth: "*An objective uncertainty, held fast through appropriation with the most passionate inwardness, is the truth*, the highest truth there is for an *existing* person" (CUP 203). The portrait is of Socrates in relation to "immortality":

> He poses the question objectively, problematically: if there is an immortality. So, compared with one of the modern thinkers with the three demonstrations, was he a doubter? Not at all. He stakes his whole life on this "if"; he dares to die, and with the passion of the infinite he has so ordered his whole life that it might be acceptable—*if* there is an immortality. Is there any better demonstration for the immortality of the soul? But those who have the three demonstrations do not order their lives accordingly. If there is an immortality, it must be nauseated by their way of living. . . .
> (CUP 201)

---

[7]Merold Westphal, *Becoming a Self: A Reading of Kierkegaard's "Concluding Unscientific Postscript"* (West Lafayette IN: Purdue University Press, 1996) 116.

A nauseated immortality: *this* is Climacus—and Kierkegaard.

"I am indeed a poor existing spirit like all other human beings" (CUP 189-90), Climacus confesses over and over again; and to be a poor existing spirit imposes restrictions. "To be in existence is always somewhat troublesome . . . " (CUP 452). To forget one's existential predicament is "fantastically" to "become something such as no existing human being has ever been or can be, a phantom . . . " (CUP 189). Many kinds of phantoms are to be found—and to be found out. Climacus employs *phantastisk* and variations some nine times in the first five pages of the chapter. This is an example of an important aspect of Kierkegaard's style which might be called "word-skipping." Not leaving out: Kierkegaard rarely does this. No, word-skipping as in skipping a stone in water. Kierkegaard's word-rocks will not sink. They stay alive and skip, jump, hop, *leap* thematically from life to life—movement, momentum, acceleration.[8]

Climacus distinguishes between "essential knowing" and "accidental knowing" (CUP 197). Essential knowing is knowing essentially related to existence (CUP 197); and we must remember that this is the kind of knowing—and truth—of which Climacus is writing: "only ethical and ethical-religious knowing is essential knowing" (CUP 198; see 199n.). Hindrance to fanaticism emerges in two words: *objective uncertainty*. Here "the road swings off" ("*Veien svinger af*"). Climacus is fond of this image, and the road swings off several times in these pages. The road swings off from the "leisurely" road of "approximation" to "objective knowledge" to the passionate, desperate road to "subjective knowledge" where "every delay is a deadly peril" (CUP 200), where approximation is procrastination—and yet: objective uncertainty.

After giving the definition of truth when subjectivity is truth, quoted above, which includes "a memento of the fork in the road" (CUP 203) where the road swings off, Climacus proceeds:

> Objectively he ["an *existing* person"] then has only uncertainty but this is precisely what intensifies the infinite passion of inwardness,

---

[8]Another instance of word skipping is the "suppose" (*Sæt*) sequence, CUP 213-16. See also CUP 220-21, 226, 231-32, 242. There is also much phrase skipping, e.g., "Whether speculative thought is in the right is an entirely different question" (CUP 222-24).

and truth is precisely the daring venture of choosing the objective uncertainty with the passion of the infinite. I observe nature in order to find God, and I do indeed see omnipotence and wisdom, but I also see much that troubles and disturbs. The *summa summarum* [sum total] of this is an objective uncertainty.

(CUP 203-204)

Compare this with Climacus in the *Fragments*:

Or are the wisdom in nature and the goodness or wisdom in Governance right in front of our noses? Do we not encounter the most terrible spiritual trials here, and is it ever possible to be finished with all these trials? But I still do not demonstrate God's existence from such an order of things, and even if I began, I would never finish and also would be obliged continually to live *in suspenso* lest something so terrible happen that my fragment of demonstration would be ruined. (PF, 42)

This is but one form of repetition in an authorship replete in repetitions. "Repetition" (*gentagelse*, again taking) is a vital concept in Kierkegaard. Kierkegaard writes *about* it. Constantin Constantius writes a book about it: *Repetition: A Venture in Experimenting Psychology*. But Kierkegaard also *writes it*. He writes repetition. One loses one's way in discourses of the same title, working with the same scriptural texts.[9] Yet in these discourses one encounters new treatments, new testaments, new turnings, the adventures of the text. Repetition gives the baseline for bounce, for buoyancy, breathing in and breathing out, systole and diastole of blood-beating bite and beauty.

Back to Climacus in the *Postscript*:

But the definition of truth stated above is a paraphrasing of faith. Without risk, no faith. Faith is the contradiction between the infinite passion of inwardness and the objective uncerta(CUP 204)

How to put objective uncertainty and a kind of certainty ("a struggling certainty," CUP 226) together is a major concern of Kierkegaard, as Holmer recognizes: "To keep oneself ethically

---

[9]See, e.g., "Love Will Hide a Multitude of Sins" (1 Peter 4:7-12), EUD 55-68, 69-78, and "Every Good Gift and Every Perfect Gift Is from Above" (James 1:17-22), EUD 125-39, 141-58.

decisive while admitting intellectual uncertainty was part of
Kierkegaard's admonition towards the good life."[10] This is Climacus's attempt. Objective uncertainty and its risk are hindrance to
fanaticism. Paradoxically, they make faith possible—never
probable.[11]

Now Climacus goes to work out over those famous "70,000
fathoms of water" (CUP 204). The tension—Climacus has just
written "the contradiction" (*Modsigelsen*)—between existential
urgency and the risk of objective uncertainty: Climacus and
Kierkegaard draw upon a kind of "psychological physics," which
involves a *Kraftmaaler* (power meter).[12] The idea, which clearly
intrigues Climacus and Kierkegaard, is the tension, the pressure, the
paradox produced by the gap between subjective passion and
objective uncertainty.[13]

---

[10]Paul L. Holmer, "Kierkegaard and Theology," *Union Seminary Quarterly
Review* 12/3 (March 1957): 24-25.

[11]See the treatment of faith in relation to "probability" (*Sandsynligheden*) and
"improbability" (*Usandsynligheden*), CUP 232-33.

[12]The Hongs translate "dynamometer." Swenson and Lowrie translate
"measure."

[13]Climacus is not as helpful here as he might be. He says the truth is a paradox
and that the paradox is objective uncertainty (CUP 201-205). Then, more clearly,
"Nevertheless the eternal, essential truth is itself not at all a paradox, but it is a
paradox by being related to an existing person" (CUP 205). The truth is a paradox.
The truth is not a paradox. At this point in the dialectic, the latter is correct—but is
Climacus in a position to know this on his own terms? Climacus is on the way to
magnifying qualitatively this tension. Another outcropping of "psychological
physics" occurs in *The Crisis and a Crisis in the Life of an Actress* when *Inter et Inter*
characterizes the actress who "*is in proper rapport with the onstage tension.*" A weight
can press something down, but it can also inversely conceal that it is pressing down
and express the pressure by the opposite, by lifting something up. . . . the light
hovering of faith is precisely by means of an enormous weight. . . . But the onstage
illusion [*Illusion*] and the weight of all those eyes are an enormous weight that is
laid upon a person. . . . where this fortunate rapport is present, the weight of the
burden continually transforms itself into lightness" (C, 312). Or again in *On My
Work as an Author*, Kierkegaard describes "the dialectical method: in *working* also to
work against oneself, which is reduplication [*Redupplikation*]. . . . To endeavor or to
work *directly* is to work or to endeavor directly in immediate connection with a
factually given state of things. The dialectical method is the *reverse*: in working also
to work against oneself, a redoubling [*Fordoblelse*], which is 'the earnestness,' like
the pressure on the plow that determines the depth of the furrow" (PV, 9n.).

Not so incidentally, where are we? Is this the sphere of Religiousness A or Religiousness B (Christian faith)?[14] Socrates is dominant. A crucial statement:

> Socratic ignorance is an analogue to the category of the absurd [*det Absurdes Bestemmelse*, SKS, 7, 188], except that there is even less objective certainty in the repulsion exerted by the absurd, and for that very reason there is infinitely greater resilience in the inwardness.
> (CUP 205)

"The absurd" marks the Christian. Meanwhile, Climacus and Kierkegaard are in love with *uendelig* (endless, infinite). The qualitative and not the quantative is signaled. Crucially, "even less objective certainty" does not depart the domain of objective uncertainty. Uncertainty is not certain nonsense. Even less objective uncertainty is less likely — goodbye probabilities — but is not and must not be nonsense. Or uncertainty is gone. Risk is gone. Room for faith — Christian faith — is gone. But in introducing "the absurd," Climacus is getting ahead of himself.

Climacus reiterates: "Viewed Socratically, the eternal essential truth is not at all paradoxical in itself, but only by being related to an existing person" (CUP 205). Again and on his own terms, is he in a position — poor existing spirit that he is — to know this? The paradox of existential urgency and objective uncertainty endures.

Suddenly "recollecting" (*en Erindren*, SKS, 7, 188) enters the discussion. And suddenly Socrates and Plato are played off against one another regarding existence. A game of existential urgency — "I take existence more seriously than you take existence" — emerges. Socrates wins. Climacus and Kierkegaard sharpen, deepen, intensify, accentuate, emphasize *existence*. Recollecting robs existence of its urgency. In a long and important note, Climacus distinguishes his treatment of Socrates in the *Fragments* from his treatment now and in so doing distances Socrates from Plato: "To emphasize existence, which contains within it the qualification of inwardness, is the Socratic, whereas the Platonic is to pursue recollection and immanence" (CUP 206n.).[15] The Socratic becomes analogous to that which

---

[14]Merold Westphal proposes a "Religiousness C." See, e.g., Westphal, *Becoming a Self*, 194-200.

[15]Climacus makes this jarring claim: "the only consistency outside Christianity

goes beyond the Socratic in the *Fragments*. The tension between and the paradox of yoking together existential urgency and objective uncertainty becomes analogous to the "paradox *sensu eminentiori*," and "the passion of inwardness in existing is then an analog to faith *sensu eminentiori*" (CUP 206n.). What is this "eminent" pair, paradox and faith, which finds an analogue in the Socratic, though "the difference is infinite nevertheless" (CUP 206n.)?

Just as objective uncertainty is qualified and complicated as "the absurd," so the poor existing person is about to be qualified and complicated as sinner. Socrates believed he was whole: "the knower is essentially *integer* [uncorrupted]" (CUP 205). But now Climacus makes a weighty move:

> So, then, subjectivity, inwardness, is truth. Is there *a more inward* expression for it? Yes, if the discussion about "Subjectivity, inwardness, is truth" begins in this way: "Subjectivity is untruth." . . . subjectivity is in the predicament of being untruth. Thus the work goes backward, that is, backward in inwardness.   (CUP 207)

Just as we think we are about to hear the gun and run the race, we discover that we are not even at the starting line. We are unqualified, if not disqualified:

> The Socratic paradox consisted in this, that the eternal truth was related to an existing person. But now existence has accentuated the existing person a second time; a change so essential has taken place in him that he in no way can take himself back into eternity by Socratically recollecting.   (CUP 207-208)

---

is that of pantheism, the taking of oneself out of existence back into the eternal through recollection, whereby all existence-decisions become only shadow play compared with what is eternally decided from behind" (CUP 226). "Pantheism" seems to suggest an assured connectedness with the eternal, with truth, with the divine "from behind." Existence is undermined. With Christianity, the eternal is to be encountered in time or not at all. The safety net of existence beneath one and the umbilical cord of existence behind one are excised, withdrawn, severed. See David Cain, "Treasure in Earthen Vessels: Johannes Climacus on Humor and Faith," *Irony and Humor in Søren Kierkegaard, Liber Academiae Kierkegaardiiensis* VII, ed. Niels Thulstrup and Marie Mikulová Thulstrup (København: C. A. Reitzels Forlag A/S, 1988) 83-86.

Socrates thought he had this option but in the name of existence chose not to take it. Now the option is gone: "Let us now call the individual's untruth *sin*" (CUP 208).

Fundamental to grasping this dialectic is rightly relating "subjectivity is truth" and "subjectivity is untruth." Kierkegaard is, of course, known for the former formulation;[16] but the latter must not be forgotten.[17] Decisive in this right relating is the word "begins": "if the discussion about 'Subjectivity, inwardness, is truth; *begins* in this way: 'Subjectivity is untruth.'" Subjectivity is not abandoned, but untruth stands *at the beginning*. Later, Climacus reviews the ground covered: "It cannot be expressed more inwardly that subjectivity is truth than when subjectivity is *at first* [*Første*] untruth, and yet subjectivity is truth" (CUP 213; italics added).

Having wrought havoc with the poor existing person, Climacus proceeds to wreak havoc, as it were, with objective uncertainty and with the truth by returning to "the absurd":

> Let us now go further ["going further" is often ironic in Kierke-gaard's authorship—but not here]; let us assume that the eternal, essential truth is itself the paradox. . . . The eternal truth has come into existence in time. . . . When the paradox [clinging to objective uncertainty] itself is the paradox [the eternal in time, Incarnation], it thrusts away by virtue of the absurd, and the corresponding passion of inwardness is faith.   (CUP 209)

Regardless of where we were before, we are now in the domain of the decisively Christian. Here we have the paradox *sensu eminenti-ori* and faith *sensu eminentiori*[18]—and hindrance to fanaticism *sensu eminentiori*. Human beings are broken backward in sin; God is broken forward in time. We are in "the extremity of existence" [*Existentsens Yderste*]: "Subjectvity culminates in passion, Christianity

---

[16]I want to suggest that one reason why "truth is subjectivity" causes so much difficulty is that different senses of "truth is subjectivity" —I call them "reduplica-tive," "constitutive," and "adjudicative" —are operative in the authorship, with "reduplicative" truth is subjectivity being the most encompassing.

[17]Remarkably, many fine studies of Kierkegaard content themselves with "truth is subjectivity" with no mention of "subjectivity is untruth."

[18]Climacus writes also of faith "*sensu strictissimo*" (CUP 210) and of "the paradox *sensu strictissimo*, the absolute paradox" (CUP 217).

is paradox; paradox and passion fit each other perfectly, and paradox perfectly fits a person situated in the extremity of existence" (CUP 230). Climacus fulfills his resolve made that Sunday afternoon at the café — Restaurant Josty — in Frederiksberg Gardens "to make something more difficult"[19] (CUP 186):

> But without risk, no faith, not even the Socratic faith, to say nothing of the kind we are discussing here [Christian faith]. . . . Instead of the objective uncertainty, there is here the certainty that, viewed objectively, it is the absurd, and this absurdity, held fast in the passion of inwardness, is faith. . . .
>
> What, then, is the absurd? The absurd is that the eternal truth has come into existence in time . . . the absurd is the dynamometer of faith in inwardness [*Troens Kraftmaaler i Inderlighed*].
>
> (CUP 210-211; SKS 7, 193)

Climacus refers to his goal "to get the absurd clear" (CUP 212), indicating that this is an absurd which one can "get clear" — that it is the absurd, which, again, is not clearly nonsense; for "it is indeed *just possible* [*jo dog muligt*] that Christianity is the truth" (CUP 234; italics added).

So much more is here. Kierkegaard still matters because of this "more," including the lovely, haunting passage on "the garden of the dead" with its "audible soundlessness of the dew" and "semi-transparency of the nocturnal mist" (CUP 235): the old man and the child at the new grave of the man's son, the boy's father, a dramatic-poetic rendering of the dialectic we have considered (CUP 235-39). "I owe it to the truth to confess that this was the most heart-rending scene I have ever witnessed," avows Climacus (CUP 238). But Climacus does not rush forward to express his pathos directly: "But pathos in the form of contrast is inwardness; it remains with the communicator even when expressed, and it cannot be appropriated directly except through the other's *self*-activity, and the contrastive form is the dynamometer of inwardness" (CUP 242). "The other's *self*-activity" involves "respect for the learner" (CUP 242).

The topic is now communication. Parallels emerge between Climacus's reflections on communication and God's form of communication. Indirect communication is the issue: "Oddly

---

[19]See CUP 213, 241.

enough, although there is so much clamoring for the positive and for the direct communication of results, it does not occur to anyone to complain about God . . . " (CUP 243). Climacus recognizes reason for protest against God. Why does not God communicate more directly, reveal Godself more clearly?

Nature is certainly the work of God, but only the work is directly present, not God. With regard to the individual human being, is this not acting like an illusive [*svigefuld*] author [such as Climacus?], who nowhere sets forth his result in block letters or provides it before-hand in a preface? And why is God illusive [*svigefuld*]? Precisely because he is truth and in being illusive [*det*] seeks to keep a person from untruth. (CUP 243-44)[20]

What is this "untruth"? It is a direct relationship which does not allow room for the truth as "the self-activity of appropriation, which a result hinders" (CUP 242):

> Consequently, the form had to be indirect. . . . Inwardness cannot be communicated directly, because expressing it directly is externality . . . the tension of the contrastive form is the dynamome-ter of inwardness . . . there is inwardness when what is said belongs to the recipient as if it were his own—and now it is indeed his own. To communicate in that way is the most beautiful triumph of resigned inwardness [*den resignerede Inderligheds skjønneste Tri-umph*]. Therefore no one is as resigned as God, because he commu-nicates creatively in such a way that in creating he *gives* independ-ence vis-à-vis himself.   (CUP 260; SKS, 7, 236)

Divine resignation: God withdraws or otherwise allows room for poor existing persons to lean forward, to venture forth, to explore existence, to become, to deepen, to expand in inwardness.

In a wonderful image:

> If God had taken the form, for example, of a rare, enormously large green bird, with a red beak, that perched in a tree on the embank-ment [*Volden*, the rampart as in Kierkegaard's Copenhagen] and

---

[20]This passage is central to my reading of Kierkegaard, and I have long wrestled with the translation of *svigefuld*. Swenson-Lowrie translate "elusive," which seems to point in the appropriate direction but is not an appropriate translation. My best attempt is "deceptive": "And why is God deceptive?" ("Og hvorfor eer Gud svigefuld?" [SKS, 7, 221]).

perhaps even whistled in an unprecedented manner—then our
partygoing man would surely have had his eyes opened.

(CUP 245)

God is deceptive in order to avoid deception:[21]

> The observer does not glide directly to the result but on his own
> must concern himself with finding it and thereby break [bryde] the
> direct relation. But this break [Brud] is the actual breakthrough
> [Gjennembrud] of inwardness, an act of self-activity, the first
> designation of truth as inwardness.   (CUP 244; SKS, 7, 221-22)

The contemporary Irish poet Micheal O'Siadhail reflects upon
"[t]he necessary absconding of the sacred."[22] Climacus offers insight
into the absconding—if not "necessary" then gracious, loving—of
God. Is "absconding" a possible rendering of "svigefuld"?

* * *

Why Kierkegaard still matters? Kierkegaard declares and
explains why "in faith there is always fear and trembling" (PV, 141).
"Without risk, no faith": hindrance to fanaticism. This is one cut—
any number of others could be chosen (those eight paths out of the
Nook)—into the gold veins that are Kierkegaard.

Kierkegaard still matters because we do not outgrow the
fundamental matters of human existence—"no generation has
learned to love from another." We may not have to "reinvent the
wheel," the wheel of rolls; but we poor existing persons do need to
reinvest in the wheel of roles, be it fortune or fire, fortune and fire:
"Fortune, good-night! Smile once more; turn thy wheel!" (Shakespeare, King Lear II.ii.180; Kent in stocks). And Lear, awakened, to
Cordelia,

---

   [21]What Kierkegaard writes of "deception" is relevant: "But a deception, that is
indeed something rather ugly. To that I would answer: Do not be deceived by the
word deception. One can deceive a person out of what is true, and—to recall old
Socrates—one can deceive a person into what is true" (PV, 53). The word translated
"deception" here is Bedrag.
   [22]Micheal O'Siadhail, "Crosslight," Essentials of Christian Community, ed. David
F. Ford and Dennis L. Stamps (Edinburgh: T.&T. Clark, 1996) 56.

"You do me wrong to take me out o' th' grave.
Thou art a soul in bliss; but I am bound
Upon a wheel of fire, that mine own tears
Do scald like molten lead."   (*King Lear* IV.vii.45-48)

The wheel of *Lear*. The wheel of life — existence. The wheel of Kierke-gaard, with a possible, daring leap to weal.

"The gleam of an indication" — adventures of the text: Kierke-gaard still matters because he knows how to write.

4

Why Kierkegaard Still Matters

George Connell

While much is elusive and ambiguous in Kierkegaard's authorship, at least one theme comes through clearly and persistently: self-justification is self-defeating. Johannes Climacus quotes with approval the aphorism, *"Qui s'excuse, qui s'accuse,"* calling into question the project of Christian apologetics (CUP 1:529). Anti-Climacus is more blunt, terming any such apologist "Judas No. 2" and stating, "To defend something is always to disparage it" (SUD 87). In the same vein, Judge William admits that his defense of marriage is a dubious undertaking: "Indeed, rather than earning me the gratitude of actual or prospective husbands, it would probably make me suspect, for he who champions accuses" (EO 2:6).

Given such Kierkegaardian doubts about self-justification, one takes up with trepidation the question of why Kierkegaard matters. For those of us who have learned a minor European language, spent years reading and rereading a remarkably ambiguous and demanding body of writings, made pilgrimages to Copenhagen and Northfield to gather with similarly obsessed colleagues, and even contributed to (much less edited!) a twenty-four-volume collection of articles about this peculiar, melancholic, and unclassifiable figure, such a statement of why Kierkegaard matters could take on a self-defensive tone, one that could confirm the suspicions of colleagues, deans, and family members about how we have been spending our time.

To make matters worse, Kierkegaard preemptively blocks our professorial assertions that he matters. He avoided taking on the socially authoritative roles of priest or professor, choosing rather to play the part first of an irresponsible dandy and later of a derided social outcast and immoderate critic. In many of his writings, he disappears behind a variety of outlandishly named pseudonyms who write oddly titled and unconventionally formed texts. And he grimly predicted that, no matter how often he ridiculed them, the private docents would descend upon his literary remains when he had left the scene. Anyone who gathers himself or herself to make a grand statement about why Kierkegaard matters ought to recall the disclaimer with which the self-described loafer, Johannes Climacus, opens *Philosophical Fragments*:

> What is offered here is only a pamphlet, *proprio Marte, propriis auspiciis, proprio stipendio* [by one's own hand, on one's own behalf, at one's own expense], without any claim to being a part of the scientific-scholarly endeavor in which one acquires legitimacy as a thoroughfare or transition, as concluding, introducing, or partici- pating, as a coworker or as a volunteer attendant, as a hero or at any rate as a relative hero, or at least as an absolute trumpeter. It is merely a pamphlet even if I, like Holberg's *magister*, were *volente Deo* [God willing], to continue it with seventeen others. (PF 5)[1]

And yet, alongside such comic self-effacement, such insistence that we not fall prey to the illusion that Kierkegaard or his pseud- onyms or their texts matter, we find many other passages that are full of urgency, that implore us to grasp the gravity of the matter at hand, that break with the diffidence of most philosophical writing in order to convey Kierkegaard's sense that what he is discussing could not possibly matter more, that, in Pascal's terms, the stakes are infinitely great. Anti-Climacus, the pseudonymous author of *The Sickness Unto Death*, writes:

> There is so much talk about human distress and wretchedness—I try to understand it and have also had some intimate acquaintance with it—there is so much talk about wasting a life, but only that person's life was wasted who went on living so deceived by life's joy or its sorrows that he never became decisively and eternally conscious as spirit, as self, or, what amounts to the same thing, never became aware and in the deepest sense never gained the impression that there is a God and that "he," he himself, his self, exists before this God. . . . What wretchedness that so many go on living in this way, cheated of the most blessed of thoughts! . . . I think that I could weep an eternity over the existence of such wretchedness. (SUD 26-27)

---

[1]Compare the similar disavowal by Johannes de Silentio in the introduction to *Fear and Trembling* (FT 7-8).

While both of these passages are by pseudonyms, they each reflect deep and important aspects of their creator. The challenge, then, in speaking appropriately to the question of why Kierkegaard matters is to find a way to hold together his comic self-effacement — his insistence that he and his writings do not matter — with his pathos-filled urgency — his sense of himself as divinely commissioned to recall his readers to what does matter: their existence as selves before God. As it happens, Kierkegaard, through his pseudonym, Johannes Climacus, addresses precisely this dialectical tension:

> That a subjective existing thinker is just as positive as negative can also be expressed by saying that he has just as much of the comic as of pathos. According to the way people exist ordinarily, pathos and the comic are apportioned in such a way that one has the one, another the other, one a little more of the one, another a little less. But for the person existing in double-reflection, the proportion is this: just as much of pathos, just as much of the comic. (CUP 1:87)

It is no doubt paradoxical to speak to the significance of a massive authorship by reflecting on a single short passage, but, in keeping with Kierkegaard's fondness for paradox and his own practice of focusing on short bits of text, I propose to do just that. In what follows, I will suggest three ways in which the above passage points us toward an appropriately dialectical sense of how and why Kierkegaard matters.

1. Kierkegaard matters because he is Socratic

It is difficult to read very far in Kierkegaard's writings, whether published or journal, whether pseudonymous or not, whether early or late, without coming across a reminder of how large Socrates looms in Kierkegaard's thought. While the passage I've singled out does not mention Socrates explicitly, one hears in it an unmistakable echo of the final scene of Plato's *Symposium*. With cocks crowing the new day and the last symposiasts, Agathon (a tragic poet) and Aristophanes (a comic poet) fading fast, Socrates presses his argument that "authors should be able to write both comedy and tragedy: the skillful tragic dramatist should also be a comic poet" (223D).

By echoing this passage in his description of the subjective thinker as combining comedy and pathos, Climacus indicates implicitly what he often states explicitly: Socrates is his model for the subjective thinker. Through his discussions of Socrates and even more emphatically by finding his own ways to think and write socratically, Kierkegaard retrieves Socrates from an effective oblivion (or perhaps better, ostracism) to which the philosophical establishment conveniently consigns him. It isn't that Socrates is simply and totally forgotten or banished. He continues to serve a useful a figurehead as the honored originator of and martyr for the enterprise of philosophy. But philosophers have a way of depriving the gadfly of his sting. For example, Leibniz depicts him as a continental rationalist *avant la lettre*, while Berkeley invokes him against materialism and atheism.[2] In these and other cases, Socrates serves simply to validate whatever philosophical position has need of him. Kierkegaard matters not least because he, along with other iconoclastic thinkers such as Hamann and Nietzsche, make Socrates himself a pressing philosophical question, struggling to recover what it was about Socrates that led Alcibiades to describe him as "bizarre" (221D).

But what does Socrates mean for Kierkegaard? After all, as Kierkegaard himself notes, his various depictions of Socrates are mutually incompatible. In *The Concept of Irony*, Kierkegaard presents Socrates as a purely negative figure. In contrast, in *Philosophical Fragments*, Johannes Climacus gives us a Socrates who is a symbol of inner riches, of immanent god-relationship. Then, in *Concluding Unscientific Postscript*, the same Climacus backs away from his earlier depiction of Socrates as "dubious," even while critiquing "Magister Kierkegaard" for his one-sided portrayal of Socrates (CUP 1:206-207n.). During Kierkegaard's unpleasantness with the *Corsair* and his confrontation with the established church, Socrates' oppositional stance to his own society comes to play a larger role in Kierkegaard's depictions of him.

---

[2]Leibniz, *Monadology*, §26; Berkeley, *Siris*, §331. It is interesting to note that Leibniz makes no effort to distinguish Socrates from Plato. He speaks of *Plato* leading a boy through short steps to difficult geometrical truths. Such a failure to distinguish Socrates from Plato is surely the most common way of effectively erasing Socrates from the philosophical tradition.

This is hardly the place to sort out Kierkegaard's evolving and complex understandings of Socrates, but it is clear that Socrates continually matters to Kierkegaard because of at least two key themes: existential appropriation and communicative humility.

(a) *Existential appropriation.* While some features of his portrayal of Socrates vary, Kierkegaard's Socrates is always the thinker who reduplicates his thought in his life. "The thesis that subjectivity, inwardness, is truth contains the Socratic wisdom, the undying merit of which is to have paid attention to the essential meaning of existing, of the knower's being an existing person" (CUP 1:204). As philosophy moved relentlessly in the nineteenth century into the age of the professor, Socrates represented for Kierkegaard the antiprofessor, the antithesis of the credentialed professionals, the intellectual salary men, the spokespersons for the ideal who live conveniently bourgeois lives, the utterly unironic producers of "easily understood surveys and brief publications about everything worth knowing and . . . true benefactors of the age who by virtue of thought systematically make spiritual existence easier and easier and yet more and more meaningful" (CUP 1:186). Kierkegaard could never make peace with philosophy's institutionalization within the university, but a great many of us writing the essays in this volume have. To be honest, many of us (myself included) fit more comfortably into the academy than we could imagine ourselves fitting into any other contemporary workplace. And that is precisely why it is so important to let Kierkegaard disturb our comfort, to allow him to hold the figure of Socrates before us as an ongoing challenge, to remind us that philosophy through much of its history has been a demanding way of life rather than a department on the humanities end of the college quad.

(b) *Communicative humility.* As Kierkegaard sees it, Socrates' focus on appropriation mandates his indirect manner of communication.

> Wherever the subjective is of importance in knowledge and appropriation is therefore the main point, communication is a work of art; it is doubly reflected, and its first form is the subtlety that the subjective individuals must be held devoutly apart from one another and must not run coaguatingly together in objectivity.
>
> (CUP 1:79)

Another way to put this is that one human being can never have essential importance for another:

> Between one human being and another, this is the highest: that the pupil is the occasion for the teacher to understand himself; the teacher is the occasion for the pupil to understand himself; in death the teacher leaves no claim upon the pupil's soul, no more than the pupil can claim that the teacher owes him something.   (PF, 24)

For Kierkegaard, no one better understood this point or better appropriated this understanding in his interactions with others than Socrates. And so, for Kierkegaard, Socrates matters because Socrates understood that he does not matter. The simple wise man of ancient Athens understood that while *what* he discusses — virtue and living a virtuous life — matters infinitely, he himself as the occasion of those discussions cannot and should not matter. And so, when Kierkegaard uses his elaborate pseudonymous ruses and other devices of authorial evasion to block our "socializing soulfully" (PF, 24) with him, he reminds us that he matters as an author and thinker preeminently because he always remembered that, like Socrates, he did not matter, that his subject matter — living as an existing human being before God — not he, himself, is what matters.

2. Kierkegaard matters because he is Platonic

If Climacus's description of the subjective thinker as combining pathos and comedy echoes Socrates, it *eo ipso* also echoes Plato. For the Socrates echoed by Climacus is the Socrates of the *Symposium*, a dialog Kierkegaard and others see as a work of Plato's philosophical creativity rather than as a reflection of the historic Socrates. Nonetheless, to say that Kierkegaard matters because he is Platonic is certain to give rise to far more perplexity, consternation, and offense than to describe him as Socratic. The precise character of these negative reactions would, however, vary considerably according to the listener, for the name, "Plato," means such a variety of things. As Saussure notes, a sign only signifies by virtue of its differentiation from other signs. And so, "Plato" means different things in different contexts depending on what is paired with it as an antithesis. For Tertullian, "Plato" epitomizes Athens as contrasted with Jerusalem, while for Karl Popper, "Plato" stands for opposition to open societies.[3] In *The Concept of Irony*, Kierkegaard sets Plato against Socrates as a way to contrast speculative forgetfulness of our temporal condition with a constant mindfulness of and existential reflection on the limits and negativity of that condition. John Caputo, in turn, sets Kierkegaard as a "friend of the flux" over against Plato, who represents the paradigmatic metaphysical equation of the real and the unchanging.[4] In none of these oppositions is Kierkegaard plausibly labeled as Platonic. And he is emphatically not Platonic when "Plato" is defined in terms of the conflict with Homer for the soul of Greece, the perennial battle between philosophy and poetry. But, ironically, when the name Plato gets its meaning through opposition to his student Aristotle it stands not for the exclusion of the poets from the city but the expression of philosophical ideas in literary form rather than in nonliterary prose. In describing Kierkegaard as "a kind of poet" and affirming that, "whatever philosophy or theology is in Kierkegaard is sacramentally transmitted 'in, with, and under' the poetry," Louis Mackey specifically links Kierkegaard to Plato:

> Philosophy is not only dialectic, producing conviction. It is also rhetoric, aimed at persuading. All actual philosophical discourse is addressed, not to a putative pure rational "anyone," but to a particular "someone" in a particular context. It takes account, as pure dialectic would not, of the diversity of persons and situations: witness Socrates in the dialogues of Plato. Moreover, in order to effect persuasion and conviction, philosophical discourse must first produce understanding, in the sense of imaginative and affective comprehension. This is its poetic aspect. Witness again Plato.[5]

When I say that Kierkegaard matters because he is Platonic, I follow Mackey in highlighting the seamless connection between what Kierkegaard says and how he says it, in affirming that "the literary techniques of Kierkegaard cannot be interpreted as devices

---

[3]Tertullian, *On Prescription against Heretics*, chap. 7; Karl Popper, *The Open Society and Its Enemies*, vol. 1: *The Spell of Plato*, 5th rev. ed. (Princeton NJ: Princeton University Press, 1971).

[4]John Caputo, *Radical Hermeneutics* (Bloomington: Indiana University Press, 1989) 59.

[5]Louis Mackey, *Kierkegaard: A Kind of Poet* (Philadelphia: University of Pennsylvania Press, 1971) xii.

for the expression of a content independently intelligible."[6] Some such acknowledgement of the essential literary dimension of Kierkegaard's work is now widely accepted, in no small measure because of Mackey's important work. While many of us cannot follow Mackey's subsequent radicalization of this acknowledgement in *Points of View* where he asserts that "Kierkegaard's writings are absolutely antiphilosophical and resolutely antitheological,"[7] we must acknowledge the significance of his 1971 publication of *Kierkegaard: A Kind of Poet*. Martha Nussbaum, who was then in graduate school, writes vividly of the resistance she encountered to the very idea that literature was philosophically significant. This was no accidental oversight. Rather, a resolutely nonliterary prose style was integral to the discipline's self-understanding at that time. Nussbaum describes the

> conventional style of Anglo-American philosophical prose" that then prevailed: "a style correct, scientific, abstract, hygienically pallid, a style that seemed to be regarded as a kind of all-purpose solvent in which philosophical issues of any kind at all could be efficiently disentangled, any and all conclusions neatly disengaged.[8]

For those of us beginning our studies during the Analytic Captivity of Philosophy, Kierkegaard mattered intensely because both the what and the how of his writings bespoke an entirely different understanding of philosophy than the one then prevailing. The geometrical covers of the old Princeton translations in all the colors of a box of crayons were icons of a broader, richer, deeper philosophical inquiry than was officially sanctioned. Mackey's reading of Kierkegaard as "a kind of poet" challenged the philosophical orthodoxy directly not just by pointing to Plato as precedent for Kierkegaard's practice but also by claiming that Kierkegaard recovers our authentic philosophical legacy: "In the work of Kierkegaard the dialectic and the rhetoric are united in the service of

---

[6]Mackey, *Kierkegaard: A Kind of Poet*, 259.
[7]Mackey, *Points of View*, xviii.
[8]Martha Nussbaum, *Love's Knowledge* (Oxford UK: Oxford University Press, 1992) 18.

poetry, as I believe they are in the major philosophical tradition of the West."[9]

While the Kierkegaard community is generally a pretty congenial crew, coming to terms with this literary dimension of his thought has generated unusual acrimony. Mackey himself spoke disparagingly of "a group of writers—mostly young, mostly philosophers—determined (as I think they might put it) to 'take Kierkegaard seriously as a philosopher,' " by extracting "doctrines" from his texts.[10] Some of these writers, in turn, have accused Mackey and his fellow travelers of trying to be "trendy" and of falling prey to the very absolutized irony of the late German romantics that Kierkegaard warned against in his dissertation.[11] Kierkegaard's authorial elusiveness and the puzzle-like quality of many of his writings will leave each of us on the hook as to how best to read him. But as we struggle with the question of how to take account of the literary character of his authorship, we can take some guidance from the passage I have highlighted on the simultaneous pathos and comedy of the existing subjective thinker.

First, what Climacus says about the existing subjective thinker is fully as true of Kierkegaard as author: his writings both sound the depths of tragic anguish and scale the heights of hilarity, often within a remarkably short compass. At the very threshold of Kierkegaard's pseudonymous authorship, we find the Diapsalmata, which opens with a passage on artists' suffering and ends with a gift of divine laughter. Johannes Climacus, in turn, gives two utterly contrasting accounts of his decision to become an author: first, a thoroughly comic account of how he decided while smoking a cigar in the Fredricksberg Gardens to create difficulties everywhere as his way of serving a society all too much at ease; second, a poignant account of overhearing a graveside lament by a grandfather over his deceased son's spiritual deception by speculative philosophy (CUP 1:185-88; CUP 1:234-40). One could multiply examples endlessly.

The point is that Kierkegaard's writings encompass a remarkable emotional range and continuously juxtapose strikingly contrasting

---

[9]Mackey, *Kierkegaard: A Kind of Poet*, xii.

[10]Mackey, *Points of View*, xii.

[11]See, e.g., C. Stephen Evans, *Kierkegaard's Ethic of Love: Divine Commands and Moral Obligations* (Oxford UK: Oxford University Press, 2006) 35.

states of mind. It is hard to imagine how he could have achieved this within the strictures of conventional philosophical prose. Most such texts are emotionally distant and relatively monochromatic. Martha Nussbaum, who has paid particular attention to the question of philosophical style, thinks that philosophical writing would not be so colorless if philosophers recovered a sense of themselves as addressing nonexpert readers on matters of urgent concern, but she also argues that "certain truths about human life can only be fittingly and accurately stated in the language and forms characteristic of the narrative artist."[12] Kierkegaard's understanding of human existence as simultaneously tragic and comic is one such truth. Only by drawing on elements of character, which involves distinctive history, perspective, and interest, of situation, of plot, with its elements of reversal and fulfillment, could Kierkegaard have captured as he does, the conflicted, juxtaposed character of human existence. Just as his favorite playwright, Shakespeare, mattered to Kierkegaard because he was a master of both comedy and tragedy and kept the two in constant contact, so Kierkegaard matters to us as a philosopher who marshals the full resources of literary expression in order to do justice to the complex realities of human life.

Second, by employing terminology, pathos, and comedy, with strong literary associations, Kierkegaard fundamentally reshapes the way some key issues are framed. Consider specifically the problem of evil. The standard philosophical framing of the issue makes it an issue of consistency: Can the existence of suffering be reconciled with belief in an all-powerful and benevolent God? This traditional theodicy problem has no place in Kierkegaard's writings. Rather, he frames the issue in terms of significance: Is our suffering ultimately pointless, as A suspects, or can it be incorporated into a larger structure of meaning that transfigures it? For Judge William, this larger structure is the life of ethical commitment, for Kierkegaard's humorists, suffering is revoked from a perspective *sub specie aeternitatis*, but for Kierkegaard, himself, when he writes as a Christian, suffering becomes the locus of communion with Christ and is transformed into joy as the water at Cana becomes wine (UDVS 233). Since each of these ways of making sense of suffering

---

[12]Nussbaum, *Love's Knowledge*, 5.

corresponds to a distinctive mode of discourse, they underline Nussbaum's point that "Literary form is not separable from philosophical content, but is, itself, a part of the content — an integral part, then, of the search for the statement of truth.[13]

Third, my highlighted passage points a way to reconciling conflicts in the Kierkegaard community over how appropriately to acknowledge the literary form of Kierkegaard's writings. Steve Evans, after noting criticisms of "straight" readings of Kierkegaard as a philosopher, quotes Climacus as saying, "Therefore, it is just as questionable, precisely just as questionable, to be pathos-filled and earnest in the wrong place as it is to laugh in the wrong place."[14] This passage, which parallels the passage on which I am focusing, suggests a nuanced approach to reading Kierkegaard, one which listens for substantive proposals on questions of enduring philosophical interest even while remaining ever-mindful of the Kierkegaard's Chesire Cat elusiveness. Once again, we face a paradox: Kierkegaard matters both because he puts forward substantive philosophical and religious ideas and because he never lets us accept those ideas on his authority, ever disappearing from our grasp.

3. Kierkegaard matters because he is Lutheran

Beyond any question, many of us who think Kierkegaard still matters do so because he insistently and unapologetically engages religious dimensions of human existence, even as philosophy increasingly closed itself off within the immanence of a developing secular age. There are a variety of ways in which we can name Kierkegaard's engagement with matters of ultimate import. Speaking, as I just did, of "religious dimensions" is the most diffuse way of placing his concerns and contributions. Such an encompassing term is useful in speaking of Kierkegaard's attention to multiple forms of spiritually informed existence and in drawing comparisons between Kierkegaard and nontheistic religious thinkers.[15] But for Kierkegaard, the divine is always ultimately a Thou, and so we can

---

[13]Nussbaum, *Love's Knowledge*, 3.

[14]Evans, *Kierkegaard's Ethic of Love*, 35-6.

[15]See, e.g., my essay, "Kierkegaard and Confucius: The Religious Dimensions of Ethical Selfhood," *Dao: A Journal of Comparative Philosophy* 8/2 (June 2009): 133-49.

more specifically place him as a theist. That theism, even in his intentionally nonspecific *Upbuilding Discourses*, is recognizably a theism shaped by Christian, or better, Protestant Christian sensibilities and traditions. Carrying this movement from general to more specific characterizations of Kierkegaard as a religious thinker to its conclusion, I want to claim Kierkegaard as a Lutheran thinker and to say that many features of his thought that still make him significant, philosophically as well as religiously, are best understood in terms of his own distinct if contested Lutheran identity.

Claiming Kierkegaard as a Lutheran is admittedly dubious given his denunciation of the Danish Lutheran Church, his refusal of a final communion from one of its priests, and his increasingly strident criticisms of Luther in the final years of his life. But Kierkegaard was deeply formed by the Lutheran character of his upbringing, his education, his religious participation, and (dare I say it) his Danish cultural setting. In ways beyond what he could probably see himself, Kierkegaard is Lutheran.

A listing of parallels between the two could quickly become rather long: both called for a return to New Testament Christianity out of a degraded cultural Christianity; both saw this degradation of Christianity as serving the self-interest of powerful social groups; both were deeply suspicious of the project of natural theology because of their shared sense that God's good news is "What no eye has seen, nor ear heard, nor the human heart conceived" (1 Cor. 2:9 NRSV) and thus must be revealed; both understand human reason to be deeply compromised by sin; both are theologians of the cross, identifying suffering as the particular locus for encounter with and knowledge of God; and both arguably contributed to secularization by their strong internal criticisms of religion.[16] All of these parallels deserve and many have received sustained evaluation, but here I want to mention briefly several ways in which Kierkegaard's Lutheran identity profoundly shapes his philosophical practice.

---

[16]For a very helpful discussion of "the noetic effects of sin" in Luther and Kierkegaard, see Merold Westphal, *Kierkegaard's Critique of Reason and Society* (University Park: Pennsylvania State University Press, 1991) 105-25. The International Kierkegaard Commentary contains a number of extremely helpful discussions of Luther and Kierkegaard, of which I would especially highlight essays by Lee Barrett and Craig Hinkson.

The issue of the relation between religious faith and philosophical inquiry is both perennial and contested, and this issue becomes, if anything, more contentious when there is an attempt to link philosophical practice to a specific theological tradition (as in the case of Reformed Epistemology). I submit that Kierkegaard's philosophical practice is usefully seen as Lutheran in several regards not by virtue of making particular confessional affirmations but rather in its manner and tone, its distinctive ways of approaching and considering philosophical questions.

First, like Luther, Kierkegaard is occasional and polemical rather than systematic and theoretical. Luther's writings are overwhelmingly set in particular contexts, often polemical contexts. They do not strike the anyone/anywhere/anywhen stance of purely theoretical philosophy and theology. Similarly, and as a number of scholars — notably Bruce Kirmmse, Alastair Hannay, and Jon Stewart — have helped us understand, Kierkegaard composed his authorship in intense, often polemical, dialog with his specific time and place.

Second, like Luther, Kierkegaard often takes his point of departure from specific biblical texts. Since it began to arise in the eighteenth century as a subdiscipline in the field of philosophy, philosophy of religion has been marked by a studied avoidance of specific biblical texts. William Rowe speaks of the proper topic of philosophy of religion as "restricted standard theism," that is, the lowest common denominator beliefs shared by the three principal Western monotheisms.[17] To understand this focus on generic theism and the associated avoidance of specific reference to any particular scriptural text, it is useful to consider Hume's *Dialogues concerning Natural Religion*. It is hard to overstate how significant Hume's *Dialogues* are for English-language philosophy of religion. Just as students learn what philosophy is by reading Plato's dialogs, philosophers of religion look to Hume's *Dialogues* as their paradigm. And, though he fills the *Dialogues* with quotations, both ancient and modern, Hume never cites a single biblical text. This exclusion has come to be the norm in philosophy of religion, arguably perpetuating a deist conceptualization of religion long after deism proper has

---

[17]William L. Rowe, *William Rowe on Philosophy of Religion: Selected Writings*, ed. Nick Trakakis (Farnham, Surrey UK: Ashgate, 2007) 81.

faded from the scene.[18] Kierkegaard's philosophical practice never fit this paradigm (a fact that goes some distance toward explaining the diffidence with which many philosophers of religion have treated his works). Rather, Kierkegaard frequently uses biblical texts as his point of departure for philosophical reflections. The classic example of this is, of course, *Fear and Trembling*, which approaches the relation of ethics and religion by focusing on the troubling text of Genesis 22 in which God commands Abraham to sacrifice Isaac. Such a biblical focus is pervasive in Kierkegaard and represents an important way in which he follows in the footsteps of Luther.[19]

For a third way in which Kierkegaard can be seen as a profoundly Lutheran thinker, I will return to the passage selected as the focus of these meditations, Johannes Climacus's insistence that the subjective thinker has "just as much of the comic as of pathos" (CUP 1:87). Considered formally, this assertion represents that most characteristically Kierkegaardian trope: the paradox. For Kierkegaard, life as a whole is paradoxical, shot through with irresolvable dialectical tensions. Further, into this conflictual existential scene, God introduces the Absolute Paradox: the God in time, the highest taking the form of the lowest; the mightiest, the weakest; the richest, the poorest.[20] Kierkegaard's comfort with and attraction to paradox powerfully manifests his deep Lutheran identity. At the center of the Lutheran theological vision is the principle, *simul justus et peccator*, the affirmation that we are at one and the same time sinners and redeemed. Other closely associated paradoxes follow this central paradox: we are at one and the same time participants in two different kingdoms, the Kingdom of God and the kingdom of this world; we are at one and the same time perfectly free lords of all, subject to none, and perfectly dutiful servants of all, subject to all.[21] And, finally, for both Luther and Kierkegaard, the central paradox

---

[18]See Peter Byrne, *Natural Religion and the Nature of Religion: the Legacy of Deism* (London: Routledge, 1989).

[19]See Timothy H. Polk, *The Biblical Kierkegaard: Reading by the Rule of Faith* (Macon GA: Mercer University Press, 1997).

[20]See Sylvia Walsh, *Living Christianly: Kierkegaard's Dialectic of Christian Existence* (University Park: Pennsylvania State University Press, 2005).

[21]Martin Luther, *The Freedom of a Christian*, trans. W. A. Lambert, in *Three Treatises* (Philadelphia: Fortress, 1970) 277.

is that in the gruesome death of Christ, the ultimate manifestation of the tragic, we also find the ultimate revelation of God's love and saving action. Given that comedy has been defined as achieving transcendence over tragedy, we can read Climacus's assertion that the subjective thinker has just as much of the comic as of pathos as a version of the paradoxical vision Luther expresses graphically in his seal: the black cross in the red heart symbolizing Christ's suffering is superimposed on a white rose against a blue field symbolizing hope and joy.[22]

4. Conclusion.

As I acknowledged at the start of these reflections, it is more than a little perverse to address the large question of why Kierkegaard still matters by focusing on a single short passage from a large book in the midst of an even larger authorship. That confession made, I offer these reflections as tokens of my sense of the profound overdetermi-

---

[22]In 1530, Luther wrote the following explanation of his seal in a letter to Lazarus Spengler, "Grace and peace from the Lord. As you desire to know whether my painted seal, which you sent to me, has hit the mark, I shall answer most amiably and tell you my original thoughts and reason about why my seal is a symbol of my theology. The first should be a black cross in a heart, which retains its natural color, so that I myself would be reminded that faith in the Crucified saves us. 'For one who believes from the heart will be justified' (Rom. 10:10). Although it is indeed a black cross, which mortifies and which should also cause pain, it leaves the heart in its natural color. It does not corrupt nature, that is, it does not kill but keeps alive. 'The just shall live by faith' (Rom. 1:17) but by faith in the crucified. Such a heart should stand in the middle of a white rose, to show that faith gives joy, comfort, and peace. In other words, it places the believer into a white, joyous rose, for this faith does not give peace and joy like the world gives (John 14:27). That is why the rose should be white and not red, for white is the color of the spirits and the angels (cf. Matt. 28:3; John 20:12). Such a rose should stand in a sky-blue field, symbolizing that such joy in spirit and faith is a beginning of the heavenly future joy, which begins already, but is grasped in hope, not yet revealed. And around this field is a golden ring, symbolizing that such blessedness in Heaven lasts forever and has no end. Such blessedness is exquisite, beyond all joy and goods, just as gold is the most valuable, most precious and best metal. This is my *compendium theologiae* [summary of theology]. I have wanted to show it to you in good friendship, hoping for your appreciation. May Christ, our beloved Lord, be with your spirit until the life hereafter. Amen." *Luther's Works*, 55 vols., various translators (Minneapolis: Fortress Press, 1957–1986) CD-Rom edition (2001) 49:356-59.

nation of Kierkegaard's writings. As we read and reread these texts, they constantly open up new levels of significance and offer new challenges, both intellectual and existential. And that, to my mind, is why Kierkegaard still matters.

5

Accidental Devotion and Gratitude:
Kierkegaard in My Life-Story

John Davenport

I. Before Kierkegaard:
My Path from the Aesthetic to the Ethical

As a recent critic of claims made for the importance of narrative unity has said, rarely do we reflect on our life "as a whole." That's quite true; usually we do not need to. But here I will risk doing just that. My personal story has been bound up with Kierkegaard in surprising, perhaps even miraculous ways that I never expected and never planned — which itself is an accurate reflection of the limits of our autonomy. Since I never meant to become a "Kierkegaard scholar" (if that phrase isn't an oxymoron), I have once or twice asked myself whether there is something in my past that caused Kierkegaard's themes to resonate with me so personally, as they have for many others, but my answers to myself were brief and vague. Now that I really think about it, the story is strange; it includes amusing twists and perhaps something else — something I could only (at great risk) call "'destiny." To explain it at all, I must reveal some personal secrets, though I will endeavor not to embarrass anyone who knows me.

At the outset, it's worth admitting that my development does not exactly conform to Kierkegaard's three stages, at least at first glance, though maybe it does at a deeper level. (More on that later.) I began life as the eldest of three boys; we lived in lovely Lancaster, Pennsylvania, where my father worked in finance, and our lives were as typical of middle-class America in the 1970s as could be. Up to age ten, my sense of the world, my family, and myself were almost entirely in the kind of dreaming consciousness that is both innocence and ignorance according to Vigilius Haufniensis (CA 37). My only sense of the noble in life came from Captain Kirk of *Star Trek*, and the only hint of things to come was that once I had the temerity to protest to the minister at our Methodist church that what he had said about "sin" was unfair since *I* had certainly done nothing wrong. His reply was ominous: "Maybe not yet, but you will!" Although I resolved then in childish naivete never to commit a single offense, unfortunately he was right.

In April 1977, the bicentennial year, we moved to Britain; we lived about an hour west of London on a hilltop with a few other houses between two towns. That woke me up from the dream in which I was unaware of "spirit." The different mores and manners of the local British school were a shock, but I adjusted and made good friends in school and on my hilltop. But things turned for the worse in the fall when my parents enrolled me in a nearby private school with a great reputation, the Reading Blue Coat. Though many of the teachers did their best to counter it, the Blue Coat School was run on a system that emphasizes "manliness" understood as taking hard knocks and following a pecking order with prefects at the top — prefects who were given quite large powers over younger boys. This made too many students hateful, cruel, or cowardly and depressed by turns, largely because of the abuses by older students, and the generally adversarial environment that the school fostered. It affected everyone, not only the direct victims. One of my friends, who never seemed to have any problems — he was captain of the rugby team and the cricket team, best at everything, and among other admired positions — made a suicide attempt at age fifteen. A boy I'd known only as one of the most spiteful bullies on campus showed up at my house years later with an older Jehovah's Witness preaching redemption; he was recovering from a serious drug addiction and looked like a wreck.

The school's Nietzschian tone was set by a few of the leading staff and followed by most (not all) of the prefects. The atmosphere of the school inculcated the assumptions that one person's gain must always be another's loss, and that care for others equals weakness. In particular I remember the terrifying inhumanity of the headmaster, Mr. Sanders, who ignored bullying when he saw it, tended to blame and criticize the victims, and humiliate some of the weakest and most vulnerable boys during all school meetings. But he liked to lead long religious services at all school meetings, during which larger boys would frequently torment smaller boys in many ingenious and subtle ways, knowing that the latter could not protest without getting in big trouble for interrupting the solemnity of the occasion. When Sanders retired years later, he was ordained as an Anglican minister, despite my letter of protest to the Archbishop of Canterbury. Perhaps this explains why I've always shared some of Kierkegaard's doubts about organized religion.

Though I was not actually a direct victim of bullying, several of my friends were, and my reaction to that shocked me. Now comes the first confession. I found myself taking revenge, overtly and covertly, in ways I could never have imagined before. One especially annoying bully who was not as strong as he thought I flattened with a stroke that must have nearly broken his jaw; I knew he would not tell. When his friends attacked me in return, I was more stunned by the fact that he looked so seriously hurt, though I still took satisfaction in his pain. On another occasion, one of the cruelest repeat offenders found most of his clothes missing from his locker after gym class. But this time, his tears of anger and embarrassment as the others laughed surprised me: could I really be the author of this suffering? When another seriously injured himself by falling into a glass door during a game, I was again filled with vindictive pleasure — but then hardly recognized myself. How had I come to this? I alternated in this inconsistent way for some time, experiencing malice yet not fully identifying with it, being moved to act yet not knowing how to.

Things finally came to a head. One day, the kindly old man who taught us second-years both Religion and Music was several minutes late arriving for our instrument lessons. I still remember with vivid clarity the beautiful oak-paneled walls of the music room in the school's old main building, and the look of my friend trapped and crying under the grand piano as four other boys tried to poke and slap him with various instrument parts. Something that in my family we call the "anger gene" was activated, and I started locating a couple of heavy blunt objects I could use to crush their skulls. Thankfully though, something stopped me; something in me (or out of me, I do not know) said: leave now, for God's sake. I had a second to choose, and I followed this counsel: I walked out of the room, left my friend without aid, quite literally for fear that I would kill his tormentors. There was real Sartrean angst in this experience — a dread of my own freedom. I wandered the school until it was pickup time. Later, not knowing what to do about skipping class or how to explain the necessity, I forged a note to the teacher saying I had to leave early for a doctor's appointment. But I was never a good artist. This teacher, who had been friendly to me, was heartbroken to have to turn me in. I wish I could find both the teacher and friend to apologize, since I'm sure they never understood.[1] That was near the end of my second year, the equivalent of American sixth grade.

In fall of 1978, I was transferred to TASIS England, a relatively new international school with an American curriculum, run on a philosophy precisely the opposite of the Blue Coat's. The school had a diverse student body; although there were many children of American expatriates, there were also European students whose parents often have American connections, as well as many Islamic students from Middle Eastern nations. It was and still is a wonderful place, led by a generous and charismatic staff: though its facilities were still quite rough around the edges when I attended, the school taught students to care for each other and for the world around them. Justice was valued as a central virtue. I flourished there, again to my own surprise, though I still had some bad habits. And the contrast was stark in my mind: I had become aware of the difference between wrong treatment that corrupts and right treatment that brings out the best in people. The impression was indelible, and worth whatever I suffered.

Now this does not look much like the way that in *Either/Or* Kierkegaard's Judge William encourages the aesthetic young man *A* to enter "the ethical" orientation to life. *A*'s problems have more to do with fear of commitment and skepticism that anything is worth caring about. These problems are somewhat unusual, and distinguish *A* from the many who are "tricked" out of selfhood by the temptation to conform to a comfortable mass society or cozy life (SUD 34). A also pursues various desires for pleasure, but in a detached way; he is cynical about polite society and doubts that there is any point in its customs. But at bottom, he is just *selfish*, a shrewd society man who cares only for money and status, or a hedonist who pursues a party life. As the Judge says in his first

---

[1]There is more to this story involving the headmaster. No, it does not involve physical abuse, though I think it might have if I had not been an American student. The abuse was rather intensely psychological, but it is in the past, and I will leave it there.

letter, the sin of the "flesh" is not "the sensuous—it is the selfish" (EO 2:49). And the Judge tells *A* that his enjoyment is egotistical: "You never give of yourself, let others enjoy you" (EO 2:24).

   This was a danger I faced, since the environment at the Blue Coat was teaching me that it's "every man for himself." But the teachers I admired there were counterexamples who clearly cared about others for their own sake, and I recognized something right in my own indignation too, however misdirected its expressions. As the Judge's analysis predicts, this went hand in hand with a new kind of *self-awareness* or concern about my agency. In response to my experiences, I had started to "venture" myself and become "aware" of myself, as Anti-Climacus describes the Judge's virtual choice to become an ethically serious chooser (SUD 35). But I did this in a way that the Judge's analysis technically allows yet does not pursue in detail: I *hated*, I willed harm, and then discovered that this was terrible. I discovered myself *as* evil: I had a character constituted by my will, but it was a character formed in the image of the very malice I despised. Perhaps Levinas would say that I discovered in the face of the other that it was wrong to take pleasure in harming even one who has done wrong. But I could not articulate it that way at first: I had to learn to oppose the moral wrong in actions, prac- tices, and institutions, rather than despising the people who commit these wrongs. Of course I did not learn this from the basic exercise of my will in fighting back or leaving the room; from this experience, my conscience could only discover that something "spiritual" was at stake, and that I was messing up—that I clearly had little idea what I was doing in the spiritual world, or what kind of person I should be. Perhaps the capacity for that much conscience is innate; but the natural tendency at that point is to look for some clear conception of the ethical, some stark distinction between good and evil, to make sense of what is spiritually at stake. Most people will then seize on the ethics of their surrounding society.

   That was partly true for me, since I had started attending a youth group at our local Anglican church. But I had other sources for ethical understanding that Kierkegaard could not have anticipated — namely, the fantasy literature of C. S. Lewis and J. R. R. Tolkien. It's said that many a scholar of early British and Irish literature began by loving Tolkien's *Lord of the Rings*; I wonder how many fans of Kierkegaard also have some early inspiration in spiritual fantasy literature. Though Kierkegaard seems to have had little love for mythology, or at least Andersen's version of it, the genre revived or recreated by Tolkien excels in the kind of imaginative variation of psychological types that Climacus and other pseudonyms recommend as a way of understanding possible forms of the mind and will.[2] As I moved on to some of Lewis's essays for adults, and by age fifteen to the epic fantasy works of Stephen Donaldson, I began to formulate a metaphysics of good and evil, an explicit theoretical conception of right and wrong motives and their spiritual effects.

This is not the way that Kierkegaard's Judge expects a reformed aesthete to understand ethical obligations and ideals as he starts to live by them. But it definitely exhibited an extreme version of what many recent critics have taken to be the Judge's limitations and hubris: by age sixteen I really believed I understood good and evil in abstract, as absolute principles; I had seen through to the heart of things and understood the spiritual realities I had encountered in my first confusion as a boy of twelve. I knew what was right with certainty, and would tolerate no opposition. I do not blame this on Lewis, Tolkien, or Donaldson, whose work is full of nuance that I missed the first time round; the fault was mine for being too desperate to master the spiritual matters at stake in life into which I had so rapidly stumbled. I wanted to master them to avoid erring again. That was my "pact" with the ethical: in certainty never to be confused again, and to stand up for the right at all costs. In that way, I would oppose not one particular headmaster but the essence of the injustice he represented. There was something noble in this (I hope), despite my naive self-righteousness. I wonder how many a teenager has entered the ethical in this overly rigid way, taking assurance of their firm identity from the eternal in it just as the Judge said. What nobility there is in this state is found in its similarity to infinite passion; it is a genuine "concern" but it is not the same as "ventur[ing] wholly to become oneself, . . . this specific individual human being, before God" (SUD 5). For it conflates understanding the universal with acceptance of being a specific individual with concrete tasks.

---

[2]And Lewis and Tolkien may even have heard of Kierkegaard and some of his ideas in the 1940s from their friend, Charles Williams, who was involved in publishing the first English translations at Oxford University Press.

In this state, speculative theory was quite a temptation to me. I began reading philosophy in high school not with Socrates's ironic correctives, but instead with Bertrand Russell's quick summaries of great thinkers and Stephan Körner's systematic introduction to metaphysics and epistemology. The game of philosophy, it seemed to me, was a kind of systematic mastery of answers to the most fundamental questions—and this was thrilling, empowering. I imagine that the young Hegel must have felt something like this (though his talents and knowledge were far beyond mine at the same age). My feet stayed on the ground only because my interest in the world of theories opening to me was still motivated primarily by my hope to justify ethical standards and principles and thus advance 'my cause.' While my naive belief in the superiority of my own nascent theories only grew as I read Russell's (rather shallow) critiques of past philosophers, at least I did not quite succumb to the illusion that winning the contest of theories was equivalent to improving the real world. I cared enough about that to warm to Mill when I read him. Reading Willie Brandt's book on poverty through-out the global South also helped me here, but the main obstacle to my theory-spinning was learning about the Holocaust. Of course I had heard about it before; quite a few friends and family acquaintances in Britain had parents or grandparents who had lived through World War II, and had stories to tell. But when I really concentrated on the Holocaust—really took it in—the enormity was so overwhelming that I was at a near total loss. While the conception of radical evil and agapic virtue that I had already learned from spiritual fantasy applied all too well here, it was also obvious that the horror of the Holocaust transcended any formulaic understanding; next to this greatest of atrocities, the paucity of all theories was clear. There is a sense in which my philosophical ambitions never recovered from this shock.

I did not clearly realize this for many years, however.[3] At first, my response was twofold, partly philosophical and partly volitional. I focused more intensely on the problem of evil and various

---

[3]In fact, I think it was not until I saw the film *Sophie's Choice* after my undergraduate years that I realized how much I identified with the madness of Sophie's lover in his room full of photos and news clippings about the Shoah. His insanity seemed to me to be an appropriate response, though I needed a better one.

theodicies. The poor vicar of our local church, who had always encouraged me, put up with quite a bit in those days—for example, more than one youth group discussion meeting with me arguing for the inadequacy of various biblical explanations of evil, critiquing C. S. Lewis's theodicy and others. I had help from other adult leaders of the youth group as well, who really cared for the spiritual progress of us teenagers, and who occasionally and gently tried (in vain) to get me to see the dangers of pride and dogmatism in my sense of theoretical superiority. But worse, in Kierkegaard's terms, there was no real "faith" in my debates and exercises; although I considered myself a Christian, my interests were purely ethical—religious truth, suitably interpreted through the lens of a priori metaphysical knowledge, was to be a foundation for an objective ethics. Looking back, my state then appears almost to be a perfect caricature of the "ethical stage" without any personal (nonspeculative) sense of its limits in mystery and the transcendent. I only give myself this much credit, though, because underneath this theoretical questioning was a new conviction that global justice—a way of ensuring that there would be no more Holocausts—was worth dying for. I had not gone deep enough in opposing my will to the headmaster's. What I had suffered was nothing compared to the sufferings that result from tyranny around the world. The victims required something more from me than philosophical proofs; they required a firm devotion to justice, to do whatever could decently be done to ensure that tyranny would never rise again or succeed in doing so much harm.

Doubtless there was more than a dash of vainglory in this new commitment (if it was that). Doubtless I was as much taken with the thought of epic greatness as moved by pure ethical concern. The warnings against this trap in Kierkegaard's "Purity of Heart" discourse were entirely unanticipated in my thought. I began considering a career in politics, although I declared myself a Philosophy major as soon as I started college back in the United States. It took to the end of my freshman year for me to begin to comprehend how little I really knew about Philosophy, let alone other subjects. This was not like a bubble bursting, but rather like a giant balloon slowly deflating. For this, I have not only my freshman-year teachers, but also my college friends, and some others to thank.[4] Finally humbled a bit, I returned sophomore year to my first course on Existentialism.

II. Discovering Kierkegaard: Almost Everything Rearranged

In the fall of my second year of college, I encountered Kierkegaard along with Nietzsche, Heidegger, and Sartre in a large lecture course on Existentialism taught by George Schrader. The fact that Schrader focused on *Either/Or* rather than *Fear and Trembling* has doubtless been important for my subsequent path. His lectures on Kierkegaard were the best in the course; his explanation of the Judge's insights and shortcomings, and his critique of the aesthetic, were truly amazing. But for me, the idea that there was a "choice" between the aesthetic and ethical, *before* the choice between good and evil, was a fundamental challenge to the whole conception of ethics I had built up for myself in the previous five years. I had to come to grips with it and figure out whether it was correct or incorrect. Schrader and my TA directed me to MacIntyre's critiques and another commentary, but the more I considered *Either/Or*, the more convinced I was that a deep insight lay here — unfortunately, since that meant I had to rethink everything. The insight that could not be denied had to do with freedom and the importance of willing something worthwhile as opposed to neutrality, detachment, or a life of ironic disregard; I understood it on an implicit level based on my own experience. In other words, the Judge's insight rang true for me.

Although Schrader had more than a hundred students in this course, he met with some of us in office hours. I probably talked with him about Kierkegaard and his debts to Kant four times. In December, Schrader suggested *Fear and Trembling* for my holiday reading. I picked up the Princeton paperback with its notoriously poor binding before heading back to England. I finished reading it

---

[4]There was also a detailed letter from Cyrus Hamlin responding to a small treatise I'd sent him arguing for the superiority of New Testament ethics over various Old Testament teachings. In a few pages, he gently told me (without saying it outright) that I had no idea what I was talking about, that I was entirely ignorant of biblical scholarship. "Yours is a rather idiosyncratic view of biblical texts," he began. I've always treasured that letter.

on a family skiing trip over the winter break, and was even more shaken than before. I recognized immediately in the portrayal of Abraham the kind of eschatological turning point I'd seen in the work of Lewis, Tolkien, and Donaldson, but I could not put the puzzle pieces together. I spent many evening hours trying to make sense of it: how did the basic choice, ethical norms, and faith fit together?

Then something happened on the last evening of the trip, something I cannot easily describe. At the severe risk of sounding full of it, I'd have to say that a certain idea about the relations among the stages, came into my mind. It did not feel like I had thought them up: a new perception just appeared, a new gestalt crystallized. My former understanding of agency, ethical ideals, and religious faith was all rearranged in a way that made much more sense: faith is trust in the miracle that vindicates the ethical ideal in reality, a union of the aesthetic and ethical. The experience of this discovery was both eerie and yet joyful, as if I had been given a gift. I saw at once that I had almost completely missed the heart of the religious before; I had not seen what faith adds to good intention or ethical commitment. I'm sure my family thought I had lost my mind: I would walk around with *Fear and Trembling*, stopping to strike my forehead, laughing in a giddy way, and shaking my head at my former errors, and talking to myself. Of course they were used to my strange philosophical ways, but clearly something new was up.

I spent much of the next semester thinking about these things while studying new subjects; along the way, I found in Tolkien's essay "On Fairy Stories" confirmation of the new view to which I'd come with Kierkegaard's help. I tried to apply this understanding to other areas of philosophy. Then in the fall of my junior year, MacIntyre came as a visiting scholar to Yale and gave a couple of lectures while staying in residence. I attended the lectures and then wrote him a letter, more than ten pages long, detailing where I thought he had gone wrong both on the ethical and religious stages in Kierkegaard. There was a long discussion of *Sickeness unto Death* in the letter to confirm my interpretation. Looking back at this piece of juvenilia now, I'm chagrined that my words in describing his mistakes and fallacies, as I saw them, were nothing short of provocative; my old confidence in my views had got the better of me again. But MacIntyre dealt with it all patiently and did not say too much in

response; if he read the whole thing, then he took it with great equanimity. And if he remembered this exchange when I encountered
him again in graduate school in 1993, MacIntyre did not show it. As
much as my tone was overblown, though, the views sketched in that
1988 letter have remained my basic outlook on Kierkegaard ever
since, although much had to be added on reading later pseudonymous and signed works. Yet somehow it took me more than twenty-
two years to put those basic ideas into published form.

Kierkegaard's influence on my interests led me to further study
of comparative religion and mythology, in addition to my courses in
philosophy and global politics. Among other things, this led me to
an appreciation of Jung, Buber, Eliade, and others whose work
appeared in the once-famous Bollingen Series. In the spring before
my graduation, I sent letters to a number of scholarly publishers
hoping to find a job. I was lucky enough to end up at Princeton
University Press in July 1989. I was delighted, because the press not
only had an excellent Philosophy list built by Sandy Thatcher in his
time there, but also because it published the Bollingen Series and the
Lowrie and Hong translations of Kierkegaard. I used to dig around
in the files after hours and found amazing correspondence between
Lowrie, the Swensons, Charles Williams (now and then) and even
such literary lights as W. H. Auden.[5] I had a chance to help make
some Bollingen books into new paperbacks, though my main work
eventually became helping the Philosophy list between editors and
after Ann Wald arrived in 1990. I did little work on the Kierkegaard
series, but, I'll take credit or blame (as you like) for the Hong edition
of the *Postscript* appearing in two volumes. More importantly for the
long term, though, I met a young woman who worked for the
Literature editor and fell in love. Fall 1989 was an exciting time; the
world was changing rapidly with the fall of the Berlin Wall, and I
was in my first serious relationship; despite my meager wages, I felt
more blessed than ever.

---

[5]I eventually sent a small sheaf of copies of these letters to the Hong Kierkegaard Library at St. Olaf College. However, Oxford University Press was not able
to find any files with letters between these scholars when I made inquiries in June
1990. It may be that these would be found at the Marion Wade Center at Wheaton
College.

The situation was not easy though, because at age twenty-two, I had not been out in the world a lot, and I did not know what my direction in life would take. Having finally started to realize how little I really knew, I was somewhat lacking in confidence: how could a career ever result from my strange mix of interests and studies? However, my beloved was clearly at the point to be thinking about marriage. It was here that Kierkegaard helped me most personally, by his own example of what *not* to do, and his haunting words: "If I had faith, I would have married Regina." I thought about his mistake, and learned from it.

I also looked again at the Judge's "Aesthetic Validity of Marriage" letter and took to heart the truth in it. Though much there must look quaint or dated or even biased to contemporary eyes, there are also insights worth treasuring. Since the Judge is so quickly dismissed by critics these days, a reminder about a few of them might be in order. His first letter includes a clear rejection of Victorian prudery in favor of "the deeper eroticism that surely is the most beautiful aspect of purely human existence" (EO 2:30; compare 49); a tough critique of bourgeois views that promote grounds for marriage other than romantic love (EO 2:27 and 33-35);[6] an extended argument that erotic love can become an expression for "deeper moral, religious love filled with a vigorous and vital conviction" (EO 2:32); and a penetrating description of "first love" as an "awakening" to the unique value of a particular person leading to nonfungible regard (EO 2:42-43). But most importantly, the Judge argues that the immediate beauty of first love is deepened in the (higher-order) will "to hold fast to this love" (EO 2:47), which gives it ethical significance without ruining it by detached reflection. Because earnest romantic love wills commitment to continue it, it wants to find a stable basis for that commitment, such as an authority that can make an oath binding (EO 2:56); thus it seeks an eternal ground for the unique value it sees in the beloved who is worthy of exclusive commitment.[7] Marriage consists in the active refreshing of this

---

[6]I use the term "romantic love" here because I think for contemporary readers, this is the most apt term for what he has in mind. Sometimes he uses "romantic love" in a different way (EO 2:28), with Arthurian knights or Byron and other sentimentalist authors in mind; in this usage, "romantic" is similar to "aesthetic.™

[7]For otherwise, if the value of the beloved is regarded only as a reflection of the

passion (EO 2:9): "This rejuvenation of our first love . . . is an action" (EO 2:10). Thus "the innermost power of married life" lies in "the energy of the will" that responds to value disclosed in erotic first love (EO 2:26). In other words, marriage is the willed repetition of first love, a paradigm case of aesthetic value retained within ethically informed striving.

Kierkegaard was right. I really loved this young woman; in her, I found both beauty and goodness in a unique combination. But if this was a response to a transcendent value, was it not worth continuing? Should I abandon it because some shrewd rule of prudence says not to marry too early? If this was the real thing, wouldn't it be *downright nuts* to betray its infinite value just because it happened to come earlier than I expected or than some recipe for success in life prescribes? I had never realized how much nobility there was in marriage until that moment: it is one of the deepest kinds of loyalty to infinite value that we know. To my surprise, I was suddenly on the verge of a major decision. The perilous words "Either/Or" took on a new meaning for me. Just over a year after we met, I proposed and was accepted—and how lucky both those decisions were for me. Ever since, I've felt that I owed a personal debt of gratitude to the Danish sage.

III. After Kierkegaard?

As must now be obvious, my life has been permanently shaped by Kierkegaard's influence and I will never "past" this. A lot has happened in the last twenty years, including the publication of *Kierkegaard after MacIntyre*, thanks to Anthony Rudd's insightful suggestion. In addition, I've finally been able to explain in print the understanding of existential faith that fell into place for me while reading *Fear and Trembling* so many years ago. And I am still waiting for the right point to articulate some ideas on agapic love that are inspired by Kierkegaard. Yet in entering on an academic career, it was never my intention to focus primarily on Kierkegaard. Although

---

lover's mood (EO 2:56), the beloved is really just a prize to be won (until the next competition). In earnest romantic love, "the girl means too much to him to dare to take her . . . as booty" (EO 57:2), whereas aesthetes like *A* live "by plundering" (EO 2:10).

I went to Notre Dame in part to work with Philip Quinn on philosophy of religion, I switched focus fairly early to ethics and moral psychology. The amount of work I've subsequently done on Kierkegaard is in some ways an accident, or perhaps better, an indication of the power of Kierkegaard's prose to cast a spell on us. So many themes in both the pseudonymous and signed works have intrigued me that I've found it hard to escape them. And the great progress of Kierkegaard scholarship in the Anglo-American world flowing from the Kierkegaard Society and the International Kierkegaard Commentary series have made the field all the more entrancing. It has been wonderful to play a small part in these developments started by the Perkins.

But going forward from this point, I must make something of a change. This imperative relates to another theme in Kierkegaard's works that has a deeply personal significance for me, though it is difficult to speak about it without sounding either vain or delusional. That is the theme of personal calling or religious vocation, which Steve Evans describes as divine commands "directed to individuals as individuals" in their unique situation.[8] It seems that Kierkegaard slowly came to believe that his work as an author was, in some sense, what "governance" meant him to do. There are lots of worries we might rightly have about such a belief, despite Kierkegaard's protests that he claimed no special authority. Some of these worries might be pertinent to his final "attack" on the Danish Lutheran church before the end of his life. Yet I think Evans is right to find value in Kierkegaard's belief in callings particular to each individual, which emphasizes the moral importance of personal uniqueness.[9]

Despite his own doubts about Kierkegaard, Martin Buber also believed that people could, in relation to the divine, discover an individual mission or role that only they could play. Thus his (open-theistic) claim that human persons stand in a "free" relation with God even though we are utterly dependent on God for our being: "You need God in order to be, and God needs you—for that which is the meaning of your life."[10] This meaning is your personal

---

[8]C. Stephen Evans, *Kierkegaard's Ethic of Love: Divine Commands & Moral Obligations* (Oxford UK: Oxford University Press, 2004) 25.

[9]Evans, *Kierkegaard's Ethic of Love*, 24, 171, citing SUD 33.

[10]Martin Buber, *I and Thou*, trans. Walter Kaufmann (New York: Scribner's,

vocation. Like Anselm, Buber held that in faith, we "participate" in creation with God, "we offer ourselves to him, helpers and companions."[11] In accepting our calling, we are both free and destined. Compare Anti-Climacus's statement that despair is possible for human persons because of the freedom "in which the synthesis relates itself to itself, inasmuch as God, who constituted man a relation, releases it from his hand — that is, inasmuch as the relation relates itself to itself" (SUD 16). In other words, the "spiritual" or volitional relation to our psycho-physical composition, the exercise of which generates our "self," exists because God creates us *as free*, despite our ontological dependence.[12] And among the greatest powers of this freedom is accepting the unique work that we can do with our contingent psychophysical makeup.

To trust in faith that one has a particular calling is not the same as doxic assent to a claim that one has a certain mission in life. It is something that we "believe" beyond normal evidence, a free response to our experiences seen in light of a theistic worldview. As Evans suggests,

> It is plausible that part of my calling will demand on God's part that I make some difficult decisions for myself, relying on principles and values that I must personalize, interpret and apply to the particular situation in which I find myself.[13]

Similarly, belief that one has a calling is an act of faith that must always be open to the possibility that I have misunderstood or interposed my own wishes or fantasies in place of the true purposes given to me. Here is the essential ambiguity: a sense of calling must both fit needs that I uniquely recognize or that I am uniquely suited to meet (or both), but not fit my own predilections and daydreams too well. And if the path I perceive too easily promotes my ego, that is good grounds for suspicion that I have misunderstood. But Evans

---

1970) part III, 130.

[11]Buber, *I and Thou*.

[12]Evans seems to agree with this reading when he writes that, for Kierkegaard, "one of the characteristics God calls me to actualize is that of being a responsible chooser, who exemplifies the kind of *relative autonomy* and freedom that a finite, dependent creature can possess." *Kierkegaard's Ethic of Love*, 26; my italics.

[13]Evans, *Kierkegaard's Ethic of Love*, 26.

is surely right that a sense of calling need not involve direct super-natural experience: I can come to it from considering how I might "creatively bring my gifts to bear to accomplish what could not be done, or done so well, by others."[14] I agree though even here, we must be careful to make sure that others have their chance to contribute.

To come to the point, I have had a growing sense for some time that my efforts are needed in other domains that pertain to political philosophy and the world of popular political opinion. I'm sure that Professor Perkins, of all Kierkegaard scholars, would understand this. I'm not sure what will happen; there is little reason to think that my talents do suit this course at all well, or that there is any realistic prospect of success. But infinite resignation is not reached without making a serious effort first. My experiences in youth, and the pledge I was moved to make when I first learned about the Holo-caust, have taken on a new meaning for me, and I see now that they might mean something more. The disarray among nations that we see in our world, and the resulting suffering under the boot of tyranny and fanaticism, are evils to which, for better of worse, my history makes me peculiarly attuned. Of course no one should claim great wisdom in these matters or assume that he or she has "the" solution. Yet there is a possibility that I feel called to pursue, with growing urgency. This does not mean that I will write no more on Kierkegaard or the many philosophical, psychological, religious, and personal topics that his thought illuminates. It does mean that there are many ways Kierkegaard's insights can affect one's life other than prompting one to write about his ideas. Among these are possibili-ties for action. Again, an either/or confronts me. Although my hopes for a solution to our global problems are only hopes "by virtue of the absurd," I must now pursue them in earnest and see where they lead. Perhaps I'm still just fighting my inner headmaster, or tilting at windmills. Or perhaps my path included both the headmaster and Kierkegaard for a good reason that I must still work to discover in patience and faith.

---

[14]Evans, *Kierkegaard's Ethic of Love*, 172.

6

The Kierkegaards I Have Known

Stephen N. Dunning

The three Kierkegaards in my life roughly correspond both to the development evident in his authorship(s) and to my own development as a person. Although each of those Kierkegaards is recognizable as a familiar face of the "real" Kierkegaard, they also testify to the extraordinary diversity of the writing he produced in little more than a decade. At the same time, they demonstrate the extent to which Kierkegaard's writings are themselves a bit like the biblical mirror of James 1:23-24, an analogy Kierkegaard often exploits in *For Self-Examination*: any text can be revelatory or meaninglessness, depending upon whether or not we take away from it a clear recollection of what it has shown us about ourselves. My goal in this paper is to clarify my recollections of why and how Kierkegaard has mattered to me for most of the past five decades.

My first encounter with Kierkegaard was as a sophomore in college, and it was entirely in line with the intellectual immaturity that we associate with that year. In a course on "Existentialism," we read *Fear and Trembling* and *Sickness unto Death* as a prelude to studying Heidegger and Sartre. There are two very powerful concepts I recall from that course: the individuality of human nature and the subjectivity of both our experience and our apprehension of the truth. No doubt the professor's lectures supplemented the class reading with information from other texts by Kierkegaard. However I learned about those two concepts, I did not hesitate to internalize them with a passion that was, I fear, more sophomoric than Kierkegaardian.

As have so many interpreters of Kierkegaard, I assumed that his focus on "the single one" and becoming an individual validated the individualism that came naturally to me at that age and in our secular culture. The concept of a radically solitary being appealed to my "Romantic" mindset; indeed, I was repelled by all forms of authority or collectivism. I believe Kierkegaard unwittingly invites this (mis)interpretation, especially in his early "aesthetic" works and the two books we read in that course. I trust this is obvious in part one of *Either/Or*, but it is also true of *Fear and Trembling* and *Sickness unto Death*. The former stresses the isolation of Abraham when God incomprehensibly tells him to sacrifice Isaac, while the latter explores despair as a failure to will to be oneself and only oneself grounded (or resting) in God. In both works, God remains a point of reference who is all-powerful but has little apparent concern for the interpersonal and social aspects of human life. In other words, the individuality of the spiritual life can seem to entail a sense of social individuality, even social solitude. As I shall show below, I now believe that this was a misunderstanding on my part, and that Kierkegaard advocates individuality in a way that strongly opposes individualism.

Just as individualism is a misinterpretation of Kierkegaard's notion of individuality, so also is subjectivism (or, more precisely, solipsism) a misinterpretation of his emphasis on subjectivity. The self-absorption of the major characters in *Either/Or*, especially in part one but also to a surprising extent with Judge William, encouraged me and I suspect many other readers to go on believing that our access to the meaningful truths of life is through our own selves. Any life-truth must conform to who I am subjectively. This gives the impression that we are all so entangled in our own subjective desires and thoughts that we are unable grasp the reality, or even just the views, of others. The positive side of this sort of solipsism is often an abundance of creative energy, and so it was with me. An immediate outpouring of creativity was both productive of lyrical essays, poems, and paintings and also inhibiting to disciplined critical thinking. This energetic self-absorption lasted for over a year, and was ended only by a change of schools and a quasi-conversion to life in a college community based upon the progressive principles of John Dewey. It will come as no surprise that Kierkegaard ceased to play a central role in my thinking, and lay dormant, as it were, for the next fifteen years.

Both by circumstance and by choice, I devoted ten of those fifteen years to masters and doctoral programs in which I read a good deal of modern Christian thought, but very little Kierkegaard. The circumstance was the increasing politicization of American intellectual life in the sixties and seventies, fueled by the Civil Rights Movement, the anti-Vietnam War movement, and the emergence of social justice issues (in particular, the rights of women and gays). It's fair to say that only one among my professors had any real interest in Kierkegaard, enough to include him in a syllabus. I do not recall noticing that at the time, however, since I was intent upon reading Hegel intensively — beginning with a seminar on his *Science of Logic* (as Hegel said, "all beginnings are difficult!"), then going on to *The Phenomenology of Mind* (it was the Baillie translation back then), and finally digging into Hegel's lectures on religion and history. Soon I was proudly playing the role of "left-wing" Hegelian among my fellow students, and I viewed Kierkegaard as a distant and passing phase. Whatever interest in "inwardness" or spiritual matters I still had was directed towards India, not Christendom.

As it turned out, and to my surprise, it was Hegelianism that eventually proved to be the passing phase for me. When it came time to write a dissertation, I knew that I wanted to use that opportunity to address a nagging question about Hegel: could he in any way illuminate the phenomenon of mysticism, and thus analyze in depth the nature of religious experience as he had already analyzed so many religious ideas? Incredibly, my proposal to write a dissertation on Hegel and a yet-to-be-determined mystic was approved! I was also successful in applying for a DAAD year in Bochum at the Hegel Archive of Ruhr University. But in the spring semester before I was to depart for Germany, I began to wonder if those critics who claimed that Hegel is thin on ethics might be correct. I also began to think that I could learn more about actual religions by looking into how they function in practice than I had learned by approaching them only in theory. So I started — somewhat furtively, I must admit -- slipping into churches to listen and watch from a back pew. The church to which I had been exposed as a child, but had not been confirmed in, was the Roman Catholic Church, and it had the distinct advantage of offering daily afternoon masses during the season of Lent. The upshot was that I was confirmed that Easter.

In the process, a providential dividend was a perfect "mystic" for my dissertation. In a conversation over coffee with the instructor of a German course I had been auditing, I complained that Hegel always discusses ideas, rarely the people who have them, even when those people claim that their ideas are based upon mystical states of consciousness that they had personally experienced. His accounts were both too abstract and too short to provide me with the material I needed to assess his view of such claims. To make matters worse, all the mystics he does mention lived before the Enlightenment, which poses significant obstacles for the conversation I hoped to set up between Hegel and whichever mystic it might be. The instructor responded that Hegel had published an eighty-page review of the collected works of J. G. Hamann shortly after they were published in 1825, and that Hamann was a brilliant thinker who, deeply shaped by a profound conversion experience and by his idiosyncratic and often mystical reading of the Bible, had become one of the major critics of Enlightenment Rationalism. It was immediately clear that I had at last found a "mystic" who might help me unlock that aspect of Hegel's thinking, and I could move ahead on the dissertation.

A few years later, I published *The Tongues of Men: Hegel vs. Hamann on Religious Language and History* in the AAR dissertation series. In it I tried to show that Hegel's frustration with Hamann and his admitted failure to penetrate Hamann's understanding of history was due to their very different views of language. For Hegel, a philosopher must develop a clear conceptual language, whereas Hamann treats language as a gift from God, especially the language of the Bible. Therefore his writing constantly juxtaposes the language that he finds in modern philosophical texts with allusions to the Bible, most often expressed only by brief phrases or images, without benefit of explanation. The reader must either know the Bible very well or be willing to track down these allusions and figure out what they mean in their scriptural context. The texts that I treated in the dissertation, in addition to Hegel's review, were Hamann's *Golgotha und Scheblimini*, which deals with Moses Mendelssohn's *Jerusalem*, and "Metacritique of the Purism of Reason," which is a parody of Kant's *Critique of Pure Reason*.

I can appreciate Hegel's frustration: understanding and then translating the *Golgotha* was so difficult that one page could require several days of research for someone like myself who was relatively new to the Bible! Hegel was interested in Hamann, but not *that* interested, and, in any case, Hamann had obviously failed to perform according to Hegel's standard: the "language" he used was not clear and conceptual, but opaque, allusive, ironic, and full of meanings that could be gleaned only by engaging directly with the Bible. It combined parody of contemporary texts with scriptural references that hinted at profound – even mystical – meanings but never spelled them out in philosophically intelligible concepts. To Hegel, all of Hamann's scriptural allusions were merely "ornamental," designed to impress without conveying any substantial meaning whatsoever. Since the Enlightenment, this dismissive view of any text with numerous biblical references has become quite common, and it is no doubt sometimes justified. But not with Hamann, whose so-called "ornaments" provide the key to his meaning.

The publication of the dissertation led directly to a second providential event, an invitation that reconnected me with Kierkegaard. During graduate school I had met Merold Westphal, who suggested to Bob Perkins that, with my work on both Hamann and Hegel, I might be able to provide a historical background article for a special issue of *Thought* on Kierkegaard. This issue was in honor of the 125th anniversary of Kierkegaard's death, and Perkins was serving as Guest Editor. With some hesitation after so many years of ignoring (avoiding?) Kierkegaard, I accepted, and agreed to write a piece that became "Kierkegaard's 'Hegelian' Response to Hamann." It did not occur to me at the time that this article would set the course for most of my future scholarship, although I did realize that in Bob Perkins and Merold Westphal I was privileged to know two of the very few scholars who are fine readers of both Hegel and Kierkegaard.

At about the same time that I was working on the article for *Thought*, I was also guiding a graduate student's independent study of Kierkegaard. As we worked through Part One of *Either/Or*, I began to discern a pattern in the presentation of the relations between inner and outer and self and other. As counter-intuitive as it seemed, this pattern was very like a Hegelian dialectic. I wrote it up in article form for JAAR as "The Dialectic of Contradiction in Kierkegaard's Aesthetic Stage," and that led to an NEH Fellowship to spend 1982-83 exploring the possibility that this sort of dialectic could be found in other works by Kierkegaard. The resulting book, *Kierkegaard's Dialectic of Inwardness: A Structural Analysis of the Theory of Stages*, was published by Princeton in 1985. So, in a span of just five years or so, unusually fortuitous circumstances had combined with one or two choices to retool a sometime Hegelian into an enthusiastic Kierkegaard scholar.

In retrospect, two things stand out when I think about why Kierkegaard became so important to me once again. First is the Christian character of his writing. To tell the truth, I had come to faith not through academic study of theological doctrines but in spite of my graduate education, which seemed designed to train philosophically sophisticated critics of traditional Christian thinking. I pursued a more existential path, if I may call it that, looking for something that could anchor my life first and foremost, while also providing a path by which to pursue the long-term goal of attaining intellectual clarity about it. With his emphasis upon paradox as absolutely central to Christian thinking, Kierkegaard showed me that our lack of understanding can be a blessing to be embraced. This lesson in a new kind of agnosticism, if I may call it that, also freed me from my years of paralysis in the name of resisting any so-called "sacrifice of intellect." Second, I doubt that anyone would ever accuse Hegel of agnosticism about anything (!), but my years of studying him did not simply disappear, in large part thanks to Kierkegaard. In struggling with the ways in which Kierkegaard's thinking often took the form of Hegelian dialectic, if only in order to undermine the results of that dialectic, I learned how deeply we remain impacted by those positions we come to reject, and how important it is to appreciate this complex tension rather than force an unstable reconciliation. Indeed, one fruitful way to approach any thinker is to look for ways in which they may implicitly continue to affirm what they intend to reject. I have also tried to do this for Hegel in "Particularity Not Scandalous: Hegel's Contribution to Philosophy of Religion" (1992).

To my knowledge, Kierkegaard never associated his understanding of the paradoxes of faith with what we think of as "agnosticism," and I do not wish to be misunderstood here. By "agnosticism" what I mean is that, like Johannes de Silentio in *Fear and Trembling*, we must all admit that faith entails incomprehensible paradoxes, and that no person of faith ever attains an intellectual grasp of such affirmations as the Chalcedonian unity of the divine and the human (or, in Kierkegaardian terms, the eternal and the temporal) in Christ. The notion of "Christian agnosticism" is too rich and complex to be adequately dealt with here, but I do hope to return to it in the near future elsewhere.

The transition from a dialectical-philosophical Kierkegaard, who was the focus of my work throughout the eighties, to a third and presumably final radically Christian Kierkegaard in the nineties was gradual and somewhat circuitous. It began with a growing interest in Hermeneutics, particularly Hans-Georg Gadamer's extraordinary work, *Truth and Method*. In retrospect, I am tempted to attribute my response to this text to the way in which it combines an almost Hegelian systematic rigor with a deep Kierkegaardian grasp of the truth and power of the subjective aspect of interpretation. Be that as it may, I believe that t was Gadamer more than any other outside influence who indirectly helped me come to a deeper understanding of the important role of hermeneutics in understanding Kierkegaard's thought.

Specifically, Gadamer helped me to understand more fully that interpretation entails — indeed, requires — "application" (his term for appropriation) of the meaning of a text. I had long understood Kierkegaard's emphasis on appropriation as necessary for becoming a Christian. Now I began to see that it is vital to all interpretation, and that Kierkegaard was also making that point, most clearly perhaps in his constant references to earnestness. In returning to *For Self-Examination*, I saw that for him earnestness is far more than simply sincerity or engagement; it is nothing less than the hermeneutical demand for appropriation as the *sine qua non* of all interpretation. Kierkegaard's extended diatribe against the sort of scholarship that calls itself "interpretation" without regard for the truth of the biblical text anticipates Gadamer's explicit demand published more than a century later.[1]

There is a paradox here also, or at least an irony, that should be noted. If earnestness in interpretation entails appropriation (positively or even negatively) of the meaning of a text, then how are we to justify the way that Kierkegaard seems to hide behind a curious and fascinating caste of characters posing as pseudonymous authors of his books? Scholars have generally agreed that he adopted this method — which he famously called "indirect communication" — to steer the reader's attention away from himself as author and toward the text itself. So he concealed his own earnestness in order to empower theirs. Aesthetically, he appears to be indulging in irony

---

[1] Of many possible references, see p. 274 in the 2nd ed. of Gadamer's *Truth and Method*, and pp. 33-34 in *For Self-Examination*.

and manipulation, but ethically he is doing so out of concern for the reader's edification. Perhaps this is also a contradiction that can best be described by the essentially religious concept of paradox.

This application of paradox to the issue of communication has been enormously and personally helpful to me as a teacher. One of the most difficult pedagogical issues I have faced is whether or not a teacher ought to "come out" in the classroom about his or her own position on the often controversial matters under discussion. Understandably, this issue is unusually sensitive in Religious Studies classes, especially on campuses such as my own where there are a number of different religious groups and the dominant ethos is secular. In this situation, I have found Kierkegaard's use of what he called "indirect communication" very helpful. I fully realize that this pedagogical stance would have been anathema to my "progressive" college professors. To them, as to many students studying Kierkegaard for the first time, the use of pseudonyms appears to be dishonest. They expect a writer to speak clearly in the first person singular. Although I must concede that their hermeneutical position has a certain consistency and integrity, I believe that indirect communication can be justified pedagogically. In fact, I find this approach to education more "student-centered" than the progressive approach that I was taught in college (Dewey, with help from Carl Rogers).

I should also mention a more controversial matter—a political justification for indirect communication. In a secular institution, those who teach Religious Studies must be very careful not to do anything that might give the impression that they are using the classroom to promote religious commitment. Since many of us are at home with secular values, it is usually not an issue. But for those of us who are personally committed to a religious tradition, it can become one, especially if that tradition is one that has a history of proselytizing, as both Christianity and Islam do. Politically, it is very important that we not violate the trust invested in us by our colleagues and institutions by crossing that line. We may certainly engage in religious extra-curricular activities, if we like, but there should never be any hint of an "agenda" in the classroom. If this seems in any way dishonest to us, then we should find a religious school in which to teach. If not, then indirect communication is, I believe, the method that will most effectively make us into the very best teachers we can be in that secular situation.

Indirect communication in Kierkegaard's pseudonymous literature finds its "second authorship" counterpart in Kierkegaard's insistence that he was a writer "without authority." Whether discussing Adler's experience-based claim to authority or his own difficulties with ecclesiastical and intellectual leaders in Denmark, Kierkegaard always presented himself as an interpreter, never as a duly appointed authority, and emphatically not as one who had authority by means of inspiration. As one who has come to understand that interpretation is the central theme of all my teaching and scholarship, I mention this as yet another way in which Kierkegaard has been pedagogically important for me. As teachers, we certainly have a great deal of authority to instruct and also to evaluate our students' work. To approach that task with a focus on the students' own interpretations of texts rather than their ability to recite interpretations they have learned from us liberates us as teachers and empowers the students in exciting ways.

Appropriation is also helpful for a deeper understanding of Kierkegaard's concept of subjectivity than I had taken away from my undergraduate exposure to him. Together with his emphasis upon inwardness, some readers have been inclined to conclude that for Kierkegaard the subjectivity of truth refers to the notion that each of us can find the truth within our selves. This can easily be countered by the simple observation that Kierkegaard was a deeply committed theist, a believer in a God who is transcendent as well as immanent, a God who is known through *appropriated* revelation rather than by an exploration of one's own inwardness. In this regard, it is also important to clarify the oft-quoted phrase from *Concluding Unscientific Postscript*, "truth is subjectivity." This refers not to the abstract truths of science, which are objective, but to truths concerning the meaning of life for each one of us. We can receive such truths only by subjectively appropriating them, unlike objective truths that neither need nor allow subjective appropriation.

This clarification of the concept of subjectivity in turn illuminates Kierkegaard's concept of the individual, which is the other concept that I had (mis)understood in my encounter with him as a college sophomore. Initially, I had taken individuality to mean an autonomous self-grounding as a person—one of the main pillars of secular philosophy and culture. When years later I returned to Kierkegaard, it quickly became obvious that his "individualism" is rooted in his understanding of our religious lives, which, in order to be in earnest and authentic, must be chosen and embraced individually. Now I realize that his view of the individual is even more radical than this: it is not simply that we can approach and encounter God only as individuals, or that God addresses us only as individuals, but that *only by virtue of our relationship with God do we ever become individuals.* As Kierkegaard puts it in the famous "Purity of Heart Is To Will One Thing" discourse, our life in temporality is one of multiplicity and distraction, and so we are incapable of willing one thing. Yet the God-relationship changes all that, for "in eternity it can be done, because each one separately becomes the single individual." This claim, made almost in passing, affirms that it is the God of eternity and God alone who creates us *as individuals.* So Kierkegaard's "individualism" does not elevate us as individuals in relation to one another at all; it transfigures us into individuals by and in our relationship with God. (See *Upbuilding Discourses in Various Spirits*, 131, or *Purity of Heart Is to Will One Thing*, 189.)

If this is true, then the "individual" of modern secular thinking is a chimera, an illusion of Romantic wishful thinking. It tries to define the individual as utterly independent, related only haphazardly to such groups as family, clan, class, society, or humanity, and those very groups understand themselves only by means of distinguishing themselves from other groups. Thus secular individualism proclaims our autonomy as persons but provides no other means for self-identification than this process of distinguishing ourselves and our group over against other selves and groups. The God relationship that Kierkegaard describes is very different. In it, we are persons who receive our individual identities from God, and those individual identities rest in God even as they entail being a part of many groups. Those human relationships no longer need be understood as one over against another, since all of us are created equally by God to be in such relations. The significant distinction that defines this individuality is one that transcends all social relations within and between groups: to realize that I exist as an individual only by virtue of God's creative act is realize also that I am not God, that God transcends me as the Divine Other. But this "opposition" within the God-relationship is not unique to me; it is

in principle available to everyone. To be an individual who is constituted as such only by God undercuts any thought of self-generated
individualism and provides a new foundation for bonding with all
other persons, whatever their clan or class, and so forth.

Of course, this interpretation of Kierkegaard's theory of individuality does not turn him into a social philosopher. It merely shows
that he is not an anti-social philosopher, or even an asocial one,
given the extent to which he portrays most of the characters he
discusses (even Abraham) as selves who are deeply related to others.
(This is argued for *Either/Or*, Part One, in "The Dialectic of Contradiction in Kierkegaard's Aesthetic Stage" and *Kierkegaard's Dialectic
of Inwardness*.) The salient fact is that Kierkegaard believed his
assignment as a religious writer was to clarify the meaning of the
God-relationship. And that is what he did.

In closing, I hope this account of my journey from a sophomoric
grasp of Kierkegaard's aesthetic, poetic, and "Romantic" insights
through years of exploring his encounter with Hegelian dialectical
philosophy and now culminating in a growing appreciation of his
radically Christian views has demonstrated why Kierkegaard
matters to me. To put it even more strongly, it is almost impossible
for me to imagine the past thirty years of thinking, teaching, and
scholarship without him. His literary creativity, intellectual brilliance, and religious depth have helped to make it a rich and
rewarding journey.

7

Why Kierkegaard Still Matters —
and Matters to Me

C. Stephen Evans

This is an essay on the importance of Kierkegaard as a philosopher.[1]
I am very happy to have the chance to write it to honor Robert
Perkins, who has done more than anyone I know to foster serious
grappling with Kierkegaard as a philosopher, both through his own
writings and especially through the International Kierkegaard
Commentary. In the essay I talk quite a bit about Kierkegaard's
break with modern philosophy's obsession with epistemology.
However, it is important to recognize that Kierkegaard has valuable
epistemological insights of his own, some of which were brought out
in Perkins's own work.[2]

In this essay I shall, especially in the beginning, engage in more
autobiography than is common in the academy. I do this partly
because I have been asked to say something about what I think
about Kierkegaard, and why I think Kierkegaard is important. I do
not think I can do this without saying something about what drew
me to Kierkegaard in the first place, and also what has sustained my
interest over many years. However, I hope it will be evident that my
goal is not to tell people about my own life, but to say something
about why Kierkegaard should matter in today's intellectual
situation.

---

[1]This article is a slightly revised version of an essay that appeared in the
Kierkegaard Studies Yearbook 2010, published by DeGruyters. My thanks to the editors
of that volume and also to Mercer University Press for permission to use this
material both in the *Yearbook* and in this volume.

[2]See esp. Robert Perkins, "Kierkegaard: A Kind of Epistemologist," *History of
European Ideas* 12/1 (1990); and "Kierkegaard's Epistemological Preferences,"
International Journal for Philosophy of Religion 4/4 (1973). For a full-length treatment
of Kierkegaard's epistemology, see M. G. Piety, *Ways of Knowing: Kierkegaard's
Pluralist Epistemology* (forthcoming from Baylor University Press).

My first encounter with Kierkegaard was in my first course in philosophy as a first-year university student at Wheaton College. In an introduction to ethics courses I was assigned to read that section of *Upbuilding Discourses in Various Spirits* translated and published in English as *Purity of Heart Is to Will One Thing*. One year later, in a survey course in the history of modern philosophy I read *Concluding Unscientific Postscript*. In both cases I was overwhelmed with the richness of the ideas, the originality of the arguments, and the power of the images, metaphors, and stories. These two books effectively changed the course of my life; I switched from a major in history to philosophy, and over the next few years I read as much Kierkegaard as I could manage. I had become a lover of Kierkegaard, as well as someone who loved doing philosophy. It was, I think, Kierkegaard who helped me see that philosophy could still be understood as a quest for wisdom and not merely as an intellectual game.

In my graduate studies at Yale, I was able to continue to study Kierkegaard, working both with Merold Westphal and Karsten Harries, but I still thought of myself primarily as a philosopher who happened to love Kierkegaard, rather than someone who was primarily a Kierkegaard scholar. For one thing I did not know Danish and I knew that proficiency in the language was a prerequisite for serious scholarship on a philosopher. So I wrote my dissertation, not on Kierkegaard, but on a problem I knew Kierkegaard could help me with: the relation between subjectivity and religious belief.[3]

Two years after finishing my Ph.D., an older philosopher (sadly, I don't remember who it was) advised me to select one great philosopher from the past, and make that philosopher the focus of my research. His reasoning was that whatever field of philosophy I wanted to work in—ethics, epistemology, metaphysics, or whatever—my work would be better if I had a deep and rigorous knowledge of one of the great thinkers of the past. After some reflection, I thought that Kierkegaard should be that figure. Some time later my wife Jan and I made a visit to St. Olaf College to meet Howard and Edna Hong. Howard had graciously read my disserta-

---

[3]C. Stephen Evans *Subjectivity and Religious Belief: An Historical, Critical Study* (Grand Rapids MI: Eerdmans, 1978).

tion, which had a chapter on Kierkegaard, and the Hongs encouraged us both to learn Danish and to try to spend some time in Denmark. For two years Jan and I faithfully worked on the Danish language every day after lunch, and after scrambling to find funding from a variety of sources, including a Marshall Fellowship from the American Scandinavian Foundation, we were able to go to Denmark in 1977–1978.

I decided to focus on Kierkegaard in part because, as a Christian philosopher, I identified strongly with Kierkegaard. The history of modern philosophy certainly includes a number of thinkers who must be recognized as Christian philosophers, including Descartes, Leibniz, Locke, Reid, and Berkeley. However, I believe one may reasonably claim that Christianity plays a more central and definitive role for Kierkegaard than for any other modern philosopher, with the possible exception of Pascal. I believe the Christian philosopher has a twofold calling: he or she is called to speak as a Christian to the philosophical world, but also called to speak as a philosopher to the Christian community. Kierkegaard himself fulfilled this calling admirably: his philosophical thinking is deep and original enough to attract the interest and attention of non-Christians. However, he also has a powerful message for the church about the dangers of "Christendom" and cultural Christianity. Although I believe this latter message directed to the Christian community is extremely important and vital, in this essay I want to focus on the former message: what does Kierkegaard have to say as a philosopher to the broader philosophical world?

Initially I thought Kierkegaard's message to that world lay primarily in his account of the role that "subjectivity" (understood as passion and "inwardness") plays in the acquisition of religious truth and in the living out of that truth. I still believe that this theme embodies one of Kierkegaard's most important and enduring contributions. However, I now think this message is embedded in a deeper, more profound challenge to some of the major tendencies of modern philosophy.

I want now to try to summarize the way I understand that challenge in two of the major fields of philosophy: epistemology and ethics. After discussing these two core areas of philosophy, I will try to say in conclusion something about what unifies the challenge Kierkegaard presents in these two areas. In what follows I shall draw broadly from several of Kierkegaard's pseudonymous writings. For my purposes in this paper the important issues raised by pseudo-nymity are not very significant, because what counts is the way the ideas and arguments found in the writings challenge major trends in modern philosophy. The challenges found in these writings is undeniably present, whether one thinks of the authors as versions of Kierkegaard or (more correctly) as fictional characters he created.

Epistemology

I think one of the main challenges Kierkegaard presents to modern philosophy lies simply in the relative lack of importance he assigns to epistemology. Many commentators would agree that from Descartes and Locke onwards, many of the great modern philoso-phers have viewed epistemology as lying at the very heart of philosophy. The primacy of epistemology for modern philosophy can be clearly seen, for example, in "The Epistle to the Reader" that John Locke provided for *An Essay concerning Human Understanding*.[4] Here Locke explains that the book had its origins in a dispute between himself and some of his friends in his chambers, in which the friends, "discoursing on a subject very remote from this [episte-mology], found themselves quickly at a stand by the difficulties that arose on every side."[5] Locke's own conclusion is that, whatever the original argument was about, some basic epistemological questions must be settled first: "it came into my thoughts, that we took a wrong course; and that, before we set ourselves upon inquiries of that nature, it was necessary to examine our own abilities, and see what objects our understandings were or were not fitted to deal with."[6]

This type of approach to philosophy gives primacy to epistemol-ogy, understood as a discipline that will determine when we have knowledge and when our beliefs are justified. On such a view, before we can decide what we know about ethics, or metaphysics, or philosophy of religion, we must first settle questions about what

---

[4]John Locke, *An Essay concerning Human Understanding* (New York: E. P. Dutton, 1910; repr.: Prometheus Press, 1995).
[5]Locke, *An Essay concerning Human Understanding*, xiv.
[6]Locke, *An Essay concerning Human Understanding*, xiv.

knowledge is and what we can know. The assumption seems to be that once we resolve the "underlying" epistemological questions, we can hope to resolve the questions in other fields of philosophy. The fundamental problem with this approach is that the epistemological problems turn out to be just as intractable as the others. We have no more agreement about the proper method to follow to reach knowledge than we do about what is good and what is right, or about whether God exists or whether humans have immaterial souls. If someone defends the primacy of epistemology on the grounds that substantive claims in ethics and metaphysics always presuppose epistemological views, this can be countered by pointing out that epistemological claims about what we can understand and know equally presuppose metaphysical claims about our nature and our powers.

One of the things I find most refreshing and stimulating about Kierkegaard is that he seems almost entirely free of this tendency to privilege epistemology.[7] I do not mean to suggest that he argues against privileging epistemology, or even that he discusses the issue. Rather, I mean simply that Kierkegaard seems to philosophize in a way that shows no trace of the primacy of epistemology. In this respect he is more like the ancient or medieval philosophers, who similarly focused on primary questions of metaphysics and ethics, rather than regarding epistemological questions as somehow foundational ones that must be settled first. I by no means wish to claim that Kierkegaard has nothing important to say about epistemological questions. This is far from the case, and I will mention some of his contributions below. I mean only to say that he does not regard the quest for justification of our beliefs as somehow the foundation of all philosophy.

The reason this is so, I suspect, is that Kierkegaard recognized that what we might call "the quest for the method" is a failure. Much of modern philosophy, from Descartes to Hegel, is a quest for the proper method that will give the philosopher an objective certainty. Kierkegaard, in my view, does not hold that we humans can achieve such certainty; there is no "method" we can follow that guarantees

---

[7]For an expanded discussion of Kierkegaard's significance for epistemology, see my *Kierkegaard: An Introduction* (Cambridge UK: Cambridge University Press, 2009) particularly chap. 3.

us knowledge. (Here Kierkegaard anticipates well-known themes in Gadamer.) However, Kierkegaard does not see this inability on our part as a catastrophe. We don't need any such method or the objective certainty that is supposed to be its outcome in order to live meaningful lives and even to hold convictions with passion.

However, Kierkegaard's challenge to modern epistemology is not merely to the primacy of this field of philosophy, but extends to more substantive characteristics of epistemology. I will briefly mention four, interconnected issues, each of which deserves far more space than I can here afford.

1. *The primacy of doubt*. Kierkegaard believes that modern philosophy posits doubt as the starting point of philosophy, though he ironically expresses some sharp doubts of his own about how seriously modern philosophers take doubt. (See, for example, the preface to *Fear and Trembling* with its polemical comments about "going further" than doubt.[8]) In contrast to this privileging of doubt, Kierkegaard consistently adheres to the Aristotelian dictum that philosophy begins with wonder.[9] Kierkegaard sees no reason to privilege doubt in this way. Beginning with wonder leaves open the possibility of faith or trust.

2. *The lessons of skepticism*. Much of modern philosophy can be viewed as a response to the skeptic, an attempt to provide an argumentative refutation of skepticism. Kierkegaard thinks this is a mistake.[10] Skepticism cannot be refuted by argument — but it does not have to be refuted. It is rooted in the will and therefore can only be cured by a transformation of the will. We overcome skepticism by deciding not to be skeptics.

3. *The place of the person in knowing*. Modern epistemology tends to focus on evidence or whatever it is that provides us with objective justification for our beliefs. In ethics and philosophy of religion this goes hand in hand with a quest for objective arguments or evidence to justify our moral and religious beliefs. If we are threatened with moral nihilism or moral relativism, the solution is to man the

---

[8] *Fear and Trembling*, SV1 III, 57-60.

[9] See, e.g., *Philosophical Fragments*, where Johannes Climacus, in discussing the wonder that must accompany a recognition of what has "come into existence" approvingly cites Plato and Aristotle for rooting philosophy in wonder, SV1 IV, 244.

[10] See again, *Philosophical Fragments*, in the "Interlude," SVI IV 245-49.

intellectual barricades and provide rational support for ethics. If religious faith is declining the problem is that we need more evidence for our beliefs. Kierkegaard does not accept this picture of moral and religious knowledge. If our grasp of moral knowledge is less secure, it may be because we have become less moral. If religious faith has declined, it is not because we are now more rational and demand more evidence than people did in earlier times, but because we lack the imaginative and emotional capacities to understand the power of religious beliefs.

To put all the focus on evidence is to assume that "everything is in order" with the people who are supposed to form their beliefs on the basis of that evidence. But that assumption is highly dubious: the best evidence in the world would be of no value to people who are unable to recognize and interpret the evidence. We must therefore focus attention not just on evidence but on the character of the knower. And perhaps not all religious and moral knowledge is based on evidence at all.

This is, I think, a significant part of what is meant by the claim that "truth is subjectivity." The quest for truth, at least the truth about the most important things, cannot be divorced from the quest to become the kind of person we need to become. The primacy of epistemology implies that we must first discover the truth about morality and life, and then perhaps we can try to live out that truth. Perhaps it is true that we can only acquire the truth as part of the process whereby we learn to live out the truth.

4. *The limits of reason and the necessity for revelation.* Kierkegaard is of course well known for his claim that the Incarnation lies at the heart of Christian faith and that the Incarnation is the "Absolute Paradox" that human reason cannot understand. These Kierke-gaardian claims have often been interpreted in such a way that Kierkegaard turns out to be an irrationalist, someone who affirms that a Christian must believe what is logically contradictory and therefore contrary to reason. I have argued against this view and given an alternative reading in much of my work.[11]

---

[11]See, e.g., *Kierkegaard's* Fragments *and* Postscript: *The Religious Philosophy of Johannes Climacus* (Atlantic Highlands NJ: Humanities Press, 1983; repr.: Humanity Books, imprint of Prometheus Books, 1999) 207-45; *Passionate Reason: Making Sense of Kierkegaard's "Philosophical Fragments"* (Bloomington: Indiana University Press,

Reading Kierkegaard as an irrationalist prevents us from seeing how fundamental a problem he is grappling with: it is essentially the problem of the limits of human reason. Kierkegaard is certainly not the only philosopher to tackle this question. It is clearly central to Kant's philosophy and is also the major theme of the early Wittgenstein's thought. More recently, a number of philosophers have argued that the human mind as a conscious reality is an essential mystery for human beings, something that humans will never understand.[12] To say that human reason has limits is surely not proof of irrationality. To the contrary, insofar as humans are finite creatures, we have good reasons to think that human reason is indeed limited.

Kierkegaard happens to think that the limits of human reason are disclosed by God's paradoxical revelation. However, even those with no interest in Christianity can recognize the importance of preserving the possibility that there are fundamental mysteries that human reason cannot solve on its own.

Ethics

I turn now from epistemology to the other core field of philosophy where I think Kierkegaard still has much to teach us: ethics. Here I want primarily to discuss the book that I take to be Kierkegaard's greatest contribution to ethical thought, *Works of Love*. In the first part of this work, Kierkegaard explores the radical character of the command to love one's neighbor as oneself, with the "neighbor" to be understood as including all human beings. He clearly sees this command as the fundamental duty humans have to each other. It is a duty that comes from the Jewish and Christian Scriptures, and Kierkegaard claims that "paganism," which for him basically means the thought of ancient Greece, had no "hint" or "intimation" that "the neighbor" in this sense even existed, much less that we humans have a duty to love our neighbors.[13] Kierkegaard thus argues that a genuine or "unspoiled" pagan, who has not been introduced to

1992) 58-79.
    [12]See, e.g., Colin McGinn, *The Mysterious Flame: Conscious Minds in a Material World* (New York: Basic Books, 1999).
    [13]*Works of Love*, SV1 IX 47-48.

Christianity, will find the idea that one has a duty to love one's neighbor to be surprising and disturbing.[14]

Things are different with the "spoiled pagan," the person who in reality is a pagan but who has learned about Christian ideas. This figure embodies the kind of "worldly" thinking that Kierkegaard thinks is pervasive in Christendom: "God and the world agree in this, that love is the fulfilling of the Law; the difference is that the world understands the Law as something it thinks up by itself. . . . "[15] In effect Kierkegaard is claiming that the "world" has learned about this fundamental duty from Christianity, but has tried to show that such an ethical principle can be given a nonreligious foundation. The "world" thinks that God is no longer needed to be the foundation of the moral law, or the ground of our moral obligations.[16]

Kierkegaard's views here anticipate the arguments given by G. E. M. Anscombe in an influential article, in which Anscombe claims that the modern concept of "moral obligation" is a survival of a concept that presupposes a divine law giver:

> Naturally, it is not possible to have such a conception [a law conception of ethics] unless you believe in God as a law-giver; like Jews, Stoics, and Christians. But if such a conception is dominant for many centuries, and then is given up, it is a natural result that the concepts of "obligation," of being bound or required as by a law, should remain though they had lost their root.[17]

In this article, Anscombe argues that modern moral philosophy, whether one looks at Kantian deontological ethics or at consequentialist ethics, fails to make sense of this notion of obligation, and Anscombe actually recommends that moral philosophers today give up trying to make sense of moral obligations and instead

---

[14]*Works of Love*, SVI IX 28.

[15]*Works of Love*, SVI IX 123. Translation given is from the edition translated and edited by Howard V. Hong and Edna H. Hong (Princeton: Princeton University Press, 1995) 128.

[16]My argument in this section draws heavily on the arguments made in my *Kierkegaard's Ethic of Love: Divine Commands and Moral Obligations* (Oxford UK: Oxford University Press, 2004). See esp. 112-39.

[17]In Steven Cahn and Joram G. Haber, eds., *Twentieth Century Ethical Theory* (Englewood Cliffs NJ: Prentice-Hall, 1995) 355. Repr. from *Philosophy* 33/124 (January 1958).

turn their attention to the virtues, following the example of Aristotle, a recommendation that has borne fruit in the subsequent revival of virtue ethics.

In *Works of Love* Kierkegaard clearly anticipates Anscombe's critique of modern moral philosophy. As Kierkegaard sees things, the modern secular mind sees emancipation from God as a further step in human liberation: slavery and serfdom have been abolished, and now it is time to "go further" by liberating humans from God.[18] However, the consequence of this will be that the place occupied by God will be empty, and this has devastating consequences for modern society: "As a reward for such presumption, all existence will in that way probably come closer and closer to being transformed into doubt or into a vortex."[19]

Since Kierkegaard is not doing moral theory in the modern sense, he provides no detailed critique of the strategies modern moral philosophers have employed to base moral obligations on something other than God. Nevertheless he does provide hints of why there is no adequate substitute for God in this role. One might think that the moral law could be something society has invented, the result of something like a social contract, but Kierkegaard thinks that such a construction is impossible:

> Or should the determination of what is the Law's requirement perhaps be an agreement among, a common decision by, all people, to which the individual has to submit? Splendid — that is, if it is possible to find the place and fix a date for this assembling of all people (all the living, all of them? — but what about the dead?), and if it is possible, something that is equally impossible, for all of them to agree on one thing![20]

The Kantian strategy of having the autonomous individual legislate the moral law is dismissed cryptically in *Works of Love* as "pure arbitrariness,"[21] but the thought is expanded in a humorous journal entry:

---

[18]*Works of Love*, SVI IX 111-12.
[19]*Works of Love*, SVI IX 112, 115.
[20]*Works of Love*, SVI IX 112, 115.
[21]SVI IX 112.

Kant was of the opinion that man is his own law (autonomy)--
that is, he binds himself under the law which he himself gives
himself. Actually, in a profounder sense, this is how lawlessness or
experimentation are established. This is not being rigorously
earnest any more than Sancho Panza's self-administered blows to
his own bottom were vigorous.[22]

The problem with legislating for oneself is that what one
legislates today can be repealed tomorrow. Of course Kant did not
think this way; on his view the moral law stemmed from a universal,
timeless reason that is the same for every individual and that
provides humans with synthetic a priori knowledge, but it is very
unclear how an objective moral law can come into being if one
doubts that humans possess a timeless faculty of reason of this type.

The claim that Kierkegaard makes that moral obligations require
a God to whom the individual is accountable is rejected by the great
majority of contemporary philosophers, even by religious philosophers. (Although, interestingly enough, Kierkegaard may have
Nietzsche on his side here, since Nietzsche also seems to think that
the death of God entails the demise of objective moral obligations.)
However, the value of a philosopher's view should not be measured
by its popularity. If Kierkegaard is right in his claim that modernity
involves a kind of "mutiny" against God's authority,[23] then it is not
implausible that the mutiny would be accompanied by widespread
confusion and lack of clarity about the nature of the mutiny. Perhaps
we should take seriously Kierkegaard's claim that the moral
confusion and disarray of modern society is the result of the
"vortex" caused by precisely such a mutiny.

Conclusion:
The Crisis of Authority in the Contemporary World

I have tried to give a brief sketch of the ways in which Kierkegaard
has something of real value to say to the contemporary philosophical
world in the fields of epistemology and ethics. In both areas

---

[22]*Søren Kierkegaard's Journals and Papers*, ed. and trans. Howard V. Hong and
Edna H. Hong (Bloomington: Indiana University Press, 1967) vol. 1, entry 188, p. 76.
    [23]*Works of Love*, SVI IX 113-14.

Kierkegaard has things to say that very few others have said; he thereby calls into question assumptions that most contemporary thinkers are hardly aware of. It goes without saying that when I claim that what Kierkegaard has to say here is valuable, I am also giving voice to my own philosophical views, and those who do not share those views may well think that Kierkegaard's challenges possess little value. However, even this kind of reader might recognize the value of a philosopher who can articulate the kind of radical challenge found in a thinker who is able to call into question some of the taken-for-granted assumptions of an age. If the patterns of thought of modernity are genuinely sound, they will be able to withstand such a challenge, but they will still be better off for having undergone such a test.

In conclusion I would like to pose the question as to whether the challenges I have described in epistemology and ethics are connected in some way. Tentatively, I would like to suggest that they are indeed linked. The common threads that tie the two areas together are the recognition of human finitude and the significance of divine authority. We humans are, when all is said and done, animals and not gods. We are creatures, special creatures to be sure, made in the image of God, but creatures nonetheless. Since we are finite creatures, it is not surprising that there are limits to human reason, limits that make it necessary for humans to respond in faith to a divine revelation if we are to reach the truth about ourselves. Our creatureliness also helps us understand why we humans are unable to construct a framework of moral obligations that are genuinely binding. On Kierkegaard's view, both when we seek the truth and when we seek the good, we must do our part to end the "mutiny" and learn to rest in God in faith:

> Is not each individual under an obligation to God to stop the mutiny, not, of course, by loud noise or fancied importance, not by domineeringly wanting to compel others to obey God, but by being unconditionally obedient oneself, by unconditionally holding to the God-relationship and to God's requirement, and thereby expressing that as far as he is concerned God exists and is the only sovereign, whereas he is an unconditionally obedient subject?[24]

---

[24]*Works of Love*, SVI IX 114; Hong translation, 117.

If I am right in my contention that there is a link between Kierkegaard's epistemological and ethical views, then we can understand why Kierkegaard lavished so much time and effort on *The Book on Adler*, even though out of concern for Adler the book as a whole was never published during his lifetime. For Kierkegaard is surely right to say that the whole of *The Book on Adler* "is basically an inquiry into the concept of authority," and that the "confusions of the present age" basically stem from modernity's confusions about authority.[25]

Kierkegaard is a philosopher who is well aware of the dangers posed by claims to have a revelation from God, and the philosophical difficulties such claims pose. However, he believes that the quest for authentic selfhood requires us to risk these dangers and difficulties. Human beings are not self-enclosed monads, and they cannot achieve selfhood on their own as atomic individuals. Nor can they become authentic selves simply by conforming to the roles and norms assigned them by human societies. Rather, genuine selfhood requires us to stand before God as individuals. However, we cannot relate to God without hearing God's word, and responding to it as God's word. Authority and authentic selfhood thus go hand in hand.

---

[25]*The Book on Adler*, KW 24, ed. and trans. Howard V. Hong and Edna H. Hong (Princeton: Princeton University Press, 1998) 4.

8

Rethinking Hatred of Self—
A Kierkegaardian Exploration

M. Jamie Ferreira

Why does Kierkegaard matter today? One reason is that there is a claim in the Christian scriptures that one ought to "hate" oneself, and that claim has always been provocative. One example: "Anyone who loves his life loses it; anyone who hates his life in this world will keep it for the eternal life" (John 12:25 NJB). Another: "If any one comes to me, and does not hate his own father and mother and wife and children and brothers and sisters, yes, and *even his own life*, he cannot be my disciple" (Luke 14:26 NASV; my emphasis).[1] Such passages lead some people to reject Christianity, or to excise this claim from the 'Christian' message they do accept. The affirmation of such claims leads other people to a self-tormenting asceticism or to a diminution of self-esteem. For example, one endorsement of Kierkegaard's notion of "Christian self-hatred" insists that Kierkegaard agrees with Luther that "any self-esteem . . . is really a slander of God's honor and praise," adding that when Kierkegaard speaks positively of self-love, "he is not promoting self-esteem, self-respect, self-admiration, or self-worth."[2] I find it worrisome that Kierkegaard is ever used to support an appeal to self-hatred or self-denial that is equated with "self-deprecation,"[3] because I agree with Paul Ricoeur when he suggests that self-esteem is important precisely because someone who "detests" himself could not even hear "the injunction

---

[1]See 2 Timothy 3:2.

[2]Ronald F. Marshall, "News from the Graveyard: Kierkegaard's Analysis of Christian Self-Hatred," *Pro Ecclesia* 9/1 (Winter 2000): 28n.26, n.29, n.31.

[3]Marshall's goal is to defend "the propriety of self-hatred" (28) [which is rhetorically quite different from defending proper self-hatred]; his qualifications to the contrary notwithstanding (Marshall, "News from the Graveyard," 28n.25, n.27, n.30); he equates "appropriate self-hatred" with "self-deprecation," arguing that they both "negate the Christian" and "affirm one's love of God" (19-20).

coming from the other," and that "the effect of the 'crisis' of selfhood must not be the substitution of self-hatred for self-esteem."[4]

Throughout the course of his authorship Kierkegaard considered this Christian claim about hatred of self in relation to notions of self-denial, self-sacrifice, self-esteem, and self-love, and as long as notions of self-esteem and self-denial are important, Kierkegaard's views on them will be worth reexamining.

In particular, given Kierkegaard's commitment to the command-ment to love the neighbor "as oneself," I want to reconsider how Kierkegaard negotiates the tension between his endorsement of self-hatred and his endorsement of self-love. I aim to show that Kierke-gaard's notion of proper self-hatred appreciates the danger of "self-contempt" as a kind of faithlessness to the self. As importantly, I want to explore how his comments on self-hatred often illuminate his conception of 'proper' self-love.

Consider some of the bold, and apparently unambiguous, claims Kierkegaard makes in his own name. In 1855, the year of his death, he condemns the Christianity of "Christendom" in contrast to the admittedly "agonizing" norm of the "Christianity of the New Testament," which is "to love God in hatred of humankind, in hatred of oneself (*had til sig selv*) and thereby of all other people, hating father, mother, one's own child, wife, etc."[5] But even if we take his final diatribes with a grain of salt, we still find earlier recommendations: a blatant rigorism is found in *For Self-Examination* (1851) where he declares "not until you in love of God have learned *to hate yourself*, not until then can there be talk of the love that is Christian love"[6]; and in an 1849 Communion discourse he writes that "the strongest expression for loving much" is "to hate oneself."[7]

Sometimes, however, Kierkegaard adds crucial qualifications to such a recommendation. In the same Communion discourse in which he equates "loving much" with hating oneself, Kierkegaard adds another element to the puzzle, by implying that hatred of self and love of self are compatible: he suggests that the fact that "the

---

[4]Paul Ricoeur, *Oneself as Another*, trans. Kathleen Blamey (Chicago: University of Chicago Press, 1992) 189, 168.

[5]TM 184.

[6]FSE 84.

[7]"The Woman Who Was a Sinner," in WA 138.

woman who was a sinner" lacked "leniency" for herself meant that "she hated herself," yet he goes on to say approvingly that "there was something self-loving in this woman's love."[8] Moreover, in one of his 1844 upbuilding discourses, "Against Cowardliness," we find the perhaps surprising claim that "hatred of oneself is still also self-love, and all self-love is cowardice."[9] This equation of self-hatred with cowardice amounts to a warning against self-hatred. Both the suggestion of the compatibility of self-hatred and self-love and the warning against self-hatred raise questions about what Kierkegaard means by these terms and I suggest that we can learn much by exploring these and other relevant passages in detail.

A. Proper Self-Love and Self-Esteem

Before turning more specifically to the notion of 'self-hatred,' however, it is worth reminding ourselves about Kierkegaard's commitments concerning 'self-love.' First, in *Works of Love* Kierkegaard makes a straightforward distinction between proper self-love and improper self-love. He insists that through its emphasis on the phrase, "as yourself," in the love commandment Christianity wants to teach a "proper self-love" (18), which he later contrasts with "selfish self-love" (151).[10] This should be enough to rebut any charge that Kierkegaard simply condemns self-love as such. Although he is exceedingly sensitive to the dangers of perversions of self-love, he assumes that without proper self-love, one could not properly love anyone else: "[I]f anyone is unwilling to learn from Christianity to love himself *in the right way*, he cannot love the neighbor either" (WL 22; my emphasis). To "wrest" self-love from you must, therefore, not amount to ceasing to love yourself but rather to opening the "lock," rendering love inclusive rather than exclusive and competitive. Christianity's doctrine reminds a person to "love his neighbor as himself, that is, as he ought to love himself." Indeed, Kierkegaard even equates them: "To love yourself in the right way and to love the

---

[8]WA 138.
[9]EUD 374.
[10]WL 18, 151.

neighbor correspond perfectly to one another; fundamentally they are one and the same thing" (WL 22).[11]

It should be noted that Kierkegaard's striking claim in the upbuilding discourse "Against Cowardliness" that "all self-love is cowardice" (EUD 373) either contradicts his commitment to the possibility of a "proper self-love" or should be read as suggesting that "all (*improper*) self-love is cowardice." This latter reading is not implausible, because even in *Works of Love*, where Kierkegaard explicitly makes the distinction between "proper" and "selfish" self-love, he often omits the qualifiers and lets the context make clear which kind of self-love he means; for example, he writes that "Whoever has any knowledge of people will certainly admit that just as he has often wished to be able to move them to relinquish self-love, he has also had to wish that it were possible to teach them to love themselves" (WL 23). In other words, Kierkegaard's claims about "self-love" are often not a comment on self-love as such; the context will determine whether "proper" self-love or "selfish" self-love is at stake for him.

In *Works of Love* there are a variety of justifications for the affirmation of a certain kind of self-love — a "proper" self-love which is appropriately considered a kind of self-esteem.[12] Such love of self is legitimated by the very unconditionality of the love command — no one can be excluded, not even oneself. One formulation of the rationale for this is the equality of all before God, but in order to generate the legitimacy of self-esteem, we need to add to this the acknowledgement of the giftedness of all creation. This latter implies that we are loved into being by God to become 'something,' and we must love our own distinctiveness because it is what comes from God's hand. To the creature's silent prayer — "Let me become

---

[11]"The Law is therefore: You shall love yourself in the same way as you love your neighbor when you love him as yourself" (WL 23). In a 1948 review article, David Roberts suggests that "Kierkegaard was exactly a century ahead of [Erich] Fromm in insisting that love for mankind (the neighbor) is conjunctive with self-love, which is the opposite of selfishness" ("*Works of Love*: A Review Article," in *Review of Religion* 12 (1948): 383.

[12]Admittedly, there is an improper kind of self-esteem, an inappropriate feeling about the self, which Kierkegaard calls "the intoxication of self-esteem [*selvfølelse*]" and which signals the rejection of the need for self-denial (see WL 56).

something in myself, something distinctive" — the God of love responds by helping it "to become its own distinctiveness" (WL 270). Together, equality and giftedness support self-esteem — because "distinctiveness . . . is God's gift by which he gives being to me, and he indeed gives to all" (WL 271).

Kierkegaard specifies proper self-love when he writes that "humility before God is true pride"; indeed, the "God-pleasing venture of humility and pride" is "*before* God to be oneself" (WL 271). True pride (which is true humility and true honesty) celebrates the paradox of creation: "the *Omnipotent One* . . . gives in such a way that the receiver acquires distinctiveness, that he who creates out of nothing yet creates distinctiveness, so that the creature in relation to God does not become nothing even though it is taken from nothing and is nothing but becomes a distinctive individuality" (WL 271-72).

The gift of creation also means that we are totally dependent on God, all of us equally. Such dependence, however, does not undermine self-esteem, but is expressed in the grateful cultivation of the gift of our freedom. What is true of others is true of us as well: "to become one's master is the highest — and in love to help someone toward that, to become himself, free, independent, his own master, to help him stand alone — that is the greatest beneficence" (WL 274). Such standing alone is always with and through God, but it is still a standing alone — it is not a self-annihilating disdain for the self or a groveling denial of the gift of freedom. If it is, as Kierkegaard thinks, "every human being's destiny to become free, independent, oneself," then in our self-esteem we are "God's coworker" (WL 278-79).

Illustrations of what Kierkegaard means by "selfish self-love" are found in abundance in *Works of Love*, most graphically in the discussion of the manipulative and self-serving attitudes that constitute the refusal to embrace the distinctive otherness of the other (WL 270-73). Selfishly "loving one's own" means wanting "everyone to be transformed in his image . . . trimmed according to his pattern for human beings" (WL 270).[13] Properly "loving one's own," on the contrary, is the humble/proud "venture" of valuing one's distinctiveness, and it takes courage for two reasons: first, it

---

[13]Ironically, selfishly "loving one's own" can also be expressed in not believing in anyone else's distinctiveness because one cannot truly believe in one's own (WL 272).

requires one "*before* God to be oneself" (WL 271), and so to assume a demanding responsibility for one's cocreation with God, and second, because it requires the consistency of appreciating the distinctiveness of all others. It would not be surprising then to learn that, as in the case of self-love, Kierkegaard makes a contrast between kinds of self-hatred.

B. Self-Hatred — Proper and Improper

How then is Kierkegaard's appreciation of (proper) self-love compatible with his endorsement of 'self-hatred'? What does he mean by self-hatred? What is he recommending? What is he warning against? What more can we learn about "proper" self-love by looking more closely at his comments on self-hatred? I suggest that we first reconsider three passages (two of which were noted above) in which Kierkegaard in his own name either qualifies or rejects any recommendation of self-hatred.

1. Compatibility and the Lessons It Teaches

The first passage contains the suggestion of the coexistence of both 'proper' self-hatred and 'proper' self-love. In the discourse, "The Woman who was a Sinner" (1849), Kierkegaard affirms that "loving much" is "hatred of oneself": "And what is the strongest expression for loving much? It is to hate oneself" (WA 138). What precisely the woman did who "went in to the Holy One" at a dinner "in the house of the Pharisee," where she could expect "the cruelty of the mockery that awaited her from the proud Pharisees," is summarized in the refrain repeated at the end of each of five paragraphs — "she hated herself: she loved much" (WA 138-40). We learn two important things by examining this passage further.

a. *Proper self-love and Need.* Kierkegaard first notes the possible objection to the woman who barged into the dinner that "in her need she basically still loved herself" (WA 142), and he agrees that this woman who "hated herself" also "loved herself." In fact, he responds that "there is no other way" in which she could seek forgiveness than through self-love:

> God forbid that I would ever presume to want to love my God or my Savior in any other way, because if there were literally no self-

love in my love, then I would no doubt be only imagining that I could love them without standing in need of them.   (WA 142)

Self-love is implied in our need for God — to try to do without that kind of self-love is to turn away from God. The woman who was a sinner came looking for forgiveness: "she dared to do it because one thing was unconditionally important to her: to find forgiveness" (WA 154). Indeed, Kierkegaard insists both that love of God is impossible without need and that seeking to fulfill need is, by definition, self-loving.

The same astonishing message had been offered earlier in Kierkegaard's *Christian Discourses*. In the third discourse of part three, "All Things Must Serve us for Good — *When* we Love God,"[14] he writes:

> The simple and humble way is to love God because one needs him. . . . Admittedly . . . it seems very selfish to love God because one needs him — yet the latter is the only way in which a person can truly love God. . . . the fundamental and primary basis for a person's love of God is completely to understand that one needs God, loves him simply because one needs him. The person who most profoundly recognizes his need of God loves him most truly. You are not to presume to love God for God's sake. You are humbly to understand that your own welfare eternally depends on this need, and therefore you are to love him.   (CD 188)[15]

This theme had long been part of Kierkegaard's repertoire. In an upbuilding discourse from 1844, the message is found in the title itself, "To Need God Is a Human Being's Highest Perfection." Kierkegaard elaborates this as follows: whereas paganism had suggested that a wise man needs little, "in a human being's relationship with God, it is inverted: the more he needs God, the more deeply he comprehends that he is in need of God, and then the more he in his need presses forward to God, the more perfect he is."[16]

---

[14]Part Three was written January–February 1848.

[15]Pia Søltoft considers part of this quotation for her more general argument concerning hatred of the world: "Is Love of God Hatred of the World," *Kierkegaard Studies Yearbook 2007*, ed. Niels Jørgen Cappeløern et al. (Berlin and New York: de Gruyter, 2008) 70.

[16]"To Need God Is a Human Being's Highest Perfection," EUD 303.

What precisely is the self-love implied in needing God? The sinful woman is self-loving in seeking forgiveness; we are self-loving in seeking our "own welfare." If we follow out the logic of the position in these discourses, we can infer that the self-love implied in need is a kind of perfection because it is a striving for our fulfillment.[17] Moreover, this is not just a question of religious fulfillment, because Kierkegaard reminds in *Works of Love* how important our need to love and be loved are: "[O]ur Lord Jesus Christ, even he humanly felt this need to love and be loved by an individual human being"; Christ's "craving to hear" that Peter loved him "more than these" is paradigmatic of human love: "to love humanly is to love an individual human being and to wish to be that individual human being's best beloved" (WL 155, 156). Thus, we can find a further justification for "proper self-love" in the connection Kierkegaard posits between self-love and need.

2. Proper Self-Hatred
and Our Nothingness before God

The second thing we learn is that the sinful woman's love of God is hatred of herself only in the sense that it is an acceptance of the fact that "she is capable of literally nothing at all; he is capable of unconditionally everything" (WA 140). Kierkegaard highlights how "she has forgotten herself completely" (WA 140), which he equates with her acknowledgement that she is capable of nothing without God. Proper self-hatred is a certain kind of forgetting of self, and we could say that conversely, proper self-love is a remembering that we are always and in every way dependent on God. This does not lead to a passive infantilism because, as we saw above, for Kierkegaard the human being must learn to "stand alone" with God, "to be oneself" before God.

In sum, proper self-hatred is the same as the proper self-love that acknowledges our need of God — it is not the forgetfulness of self

---

[17]Kierkegaard emphasizes our spiritual welfare when he writes that "In the profoundest sense, the question 'Do I love God?' is a question of welfare" (CD 188) and then he continues by referring to "this self-concern, this fear and trembling with regard to whether one is a believer" (CD 189). But he is clearly concerned to acknowledge the legitimacy of our need to love and be loved, e.g., in WL 155, 156.

that forfeits or despairs of forgiveness, nor the forgetfulness of the self that ignores or disdains our welfare. Proper self-hatred/self-love is not merely the fact of needing God, but rather the embracing of that need and the giving up the fight to deny or minimize it.

3. Rejection of Self-hatred in the Name of Courage

The question of what Kierkegaard understands by the recommendation to hate oneself can be further illuminated by turning back to the discourse "Against Cowardliness" (1844). The claim I noted earlier, that "all self-love is cowardice," is found in the context of a warning against self-hatred. Kierkegaard writes: "hatred of oneself is still also self-love, and all self-love is cowardice" (EUD 374). This statement accomplishes three distinct and significant things. First, it warns us against self-hatred. Second, it suggests that self-love is cowardice. Third, it suggests that (improper) self-hatred is not the opposite of self-love, but is rather a form of (improper) self-love.

Some of Kierkegaard's comments seem to point to ordinary notions of self-hatred, as when he speaks of self-hatred in relation to "purposeless suffering" (EUD 373) and as an instance of being "inventive in increasing [one's] own torment" (EUD 374). Warnings against these parallel the warnings found later in *Works of Love* where Kierkegaard writes compassionately that just as often as he feels the need to pull in the reins on one person's selfish self-love, he feels the need to open another person to proper self-love: the person who "throws himself into the folly of the moment," the person who is suicidally depressed or otherwise self-destructive, and the one who "surrenders to despair" because he has been betrayed — all these are examples of a person who "does not know how to love himself rightly" (WL 23). He concludes: "When someone self-tormentingly thinks to do God a service by torturing himself, what is his sin except not willing to love himself in the right way?" (WL 23).

It is easy to see why contrived suffering and self-torment are a kind of improper self-hatred. But it is not obvious how self-hatred exhibits cowardliness or how this cowardliness of self-hatred is also a form of self-love? We need to consider the larger context of the discourse to discern these connections.

The discourse is aimed at highlighting the cowardly ways through which we avoid the good — "cowardliness prevents a person from *doing the good*" (EUD 363) and "*cowardliness prevents a person from acknowledging the good that he does do*" (EUD 369). In general, cowardice is the enemy of "the good resolution":

> The good resolution, which corresponds to the acknowledgement of the good, is indeed to will to do everything in one's power, to serve it to the utmost of one's capacity. To do everything one is capable of doing. (EUD 361)

Kierkegaard explores with psychological astuteness the countless "evasions" and "sophistries" (EUD 366) through which cowardice undermines our achievement of the good. For example, cowardice may say that the task is "too easy" (EUD 358) — cowardice always wants to deal with "the important," so one "cheats the task, calls it a trifle, and then he abstains from accomplishing it" (EUD 365). On the other hand, cowardice may suggest that "the capability is slight," that there is "too little to begin with" and so we have an excuse for not beginning; after all, it is easier to do nothing than to fail, easier to reject everything than to begin with little, for "the person who begins nothing does not lose anything either" (EUD 359). These and many others are the ways in which cowardice keeps people from doing the good.

Such "evasions" and "sophistries" are interesting, but they are not surprising. What is more surprising is the particular turn Kierkegaard takes in this discourse: he turns away from the usual ways in which cowardice works to the peculiar and less obvious ways in which cowardice "prevents a person from acknowledging the good he does do" (EUD 369). He turns to a cowardliness that is a form of self-hatred. He is concerned not with the hypocrite who wants to appear better than he is, but rather with the "hatred of oneself that wrongs the person himself so that he is merely inventive in increasing his own torment" (EUD 374). That is, he is concerned with the subtle ways in which self-hatred manifests itself by refusing to acknowledge the good one does. Contributing to maintaining the world's low opinion of oneself is self-destructive, but Kierkegaard is at pains to show how such self-destructiveness is also self-serving, hence at the same time a form of improper self-hatred and improper self-love.

What is the context for concluding that self-hatred is also a form of self-love, both of which can be cowardly? Kierkegaard says early on that one can be "an unworthy servant even when one has done one's utmost" and one wants to avoid this sad truth; we want to avoid "resolution's solemn agreement with the good on such humiliating terms" (EUD 359). He reiterates this: "The good retains the right to make a person an unworthy servant even when he does the most" — this thought is "the most humiliating" because it "requires from a person the honest confession that he is just like every other human being, even the lowliest" (EUD 372). How can one avoid this humiliation?

Kierkegaard writes that self-hatred is a way of eliciting misunderstanding so as to promote self-importance: "When he suffers misjudgment, it is easy for him to become more self-important" (EUD 372).[18] Suffering misjudgment equals refusing to acknowledge the good one does, and this perversely is self-serving: "one becomes self-important, since someone who does the good but does not acknowledge it is still not altogether like other people" (EUD 374). Self-hatred is a self-serving way of making us stand out, highlighting our tarnished importance — it is improper self-love.

In addition, either by occasioning misjudgment or by being silent in the face of it, someone can lack "the courage to admit his weakness, [preferring] to seem evil and be hated rather than to be loved and have his weakness known to others" (EUD 373). Better to seem bad than to seem ordinary. Better to seem evil than to be seen as inadequately striving to be better. Acknowledging the good we did allows it to be seen in its meagerness as compared to giving our all.

Although it may seem that preferring to seem evil amounts to admitting one's weakness, it is not, for Kierkegaard, an admission of one's actual weakness. Rather, emphasizing one's evilness ironically keeps one's sense of one's strength intact.

According to Kierkegaard, what every human being should learn is that "he is nothing" (EUD 368), and yet one is obliged to do "everything one is capable of doing" (EUD 361). For Kierkegaard, this 'nothingness' is a nothingness before God — one's inability to do

---

[18]"it is much prouder to be conscious that one could be somewhat more than one is if one only wanted to be" (EUD 359) — but this is an example of how "pride and cowardliness are one and the same thing" (EUD 354).

anything without God. The self-hatred that is cowardly is the attitude that promotes a feigned nothingness before others, rather than our actual nothingness before God.

Self-hatred is a cowardly excuse for inaction or passivity. Kierkegaard explains this cowardliness by suggesting that "if he acknowledges the good, the world will perhaps judge him differently; it will demand something else from him, and this he perhaps cannot endure" (EUD 372).

A more general formulation of these ideas is that self-hatred is an unwillingness to acknowledge the good (in oneself, or in general). Since acknowledging the good in us entails acknowledging our unworthiness despite the good in us, when we refuse to acknowledge the good we are not acknowledging our weakness or unworthiness. The self-hatred that is to be warned against is at the same time a refusal to acknowledge the good in us and a refusal to acknowledge our unworthiness.

From Kierkegaard's twofold conclusion that self-hatred is a self-serving and cowardly attempt to avoid responsibility, as well as a self-serving and cowardly failure to acknowledge our unworthiness, we can derive something about what proper self-love is. First, proper self-love is to admit our weakness without cultivating self-importance through it; second, proper self-love is to acknowledge the good in us, while admitting that we are still unworthy. The difficulty is to acknowledge both at the same time. To acknowledge the good in us opens us to demands from those who need to see that good in action. To embrace our weakness without thereby attempting to become important by it is to be humble enough to seek God's grace to do the good we can do.

4. Rejection of Self-Contempt in the Name of Faithfulness to Self

Another indication of what is at stake for Kierkegaard in improper self-hatred and proper self-love is found in his explicit rejection of the notion of self-contempt. In "Purity of Heart Is to Love One Thing" he calls on a contrast made by a poet between self-love and self-contempt: the poet writes that "Worse than self-love is self-contempt."[19] Kierkegaard suggests that self-contempt is the "offense" (the "guilt") of "unfaithfulness to oneself or *a disowning of one's own better nature*" (93; his emphasis). He brings this up in the process of insisting that "faithfulness to oneself with respect to [one's "eternal purpose"] is the highest thing a person can do." Thus, one could say that in faithfulness to oneself there is a proper self-love — there is a kind of self-love that is faithfulness to oneself. Moreover, the courage it takes to be faithful to oneself is the courage of self-love. Self-contempt is worse than selfish self-love because self-contempt is an unfaithfulness to the self.

Rather than simply agreeing with the poet that self-love is bad, Kierkegaard offers a description of self-contempt that suggests a way in which there can be proper self-love and improper self-hatred. Proper self-hatred does not entail self-contempt. Self-contempt is improper self-hatred, and it is worth being warned against.

In his rejection of self-contempt, Kierkegaard takes up again the question about honesty before God he considered in relation to cowardliness. Here he notes that self-contempt involves having "so low an opinion of the good and beautiful and true as to believe them capable of employing everyone as a useful instrument to coax his sweet-sounding agreement — everyone, even the person who has made a mess of himself" (93-94). Self-contempt is dishonest; it is self-deceptive.[20] The refusal (embodied in self-contempt) to acknowledge the good (in us or in general) echoes the cowardly fault alluded to in the preceding section.

It is interesting that one of today's leading moral philosophers appeals to this very piece of writing by Kierkegaard in his own philosophical argument that self-love is valuable and is to be cultivated rather than feared or denounced.[21] Harry G. Frankfurt's defense of self-love in part three of *The Reasons of Love* (2004) explicitly appeals to Kierkegaard's "emphatic declaration" that "Purity of heart is to will one thing."[22] He thereby calls on Kierke-

---

[19]UDVS 93.

[20]Willing the good in truth, on the contrary, means using "sagacity *against evasions*" (UDVS 94; his emphasis).

[21]Frankfurt, *The Reasons of Love* (Princeton NJ: Princeton University Press, 2004); for Frankfurt, self-love is both "desirable and important" (96).

[22]Frankfurt, *The Reasons of Love*, 95.

gaard to provide support for his claim for the fundamental importance of what Frankfurt calls a "unified will" — the structural or
formal condition of being undivided in one's will. Frankfurt rightly
notes that for Kierkegaard, this condition is not a matter of simply
being "narrowly focused"; what is endorsed is, rather, the "integrity" of the will and its "wholeheartedness," the "quality of the will
. . . not the quantity of its objects."[23] Frankfurt elaborates: the "purity
of a wholehearted will" is valuable because it precludes the incoher-
ence and irrationality of a divided will, and it allows for genuine
freedom; volitional integrity assures volitional freedom.

Frankfurt goes further, claiming that "to be wholehearted *is* to
love oneself"; indeed, "wholehearted self-love consists in, or is
exactly constituted by, the wholeheartedness of [one's] unified
will."[24] Self-love is valuable and is to be cultivated because self-love
is loving what one loves.[25] Self-love precludes the "irrationality" of
a "self-defeating" will, and it issues in "the inner harmony" that is
"tantamount to possessing a fundamental kind of freedom."[26] For
Frankfurt, "loving ourselves is desirable and important for us
because it is the same thing, more or less, as being satisfied with ourselves," as endorsing "our own volitional identity" — in other words,
"we are content with the final goals and with the loving by which
our will is most penetratingly defined."[27] This latter bit might sound
Kierkegaardian, but Frankfurt's appeal to Kierkegaard has been
found appalling by some; why, and what can we learn from this?

Frankfurt's defense of self-love suffers from what looks like a
contradiction between a claim for its value and a claim for its value
neutrality. For Frankfurt, self-love is valuable, but wholeheartedness
is a purely formal category — "the value of what [one] loves is
irrelevant to the question of whether [one] is wholehearted in loving
it."[28] In the end, however, Frankfurt is not guilty of a contradiction:
"whatever the value and importance of self-love, it does not
guarantee even a minimal rectitude"; "the function of love is not to

[23]Frankfurt, *The Reasons of Love*, 97.
[24]Frankfurt, *The Reasons of Love*, 95.
[25]Frankfurt, *The Reasons of Love*, 97.
[26]Frankfurt, *The Reasons of Love*, 96, 97.
[27]Frankfurt, *The Reasons of Love*, 97.
[28]Frankfurt, *The Reasons of Love*, 98.

make people good" but rather to make their lives "meaningful."[29]
Self-love is good for you, but it is not morally good.

So Frankfurt's account is consistent, but is it Kierkegaardian?
Kierkegaard had, as we saw above, suggested that self-contempt is
the "offense" (the "guilt") of "unfaithfulness to oneself or a disowning of one's own better nature" (UDVS 93); moreover, he had
insisted that "faithfulness to oneself with respect to [one's "eternal
purpose"] is the highest thing a person can do." Obviously, Frankfurt took the general idea of the importance of integrity from Kierkegaard's essay without noting his divergence from Kierkegaard
with respect to the substantive constraints Kierkegaard had in place
concerning the purity of the will. What Frankfurt calls "the final
goals" and "the loving by which our will is most penetratingly
defined" are seen by Kierkegaard in terms of one's "better nature"
and one's "eternal purpose." To imply that for Kierkegaard integrity
and wholeheartedness are purely formal categories is clearly misrep-
resenting Kierkegaard — in this respect, Frankfurt and Kierkegaard
are at odds.

There is, however, a sense in which Frankfurt can still call
Kierkegaard an ally, although the details will not be found in the
essay on "purity of heart." If we look to *Works of Love*, however, it
could be argued that there is an important sense in which love, even
self-love, is not a matter of moral value. That one loves is, for
Kierkegaard, a "need" in us.[30] To love is a need in us in the sense
that to grow is a need in a plant — without it we die.

Frankfurt's claim that loving is valuable in itself corresponds to
Kierkegaard's affirmation of the need to love. Our "need" to love
renders it amoral. We do not have a choice to love or not love — our
choice lies in the 'how' of our loving. In this way, then, we have
come full circle--back to the connection between self-love and need,
which *is* a Kierkegaardian theme.

5. What Hatred of Others Teaches Us about Hatred of Self

Another entrée into Kierkegaard's views on self-hatred can be found
in an exploration of his views on hatred directed to others: that is, I

---

[29]Frankfurt, *The Reasons of Love*, 98, 99.
[30]WL 10-11, 67, 154-55, 375.

suggest that we can learn from the way Kierkegaard explicitly construes any injunction to hate mother and father etc., something about how he sees hatred of self. Kierkegaard discusses such hatred in both his nonpseudonymous and his pseudonymous writings: in *Works of Love*, in *Christian Discourses*, in *Fear and Trembling*, and in the *Concluding Unscientific Postscript*.

In *Works of Love*, Kierkegaard reminds us that it is Christianity itself (not he, Søren Kierkegaard) that teaches that the Christian "must, if required, be able to hate father and mother and sister and the beloved" (WL 108). But he immediately qualifies this requirement when he asks whether Christianity requires this "in the sense, I wonder, that he should actually hate them? *Oh, far be this abomination from Christianity!*" (WL 108; my emphasis). As he makes clearer a few pages later, we cannot be asked to "refrain from loving them"; indeed *"How unreasonable — how then could your love become the fulfilling of the Law"* (WL 129; emphasis mine). Not only can we not be asked by God to actually "hate" father or mother or beloved, we cannot even be asked by God to "refrain from loving them" — after all, we are to exclude no one from our love.

Although he does not explicitly mention hatred of self in this context, the same argument against the idea of literally hating mother or father or beloved can be applied to the idea of literally hating the self — to do so would be to fail to fulfill the unconditional commandment to love without exception; it would be to refuse to fulfill the duty never to exclude anyone from our love. That is, in *Works of Love*, Kierkegaard proposes one justification for why he could never consistently endorse a failure to keep the love commandment, and so could not consistently endorse self-hatred.

What then does this "hate" refer to? Pia Søltoft has suggested that the requirement of hating mother and father is illuminated in the second discourse in part three of *Christian Discourses*.[31] Concerning Kierkegaard's claim there that Peter *"left the faith of his fathers and therefore had to hate his mother and father"* (CD 183; Kierkegaard's emphasis), Soltoft judges that "what we have here is not a call to hatred, but a conflict between different religious and self-percep-

---

[31]Pia Søltoft, "Is Love of God Hatred of the World?" in *Kierkegaard Studies Yearbook 2007*, 65-79.

tions." Kierkegaard suggests that "If there is a difference of religion, that is, an eternal, decisive difference of eternity between father and son, and the son ardently believes with all his heart, with all his strength, and all his soul that only in this religion is there salvation — then he indeed hates the father, that is, his love for something else is so great that his love for the father is like hate" (CD 183). He continues that to believe the father is "lost" is "hating the father, or rather, it is hating him and yet loving him!" (CD 183-4). Søltoft notes that the "hatred appears only *in* love. It is only because Peter still loves his mother and father and all the others he leaves behind who share the same religious conviction; his choosing another religion can be interpreted as hatred only because his love remains."[32]

A similar explanation of the reference to hating mother and father is found in the *Concluding Unscientific Postscript* where Climacus writes:

> For the believer it holds true that outside this condition there is no eternal happiness, and for him it holds true, or it can come to hold true for him, that he must hate father and mother. Is it not the same as hating them if his eternal happiness is bound to a condition that he knows they do not accept. . . . He can be willing to do his utmost for them, to fulfill all the duties of a faithful son and a faithful lover with the greatest enthusiasm — in this way Christianity does not enjoin hating — and yet, if this condition separates them, separates them forever, is it not as if he hated them?[33]

It is easy to see how the tragedy of religious difference which is "as if" hate applies to hatred of family or beloved, but it also applies to hatred of self insofar as we can see ourselves as distant from the ideal religious stance we want to have, see how our actual self is religiously opposed to our ideal self.

Such interpretations of the injunction to hate others undermines the view that it is ever intended to be taken as asking for a break with the commandment of love. Early in his career, however, in *Fear and Trembling*, Kierkegaard had explored the possibility of a "literal" reading of such injunctions — what can we learn from that? What is

---

[32]Søltoft, KSY, 73-74.
[33]CUP 586.

a "literal" reading? Is this a divergence between de Silentio and Kierkegaard?

Johannes de Silentio starts off by arguing in favor of a "literal" reading of the well-known biblical passage from the Gospel of Luke in which Christ confronts his disciples with an ultimatum: "If any one comes to me and does not hate his own father and mother and wife and children and brothers and sisters, yes, and even his own life, he cannot be my disciple" (FT 72). This biblical formulation maintains a parallel between hatred of others and hatred of self; moreover, at the outset de Silentio purports to admire Abraham for being great in virtue of the "love that is hatred of oneself" (FT 17) — this supports the legitimacy of extrapolating what we learn here about hatred of others to hatred of self.

As is well known, the claim that one must hate father, mother, wife, children, brothers, and sisters, and "even his own life" was used by de Silentio to show what an "absolute duty to God" means (FT 72) and to illustrate the kind of resignation that is required of a knight of faith. Of this shocking passage, which shows that "God is the one who demands absolute love" (FT 73), de Silentio notes that "anyone who does not dare to mention such passages does not dare to mention Abraham" (FT75).

De Silentio insists that "if this passage is to have any meaning it must be understood literally" (FT 73). He cuttingly rejects the weak interpretations offered by biblical exegetes, diluting the requirement to that of being "less kind" or "less attentive" (FT 72). But it soon seems that he is not advocating a literal reading after all because he goes on to say, "But if he actually hates Isaac, he can rest assured that God does not demand this of him, for Cain and Abraham are not identical" (FT 74). In fact, de Silentio seems concerned to nuance his "literal" reading significantly when he insists that "the absolute duty can lead one to do what ethics would forbid, but it can never lead the knight of faith to stop loving" (FT 74). If it is not an injunction to break the love commandment, how then are we to understand what we should do — "how to hate them"?

De Silentio makes an important comment on the injunction to hate others (or self), when he suggests: "I shall not review here *the human distinction, either to love or to hate*, not because I have so much against it, for at least it is passionate, but because it *is egotistic and does not fit here*" (FT 73; my emphasis). This comment makes clear that we are in a special context, and this applies to all mentions of the injunction to hate others (or self). He had noted earlier that "the ethical in the sense of the moral is entirely beside the point" (FT 59). On the contrary, "if I regard the task as a paradox, then I understand it" (FT 73). That is, while asking "how to hate them," he suggests that the human distinction between love and hate does not apply — because "to hate" is a paradoxical task. What is it to take a "paradoxical" task literally?

Ethically, hate is not a paradoxical task (to hate ethically is not a paradoxical task). "The ethical expression for what he is doing is: he hates Isaac"; in the realm of the ethical, the universal, "he is and remains a murderer" (FT 74). De Silentio insists that Abraham's absolute duty to God can never be a duty to stop loving Isaac, so what is being asked of Abraham is not to hate *ethically*. To hate ethically is a straightforward task, and to take it literally is to see it in all its ethical horror. The hatred that is being enjoined on Abraham is not an ethical task, but rather a paradoxical task, and if it is to be taken literally, it must be taken literally as a paradoxical task. Its literality as a paradox precludes its literality as simply either pole of the paradoxical task of loving while hating.

The injunction to hate others or self can be understood in two different ways — to hate ethically (univocally) or to hate religiously (paradoxically). I suggest that de Silentio's insistence that the passage must be understood literally encompasses the need for both understandings to be "literal."

The injunction to hate others or self must first be understood ethically: the formulation is most commonly an ethical formulation, a formulation within the language of ethics. When de Silentio protests against the weak reading of the passage done by the academic exegete, he seems to be rejecting the literalness of the formulation, but he is not. He is putting the injunction in ethical parentheses, and ethically "the words are to be taken in their full terror" (FT 72). He is against the dilution of the literal, ethical, requirement: its starkness must be maintained if we are to appreciate any other possible context for fulfilling the injunction. The ethical expression for what is required is 'hate'; there is no "higher expression" of the ethical *as the universal*. "[T]he passage in Luke must be understood in such a way that one perceives that the knight of faith can achieve no higher expression whatsoever of *the universal* (*as the ethical*) in which he can save himself" (FT 74; my emphasis).

But this is not the only expression possible. There is another expression and this must be understood literally as well, namely, the injunction to keep the commandment to love while doing what is ethically seen as hate. De Silentio proposes: "The ethical is reduced to the relative. From this it does not follow that it is invalidated;[34] rather the ethical receives a completely different expression, a paradoxical expression, such as, for example, that love to God may bring the knight of faith to give his love to the neighbor—an expression opposite to that which, ethically speaking, is duty" (FT 70). The willingness to take one's son's life is the willingness to die to all earthly hopes, and to hope for what is possible only with God. Abraham is not asked to give up all hope, but rather, as Kierkegaard puts it in *For Self-Examination*, to have a "new hope," "the *hope* that is against hope" (FSE 83), a hope (in God) against "every merely earthly hope . . . every merely human confidence" (FSE 77).

Abraham is required to hate paradoxically, not to hate ethically. If the ethical can only be expressed as the universal, if there is no *telos* beyond the ethical, then Abraham can only be judged ethically. The literal understanding of hating ethically must be appreciated if we are to appreciate what acknowledging a *telos* beyond the ethical would entail literally.

The question of hatred of self is also indirectly addressed in those places where Kierkegaard speaks of being willing to be hated by others. To willingly put ourselves in the position of being hated by others is to die to our self, to act as if we hated our self. Kierkegaard speaks of willingness to be hated by others in tandem with a willingness to "as if" hate others in *Works of Love*: "love, faithful and true love, divinely understood, must be *regarded by the loved ones . . . as hate*, because these refuse to understand what it is to love oneself, that it is to love God, and that to be loved is to be helped by another person to love God, whether or not the actual result is that the *loving one submits to being hated*" (WL 108-109; my emphasis). When we cannot fulfill the other's wishes, our love will seem to the other as if

---

[34]Yet one has to ask what content the validity of the ethical maintains if the knight of faith nonetheless "transgresses" the ethical (FT 59), "violates" the ethical (FT 78), and does what the ethical would "forbid" (FT 74).

it is not love; if she does not see God's judgment as middle term, she will see our refusal to give what she asks as hatred toward her. We must not hate the other, but we must be willing to undergo "the suffering of having to *seem* to hate the beloved" (WL 109; my emphasis). Correlated with this is the suggestion that we must be willing to be hated for our love (that seems like hate). Christianity "requires only this sacrifice (admittedly the hardest possible in many cases and always very hard): willingly to endure being hated as a reward for one's love" (WL 114). Kierkegaard ties both these issues about hatred together, when he ends sadly:

> I wonder if [in worldly wisdom] you find the suffering of having to *seem to hate the beloved*, of having to have hate as the final and sole expression of one's love, or of *having to be hated by the beloved* as a reward for one's love because there is the infinite difference of Christian truth between what the one and what the other understand by love? (WL 109; my emphases)

This willingness to be hated by the beloved can be seen as one way in which the recommendation of self-hatred can be understood.

Concluding Comments

What then have we learned about Kierkegaard's understanding of the injunction to hate oneself? It is true that it means for him self-denial,[35] self-renunciation, and dying to the self, but these are all misunderstood if one thinks of them as involving "self-deprecation," since this comes frighteningly close to the notion of "self-contempt" which Kierkegaard himself explicitly rejects. So it is important that we have learned that whatever is being recommended by Kierkegaard as self-hatred cannot require one to refrain from whatever proper self-love involves. Everything we learn about proper self-love tells us something about how *not* to interpret proper self-hatred.

At the very least, *Works of Love* tells us that proper self-love involves a valuing of oneself (one's distinctiveness, one's freedom, one's potential, one's equality with others) that is a kind of self-esteem. It tells us that we cannot exclude ourselves from the

[35]"What Is self-denial? It is giving up the moment and the momentary" (WL 369).

commandment to love without exception what is God's; it tells us that gratitude for God's gift implies self-love. It also tells us that we have a created, and therefore legitimate, need both to love and to be loved. Acknowledging those Kierkegaardian commitments is a prerequisite to fruitfully reexamining any passages in which Kierkegaard endorses hatred of self.

The reexaminations I have undertaken have given some substance to a Kierkegaardian distinction between proper self-hatred and improper self-hatred. Proper self-hatred involves recognizing one's "nothingness before God." This is nothing more, and nothing less, than an appreciation that one is incapable of doing anything without God. Proper self-hatred is not self-deprecation: it is the honest affirmation of one's inability to do anything without God, not the tormenting and despairing insistence that one can do nothing, full stop. Proper self-hatred involves "forgetting" self; this amounts to remembering our utter dependence on God and refusing to try to do things without God. Neither of these tasks (the forgetting or the remembering) entails "self-contempt" which is a kind of faithlessness to oneself. Proper self-love can be seen as a kind of faithfulness to oneself: proper self-love is being faithful to our created need to love and to be loved.

Kierkegaard also specifically aligns self-hatred with a variety of cowardly and self-serving denigrations of self, ways in which we fail to acknowledge the good in us. True, Kierkegaard asks for self-denial and dying to the self, but these are a "transformation" of the self—not a petulant, childish rejection of the good in us.

Finally, those passages in which Kierkegaard parallels hating self with hating mother and father, etc., illuminate something of the way in which proper self-hatred is a kind of dying to the self, an infinite resignation. They suggest that self-denial that comes in the process of following the path of Christ. Kierkegaard's best illustration is how the self-denial of parents begins when the child is born (EUD 281).[36] He is suggesting that it is never a question of self-denial for the sake of self-denial: there will be enough opportunities along the path of discipleship—one need not create more. In addition, these passages

---

[36]The "yoke of self-denial" (EUD 305) is at the same time "the joy of self-denial" (EUD 287).

highlight the self-denial that consists in the willingness to be hated for the sake of Christ, when necessary.

But when all is said and done, one cannot properly appreciate what the self-denial of self-hatred means for Kierkegaard unless one appreciates the second movement of faith. Improper self-hatred stops at the first movement. Proper self-hatred is at the same time proper self-love. Proper hatred of self is not self-reflexive: "he who loves God without faith reflects upon himself; he who loves God in faith reflects upon God" (FT 37). 'Literal' hatred of self is precisely that willingness to resign all (while continuing to love and cherish what is resigned) for the sake of a *telos* beyond the ethical. But it is also the case that the recommendation of hatred to oneself amounts to reflection on the God of love who is "commensurate with actuality," and hence gives us reason for the impossible hope that allows us to take joy in the finite which we have resigned. The paradox at issue is the same one that informs the other scriptural revelation, namely, that "Whosoever shall seek to save his life shall lose it; and whosoever shall lose his life shall preserve it" (Luke 17:33 KJV). From the story of Abraham we learn that it was not a question of renouncing the temporal realm in order to gain eternity (FT 49): Abraham had "faith for this life" (FT 20). As de Silentio intuits about "relinquishing" in the religious sense, "this having after all is also a giving up" (FT 47), or conversely, the giving up is also a having. De Silentio makes a contrast between the "purely human courage" it takes to renounce the whole temporal realm in order to gain eternity" and the "paradoxical and humble courage" it takes to grasp the whole temporal realm now by virtue of the absurd" (FT 49). One could argue that a purely human self-denial is a simple negative movement, while Christian self-denial is the double movement.[37]

---

[37]In *Works of Love*, Kierkegaard interprets the contrast between "Christian self-denial" and "merely human idea of self-denial" (WL 194) in another way — namely, that the latter assumes that you will be honored for denying yourself; Christian self-denial assumes you will suffer for it. Kierkegaard writes: "It is human self-denial when the child denies himself while the parents' embrace, encouraging and prompting, opens to it. It is human self-denial when a person denies himself and the world now opens to him. But it is Christian self-denial when a person denies himself and, thrust back by the world precisely because the world shuts itself to him, he must now seek the confidential relationship with God" (WL 195).

Proper self-hatred is not hating oneself as such, but restricting one's selfishness, including the selfishness of wanting to be able to do without God. The point of voluntarily dying to "selfishness" is to die to confidence in human help (FSE 82): to "die to every merely earthly hope, to every merely human confidence; you must die to your selfishness, or to the world, because it is only through your selfishness that the world has power over you" (FSE 77). The point is not to stop loving the self, but to stop loving *anyone* "selfishly": "Not until you have died to the selfishness in you and thereby to the world so that you do not love the world or anything in the world, do not selfishly love even one single person—not until you in love of God have learned *to hate yourself*, not until then can there be talk of the love that is Christian love" (FSE 83-4).

To hate oneself properly means: to deny oneself while loving oneself, to deny oneself without disdaining oneself, to deny oneself without self-contempt; to deny oneself while being faithful to one's self. It takes imagination and courage to affirm such a possibility. To paraphrase Graham Greene: improper "hate is just a failure of imagination."[38]

Although I have so far limited myself to Kierkegaard's published writings, there is one journal reference that I must include for the way it summarizes my general conclusion that self-forgetting and self-denial and acknowledging the absolute dependence of our creaturehood are compatible with the proper self-love of self-esteem. Kierkegaard writes:

> To hate oneself. This must not be understood, however, as a demand of the law, for it is God one must love—consequently it is the expression for love. Still less is hating oneself a way of achieving perfection or even meritoriousness. . . . No, the purpose of the requirement to hate oneself is to teach one rightly to depend upon grace.[39]

---

[38]Graham Greene, *The Power and the Glory* (London: William Heinemann, 1940) 170. Note that later in the novel Greene affirms a relevant Kierkegaardian sentiment when he writes: "We wouldn't recognize *that* love. It might even look like hate. It would be enough to scare us—God's love" (259).

[39]*Journals and Papers*, 3:3772.

In this respect, Kierkegaard could easily agree with the profound comment by Georges Bernanos's country priest that

> It is easier than one thinks to hate oneself. Grace means to forget oneself. But if all pride were dead in us, the grace of graces would be to love oneself humbly, as one would any of the suffering members of Jesus Christ.[40]

---

[40]"Il est plus facile que l'on croit de se haïr. La grâce est de s'oublier. Mais si tout orgueil était mort en nous, la grâce des grâces serait de s'aimer humblement soi-même, comme n'importe lequel des members souffrants de Jésus Christ." Georges Bernanos, *Journal d'un Curé de Campagne*, Bernanos Oeuvres 4 (Paris: Plon, 1947) 233.

9

Silence, "Composure in Existence," and the Promise of Faith's Joy

Sheridan Lynneth Hough

Temporality, finitude: that is what it is all about.[1]

This is a love story. And, as with all profound loves, there is a mystery at its heart. . . .

No, I am not in love with Kierkegaard the author. What could *that* possibly mean? To be smitten with his maddening hall-of-mirrors multifariousness, the duplexity of even his most straightforward voices? No, not at all and never. Anyone captivated with Kierkegaard's authorship, taken whole, must immediately rent out a vast estate of many rooms, filled with every imaginable human (and some nonhuman) manner of prolixity: Christian brothers and love-struck women, mermen and tax collectors, talking birds and worried lilies, fashion designers and judges, seducers and apostles.

Then again, mine is perhaps an even stranger profession of love: since my first reading of *Fear and Trembling* I have been taken with one of Kierkegaard's pseudonyms, and *his* own marvelous meditation on the very frame and nature of human existence.

Who is he?

His reticence names him: Johannes de Silentio, "John of Silence," and his silence contains a profound — and, paradoxically, of course, an exceedingly loud — account of the human self as realized in faith.

Johannes de Silentio's meditation focuses on the paradigm of the faithful life, Abraham. Three features of this life are immediately apparent. First, a person who has faith acknowledges its ineluctable demands. Abraham has a necessary task, one that is uniquely his own: "[T]ake Isaac your only son, whom you love, go to the land of

---

[1]Søren Kierkegaard, *Fear and Trembling,* trans. Sylvia Walsh, ed. C. Stephen Evans and Sylvia Walsh (Cambridge UK: Cambridge University Press, 2006) 42. Subsequent references to FT are to this version, not the KW version.

Moriah and offer him there as a burnt offering upon a mountain that I will show you" (Genesis 22:2). This task is not notional, but horrifyingly actual: Abraham must get up, saddle his donkey, prepare his servants and Isaac; he must cut the wood for the burnt offering; must travel three days, all the while mindful (in some sense) of the dreadful task — the absolutely necessary task — that he is undertaking.

Yes, but what *is* in Abraham's mind as he lives out, and bears out, this faithful assignment? Johannes of silence admits that thinking about Abraham's life presents a kind of conceptual impossibility:

> [W]hen I must think about Abraham, I am virtually annihilated. . . . At every moment I am aware of that prodigious paradox which is the content of Abraham's life . . . my thought cannot penetrate it.[2]

This, of course, is the second distinctive feature of faith, that it is opaque. Abraham's task, for all of its ineluctability, is absolutely beyond reckoning; anyone who attempts to explain what Abraham is doing, or what Abraham takes himself to be doing, has instantly distorted and diminished the deed.

> [Abraham] believed that God would not demand Isaac of him, while he still was willing to sacrifice him if it was demanded. He believed by virtue of the absurd, for human calculation was out of the question, and it was indeed absurd that God, who demanded it of him, in the next instant would revoke the demand. . . . Let us go further. We let Isaac actually be sacrificed. Abraham believed. He did not believe that he would be blessed one day in the hereafter but that he would become blissfully happy here in the world. God could give him a new Isaac, call the sacrificed one back to life. He believed by virtue of the absurd, for all human calculation had long ago ceased."[3]

Abraham cannot be understood: by Sarah, by Isaac, or even by himself. Faith's incomprehensibility, however, is preceded by a necessary final reckoning, and one that does demand utter clarity and coherence: "Infinite resignation is the last stage before faith, so

---

[2]*Fear and Trembling*, 26.
[3]*Fear and Trembling*, 29-30.

that whoever has not made this movement does not have faith."[4] Johannes's explanation of "infinite resignation" suggests both a "resigning from" and a "resigning to"; that is, a person must review life's lineaments, its possibilities and limits, and become conceptually at home with them. And what does that mean? It means, of course, that we human beings are called to make an intellectual truce with the impossibility of our undertakings: everyone we love and care for will die; the political causes we champion will fade and be forgotten; the books we write, the buildings we build — all of it is a vast and passing scene. To invest ourselves in this finite, temporal life, to attempt to express the infinite and the eternal within the mortal, is folly. "Resignation" indicates that a person has the conceptual acumen to see this truth, and understands that this temporal, corporeal situation is nothing in relation to God's timelessness; the knight of resignation abandons any notion of achieving anything of ultimate worth in this vale of tears.

Johannes elaborates on this theme by telling a love story: "A youth falls in love with a princess and the whole content of his life consists in this love, and yet the relation is such that it cannot possibly be realized, cannot possibly be translated from ideality to reality."[5] The youth realizes that the finite is not a fit place for infinite devotion: so what does he do? He translates his relationship into a conceptual one; the *thought* of the princess is one that will not waver or tarnish with the years:

> The love for that princess became for him the expression of an eternal love, assumed a religious character. . . . He keeps this love young, and it increases along with him in age and beauty. However, he needs no finite occasion for its growth. *From the moment he has made the movement the princess is lost.* He does not need those erotic palpitations of the nerves from seeing the beloved etc., nor in a finite sense does he constantly need to take leave of her, because he recollects her in an eternal sense. (Emphasis mine.)

In order to honor his infinite devotion, the youth resigns his actual, enfleshed beloved to a specter of recollection. Note that the resignation is infinite; that is, a resigned person absolutely acknowledges

---

[4]*Fear and Trembling*, 39.
[5]*Fear and Trembling*, 35.

the demands and limits of time and finitude. And so too for Abraham: a dead Isaac cannot be revived; the sacrifice of Abraham's cherished son would indeed be the irretrievable betrayal of a promise made to generations to come.

Faith, however, is able to move beyond the boundaries of resignation. Johannes de Silentio finishes his story of the love-struck youth:

> We shall now let the knight of faith appear in the incident previously mentioned. He does exactly the same as the other knight, he infinitely renounces the love that is the content of his life. . . . But then the miracle occurs . . . he says: "I nevertheless believe that I shall get her, namely, by virtue of the absurd, by virtue of the fact that for God everything is possible."[6]

Of course, the princess is still just as unobtainable: "The understanding continued to be right in maintaining that in the world of finitude where it rules it was and remained an impossibility." The knight of faith has resigned his love, but he claims that he will get her back again by virtue of the absurd: meaning, of course, he believes something that does not make any sense.

Abraham's silence is therefore not a species of reticence (as if his words would be too awesome for an ordinary listener). Abraham cannot say anything because there are no propositions, none, that can express the absurdity of his existential condition. The closest we can come to understanding what Abraham believes, says Johannes, is that he believes that he can both have, and sacrifice, his Isaac, that a sacrifice will not entail the loss of Isaac: "With God, all things are possible."

Johannes de silentio also wants us to notice that faith is utterly different from hope: hope still lives within the margins of what is, and is not, humanly possible. Johannes imagines a young girl who has made a passionate wish: "[I]f in spite of all difficulties [she] is still convinced that her wish will be fulfilled, this conviction is not at all that of faith . . . her conviction dares not look the impossibility in the eye in the pain of resignation."[7] Johannes urges us to recognize that Abraham does not *hope* to keep his cherished Isaac: his faith that

---

[6]*Fear and Trembling*, 39.
[7]*Fear and Trembling*, 40.

he will keep him is an entirely different matter. Here the silence of the incomprehensible begins.

But faith's silent opacity (when we tear ourselves away from this gripping, paradoxical scene) is also instructive. Abraham's faith cannot be understood because it is not a thought, but *a way of being in the world*. When Abraham says "Here I am," he is telling us that he is who he is as he does what he must (and, of course, what he must do — sacrifice Isaac, the sum and substance of his life — is precisely what cannot be done). Abraham's faith is in this sense immediate: it is actualized at every moment, from saddling up the donkey to preparing the sacrificial wood; it is not some *thought* about God's greatness, or Isaac's infinite preciousness, but it is constituted by those deeds in the world, deeds that can only be thought about in what Johannes de Silentio aptly calls a "lyrical dialectic,"[8] a rhythmic, deft movement between an account of what faith is not, and an unspoken suggestion of faith's impossible contours.

So: faith is ineluctable, opaque, and realized at every moment by a way of being in the world: this is what Johannes de Silentio means when he remarks, "Temporality, finitude is what it is all about"[9] — Abraham's finite circumstance, as realized in time, is the site of his faith.

But the spectacle of Abraham dazzles; as Johannes de Silentio reminds us, "Abraham I cannot understand; in a certain sense I can learn nothing from him except to be amazed."[10] The paradoxical contours of Abraham's faithful existence are visible, but the interior of that life is impossible to apprehend. Johannes's inability to make sense of Abraham certainly informs his own — and very different — kind of silence: Johannes reminds us that he knows that "God is love" but that he himself does not have the joy of faith.[11] He can articulate the puzzle of faith, he can tell us what it is not and what it cannot be, but he, Johannes, does not know what it is to dwell in faith.

And here I too have been silent. I began with a profession of love, but in fact the real object of my devotion is not the redoubtable

---

[8]*Fear and Trembling*, 1.
[9]*Fear and Trembling*, 42.
[10]*Fear and Trembling*, 31.
[11]*Fear and Trembling*, 28.

Johannes de Silentio, but one of *Johannes's own* fictional creations. This character is also silent; Johannes depicts his actions in dumb-show, and yet his existence is meant to speak to us about the crucial element in human life, the axis around which all is meant to revolve: faith. Johannes de Silentio admits that he has never met a "knight of faith," but that he can readily imagine what this person is like.

Here he is:

> "Dear me! Is this the person, is it actually him? He looks just like a tax collector" . . . I draw a little closer to him and pay attention to the slightest movement to see whether a little heterogeneous fraction of a signal from the infinite manifests itself. . . . No! He is solid through and through. His footing? It is sturdy, belonging entirely to finitude. . . . He enjoys everything he sees, the throngs of people, the new omnibuses, the Sound. . . . On the way he thinks about an appetizing dish of warm food his wife surely has for him when he comes home, for example, a roast head of lamb with vegetables . . . he does not have four beans, and yet he firmly believes that his wife has that delectable dish for him. If she has it, to see him eat would be an enviable sight. . . . If his wife doesn't have it — oddly enough, it is all the same to him. . . . Everything that happens — a rat scurrying under a gutter plank, children playing — *everything engages him with a composure in existence* as if he were a girl of sixteen . . . absolutely to express the sublime in the pedestrian — that only the knight of faith can do — and that is the only miracle. (Emphasis mine.)

This portrait stands in comical juxtaposition to the awesome mystery of Abraham. Johannes de Silentio, and indeed his readers, can barely stand to gaze at the terrible, majestic equanimity of Abraham, his calm refrain of "Here I am" always securely locating him in space and time as he proceeds with his impossible, necessary and unthinkable (in both senses) task. The tax collector, this seeming "bourgeois philisitine" (de Silentio's own comparison)[12] is, on the other hand, entirely familiar. The "faithful" tax collector (for so we are invited to think of him) sings loudly in church, enjoys his work

---

[12]*Fear and Trembling*, 28. Robert Perkins has aptly described the tax collector as "a 'gabber,' a 'hale fellow well-met' " (International Kierkegaard Commentary: *Without Authority*, ed. Robert Perkins [Macon GA: Mercer University Press, 2007] 10).

and his walks around Copenhagen; he takes pleasure in thinking about his supper.

What is so loveable—to me, at any rate—about this affable, humble character?

First, the tax collector's behavior reveals the transformative power of faith, even in the most quotidian affairs. He thinks with pleasure about a supper he might find waiting for him; of course, when he gets home he discovers that this opulent dish, lamb's-head stew, is not on offer: "curiously enough, he is just the same." Why isn't the tax collector disappointed? Clearly, he embodies the wisdom of one of Kierkegaard's favorite New Testament verses, James 1:1-17: "Every good gift and every perfect gift is from above and comes down from the Father of lights, with whom there is no change or shadow of variation." Three of Kierkegaard's discourses on this verse from James[13] elaborate on the way in which the tax collector takes up this experience: "just as God's almighty hand made everything good, so he, the Father of lights, ever constant, at every moment makes everything good."[14] The tax collector is delighted with whatever supper awaits him, just as he takes pleasure in anticipating what is ultimately denied him: "And when your wish was denied, did you thank God?"[15] This particular existential practice is necessarily comprehensive: "And when people wronged and insulted you, did you thank God? . . . We are not saying that their wrong ceased to be wrong—what would be the use of such pernicious and foolish talk! It is up to you to decide whether it was wrong; but have you taken the wrong and insult to God and by your thanksgiving received it from his hand as a good and perfect gift?"[16] The tax collector's faith gives him what I have elsewhere called "epistemic flexibility": no matter what befalls him, he is able to take it up as a good and perfect gift from God.[17] What's for supper is not

---

[13]Significantly, three of Kierkegaard's discourses on "Every Good and Every Perfect Gift" were published in the same year as *Fear and Trembling* (the first two appearing five months before, and the third seven weeks later).

[14]*Eighteen Upbuilding Discourses*, 41.

[15]*Eighteen Upbuilding Discourses*, 43.

[16]*Eighteen Upbuilding Discourses*.

[17]A lengthier treatment of these issues appears in "What the Faithful Tax Collector Saw (Against the Understanding)," International Kierkegaard Commentary: *Without Authority*, ed. Robert Perkins (Macon GA: Mercer University Press,

the issue: what does matter is God's infinite ability to transform *any* circumstance into a good and perfect gift, and that power is made available by the practice of faith.

Johannes de Silentio wonderfully describes the tax collector's faithful life as "composure in existence." His lived practice of faith limns his finite, ever-changing condition with significance; he takes joy in what is made manifest to him in the immediate moment. Life, when lived faithfully, is infinitely abundant and satisfying: at least, this is the suggestion of the tax collector's blissful perambulations around Copenhagen: entranced by rats, delighted by child's play, finding, as Johannes de Silentio says, "the sublime in the pedestrian." This happy rambler is utterly absorbed in his life at this moment, *from* moment to moment, while still indulging in wishes for the future (that delectable stew), managing his tasks with precision ("to see him one would think he was a pen-pusher who had lost his soul in Italian bookkeeping, so exact is he"[18]), yet never out of touch with the wonder of his own immediate existence, strung between (to borrow the words of another pseudonym, Anti-Climacus) the finite and the infinite, the temporal and the eternal, the necessary and the possible,[19] strung between, but always securely expressed in the unfolding existential moment. This picture of a life fully realized right now — despite the absolute limits and inevitable regrets of the past, as well as the invitations and fearful taunts of an imaginary future — both fascinates and compels: "He lets things take their course with a freedom from care as if here were a reckless good-for-nothing and yet buys every moment he lives at the opportune time for the dearest price, for he does not do even the slightest thing except by virtue of the absurd."[20]

Of course, there is a disturbing silence here, too: not the awe-inspiring, reason-defying quietude of Abraham, but a *refusal* to speak, to tell us what we need to know about him beyond the happy spectacle of his faithful life. This character, merrily living out his faith in the gritty boundaries of finitude, says nothing to us about

---

2007) 295-311.
    [18]*Fear and Trembling*, 32-33.
    [19]*The Sickness unto Death*, trans. Howard V. Hong and Edna Hong (Princeton NJ: Princeton University Press, 1980) 13.
    [20]*Fear and Trembling*, 33-34.

how he came so to live. We look on with pleasure at this depiction of an (extra)ordinary life, and yet we have little sense of its interiority. This strolling charmer is able to navigate as he does because he has earned his faithful practice: but how does he do it? What does his faithful practice actually entail?

Johannes is, of course, obliged to be silent about the nature of faith. After all, he has already told his readers that his joy is not that of faith. He does, however, offer some hints:

> [T]his person [the tax collector] has made and at every moment is making the movement of infinity. He empties the deep sadness of existence in infinite resignation, he knows the blessedness of infinity, he has felt the pain of renouncing everything, the dearest thing he has in the world, and yet the finite tastes every bit as good to him as to someone who never knew anything higher."[21]

So, merely *watching* (an imagined) "knight of faith" move blissfully about his environment in all his engrossed and ordinary splendor is, in a sense, a cheat: a view of his joyful existence does not instruct the reader about the renunciation and indeed the confession of sin that the life of faith entails.

Kierkegaard, in his later writings, certainly adumbrates the life of faith in a different fashion. He maintains that the life of faith is indeed one of joy, but Kierkegaard's later perspective sees well beyond that of his earlier pseudonym, Johannes de Silentio: Kierkegaard of the second authorship is focused on the renunciation and death to self of the faithful life:

> [T]o be a Christian is, to speak merely humanly, sheer agony . . . what Christ is speaking about—he makes no secret of it—is about crucifying the flesh, hating oneself, suffering for the doctrine, about weeping and wailing while the world rejoices, about the most heartrending suffering caused by hating father, mother, wife, one's own child.[22]

This suffering, Kierkegaard avers, is not only beneficial[23] but joyful:

---

[21]*Fear and Trembling*, 34.
[22]*The Moment* and Late Writings, trans. Howard V. Hong and Edna Hong (Princeton NJ: Princeton University Press, 1980) 189.
[23]*Upbuilding Discourses in Various Spirits*, trans. Howard V. Hong and Edna Hong (Princeton NJ: Princeton University Press, 1980) 239.

After the apostles had been flogged, "they went away joyful because they had been deemed worthy to be scorned for the sake of Christ's name" . . . in suffering, bold confidence is able to take power from the world and has the power to change scorn into honor, victory into downfall![24]

The transformational power of "bold confidence" has at least a structural resemblance to the cheerful tax collector—no matter what befalls him, it is all the same—but these faithful apostles are clearly living at the extremity of this notion: they are joyful *in* their suffering, not in spite of it.[25] Kierkegaard remarks that this joy in suffering is not a turning away from life; on the contrary, he claims that this is life most fully realized:

[I]f we wanted to find the most reliable way to express that the good always has the victory, what expression is more reliable than this: in suffering, bold confidence is able to take power from the world and has the power to change scorn into honor, victory into downfall! When we say this, we are not saying that the good person is eventually victorious in another world, or that his cause will eventually be victorious in this world. No, he is victorious while he is living; suffering, he is victorious while he is still alive— he is victorious on the day of his suffering.[26]

Kierkgaard adds that "it is not without a shudder that we look at this apostolic assurance."[27] Indeed. We are now at a considerable distance from our happily absorbed, enigmatic tax collector. This glimpse into the interior of faith from the perspective of the eternal, rather than the temporal, is a sobering reminder that the faithful life is always a practice of self denial and self hatred; it requires an ongoing practice of confession and the "will to suffer."[28] These existential demands of faith are not available to the onlooker:

Just as the ship as it lightly proceeds at full sail before the wind at the same time deeply cuts its heavy path through the ocean, so also the Christian's way is light if one looks at the faith that overcomes

---

[24]*Upbuilding Discourses in Various Spirits*, 331.
[25]*Upbuilding Discourses in Various Spirits*, 330.
[26]*Upbuilding Discourses in Various Spirits*, 331.
[27]*Upbuilding Discourses in Various Spirits*.
[28]*The Moment* and Late Writings, 294.

the world, but hard if one looks at the laborious work in the depths.[29]

The *appearance* of the faithful Christian — joyful, confident, bold — tells us nothing about the work that constitutes such a life.

And so the tax collector's perambulations really cannot teach us very much; his attentive delight in each moment conceals the work that makes his life possible.

So why am I still so intrigued by him?

Surely, it is because his cheer beckons me, and issues me an invitation. The invitation is quite specific: I am called to leave his absorbed and joyful silence and to begin listening again, and again, to Kierkegaard's many voices. As I write, as I teach, as I love and live with my family and my friends, the promise of this depiction of lived practice stays with me. The tax collector is a compelling figure — an image, nothing more — but one that always renews my conviction that the life of a self forged in faith is the only life worth living, or — more to the point — *worthy* of being lived.

---

[29]*Upbuilding Discourses in Various Spirits*, 218.

10
Kierkegaard and Our "Need" for Speed[1]

Jamie Lorentzen

Given that most modern inventions are predicated and marketed on the assumption that faster is better, Kierkegaard's comments on deception and self-deception regarding our ever-burgeoning "need" for speed are as timely in the twenty-first century as the nineteenth century — which is just another one of the many reasons why Kierkegaard still matters.

The phrase *faster is better* is perhaps marketing's crowning mantra in today's highly technological, increasingly unreflective culture. *Faster is better* is at its most reliable when results or goals of a given invention reveal no substantive harm or consequences caused by accelerating the process. But there is a physics to speed, and few are the inventions whose outcomes are not somehow ethically diminished by altering the concept and process of time for the sake of speed. There is loss or sacrifice in opting, for instance, for fast food or steroid use or speed-reading or compulsive cell phone use; the question becomes whether or not speed and ease ultimately and regularly cancel the real value and benefits of wholesome eating, healthy exercise, patiently understanding an idea, and relationships in which absence (instead of ubiquitous wireless connection) make the heart grow fonder. Few are the inventions, in other words, that raise no red flags — because ethics, not ignoring results, is nonetheless equally attentive to and skeptical of the sped-up means or processes by which results or goals are achieved. A man may be

[1]This essay is adapted from a chap. 1 section of *Sober Cannibals, Drunken Christians: Melville, Kierkegaard, and Tragic Optimism in Polarized Worlds* (Macon GA: Mercer University Press, 2010). All passages from Kierkegaard are from the Kierkegaard's Writings series, Howard V. Hong, general editor (Princeton NJ: Princeton University Press, 1978–1998) or *Søren Kierkegaard's Journals and Papers* (Bloomington: Indiana University Press, 1967–1978). Page numbers in parentheses following Princeton University Press citations correspond to *Søren Kierkegaards Samlede Vørker*.

guilty of an impulsive crime of passion that everyone witnessed, but an impulsive lynch mob punishing that man without the slow deliberation that an ethical due process demands is the greater criminal.

Ethics thus is quality control, umpire, conscience, the watchdog that follows the steps of those expecting to profit most in the end by hastily manipulating or outright ignoring process. Although ethics does not ignore *what* things are done, it is more concerned about *how* things are done, knowing that good results will follow good process, and that good process is predicated on allowing sufficient time for the process to work. Ethics is most people's worst nightmare, because ethics is about honesty that doesn't care about winning or losing but only how the game is played. Ethics applies itself with restraint on all levels of risk assessment. Its motto is "Measure twice before cutting once" because it knows itself enough not to side with the speedy and impulsive hare, but rather the slow and patient tortoise. Ethics does it right the first time because it allows for time to do it right.

In his *For Self-Examination*, Kierkegaard calls human earnestness, which relies in great part upon ethics and patience, "an honest distrust in oneself, to treat oneself as a suspicious character, as a financier treats an unreliable client, saying, 'Well, these big promises are not much help; I would rather have a small part of the total right away.' "[2] He echoes words of Socrates with which he was familiar: "I have long been wondering at my own wisdom. I cannot trust myself. And I think that I ought to stop and ask myself, what am I saying? For there is nothing worse than self-deception — when the deceiver is always at home and always with you it is quite terrible, and therefore I ought to retrace my steps and endeavor to 'look fore and aft.' "[3] Both Socrates and Kierkegaard know humans to be far too capable of self-deceptions out of simple impatience or the "need" for speed, for impatience, Kierkegaard suggests everywhere, does not mind being deceived. The operative and indicative mode for which Socrates calls is "to stop and ask," and stopping and asking require time and patience.

---

[2] *For Self-Examination*, 44 (XII 332).
[3] *The Collected Dialogues of Plato*, trans. B. Jowett (New York: Random House, 1937) 1:217 (*Cratylus*, 428d) (see also *Anxiety*, 254nn.).

Ethics knows that the con man doesn't want his prey to think but only to feel, because thinking takes time that the fast-talking con man knows to steal first so as to steal the prey's money more easily. Ethics' timetable invites doubt and skepticism into the equation, which more times than not kills the deal and sends the con man packing. If the pitch is too good to be true, it is because the dazzling prospect of the goal or result has eclipsed the time-burdened process. The phrase "get rich quick" is always suspect because the "quick" assures that a natural gestation, birthing, and developmental process yielding a healthy decision will be leapfrogged for the sake of satisfying esthetic impulse, the result of which becomes severely compromised by blindsiding natural process.

In *Concluding Unscientific Postscript*, Johannes Climacus identifies thinking about external results as objective thinking and thinking about process as subjective thinking. Impatience's impulsivity to get what it wants when it wants becomes self-fulfilled prophecy and thereby goes far to suggest how, being an easy slave to time and speed, self-deception grows: "Whereas [objective] thinking invests everything in the result and assists all humankind to cheat by copying and reeling off the results and answers [*cooking the books*, to use a modern clich] subjective thinking invests everything in the process of becoming and omits the result."[4] Climacus can afford to *appear* highly partial or one-sided here toward subjective thinking so as to serve as a corrective to a modern culture that places a far greater premium on objective thinking and results in an overconfident nineteenth century. He nonetheless suggests that process needn't worry about the result because the result is part of process, namely, its conclusion. What is gained by Climacus is the element of trust or faith capable of quelling or assuaging anxieties and despairs of the objective thinker. Climacus, in other words, knows that good and ethical process plus trust or faith in the process equals results over which a person need not be anxious nor despair. Results derived from good process *will be good* (whatever they may be) because they are *honest* and *objective* (as opposed to corrupted results from corrupted processes).

---

[4]*Postscript* I, 73 (VII 55).

A rowboat analogy that Kierkegaard employs in his *Christian Discourses* is particularly applicable to the kind of patient plying toward good results: "The one who rows a boat turns his back to the goal toward which he is working." It is always delaying and distracting impatiently to want to inspect the goal every moment, to see whether one is coming a little closer, and then again a little closer. No, be forever and earnestly resolute; then you turn whole-heartedly to the work—and your back to the goal. This is the way one is turned when one rows a boat, but so also is one positioned when one believes. Faith turns its back to [the goal] expressly in order to have it entirely present with it today."[5] Which is not to say that one ought not to, as the old folk song of hope goes, "keep your eye on the prize"; it's just that, to truly and ethically keep eyes on the prize, eyes are constituted by belief rather than by a desperation that continually looks over one's shoulder with impatience and anxiety.

Kierkegaard's Christian-oriented Climacus feels so strongly about how speed impatiently sidesteps the process for the results that he never considers himself to *be* a Christian (a result), but claims at best that he is *becoming* a Christian (a process). In his claim, the emphasis is on *how* a life is lived day-to-day rather than on the resultant and dubious pride of ownership of *what* a life is called at the end of the day. Climacus subsequently respects the infinitely patient discipline and suffering that actually *being* a Christian in the vocation of imitating Christ bears on a person. They say that practice makes perfect—yet even if this maxim is a calculated illusion designed to help a person focus upon striving toward some impossible goal, then let it be a happy illusion, for best results *in* time require paying due respect *to* time—a notion humorously offered by another pseudonym of Kierkegaard's, Johannes de Silentio, in *Fear and Trembling*:

> If someone who wanted to learn to dance were to say: For centuries, one generation after the other has learned the positions, and it is high time that I take advantage of this and promptly begin with the quadrille—people would presumably laugh a little at him.

---

[5]*Christian Discourses*, 73-74 (X 77-78).

What, then, is education? "It is the course the individual goes through in order to catch up with himself, and the person who will not go through this course is not much helped by being born in the most enlightened age."[6]

Kierkegaard thus sees any person's "need" for speed as an act of deception or self-deception that threatens the well-developed education of that person, given that speed does not allow for the kind of patient, earnest, deep, inward, readerly reflection and self-examination that Kierkegaard fosters and respects in striving to become fully human. Speed for speed's sake is certainly externally profitable for many, but it holds no intrinsic or essential worth to individuals whose lives are dependent upon reading well in an increasingly ambiguous and shifty world. And although Kierkegaard indirectly arrives at this point throughout his works, he pays particular attention to how speed renders individuals poor readers not only of books, but also of the world around them. Kierkegaard thereby warns individuals-as-readers against any impatience that invites deception and self-deception. In the first line of his preface to *Works of Love*, he notes that his following "deliberations" will be "understood slowly but then also easily, whereas they will surely become very difficult if someone by hasty and curious reading makes them very difficult for himself." Later, he appeals to the reader, "May your patience in reading correspond to my diligence and time in writing it," for, he writes further on, that "it takes no time at all to be deceived; one can be deceived immediately and remain so for a long time — but to become aware of the deception takes time."[7]

In effect, Kierkegaard recognizes the unwieldy speed at which busy modern lives move. The busyness is compounded in these modern times, what Bob Dylan calls these New Dark Ages, when what is essentially true is the ephemeral speed of virtual or digital reality.[8] In the Old Dark Ages, at least the monks kept troth by patiently dusting, reading, transcribing, and translating ancient

---

[6]*Fear and Trembling*, 46 (III 96).
[7]*Works of Love*, 3, 73, 124 (IX 7, 74, 120).
[8]Bob Dylan, *World Gone Wrong*, compact disc (New York: Columbia Records, 1993) liner notes.

books in subterranean library stalls. They knew that biding time in such ways illuminated both the meaningful possibilities *and* essential limitations that time offers the patient reader. Kierkegaard would subsequently prefer the old times to the new, not in any foolish sentimental way, but in the eminently practical way of which Johannes de Silentio speaks when he considers how a religious enthusiast is one who attempts to remind the present age of what it has forgotten.[9]

In addition, Kierkegaard constantly resists the modern and externally driven condition of busyness that puts such a stranglehold on time — a stranglehold to which human beings more times than not resign their very humanity for the sake of busily "productive" yet thoughtless lives. Such oblivious lives are lives to which Americans are particularly susceptible, at least those Americans who in the main still exemplify Henry Ford's unreflective quip that "history is more or less bunk." In *Christian Discourses*, Kierkegaard writes: "It is regarded in the world as definitely settled that people would like to know the truth if only they had the capacity and the time for it and if it could be made clear to them. What a superfluous concern, what an ingeniously fabricated evasion! Every human being truly has capacity enough to know the truth. And every human being, even the busiest, truly has time enough also to come to know the truth — if a person himself *wants* to have it made clear."[10]

And so it is up to me — and you — in our embarrassingly busy lives of quiet desperation to *want* to have the truth made clear — which is perhaps a pivotal reason why Kierkegaard still matters to each of us today. As Bob Dylan sings,

> Everything went from bad to worse,
>   money never changed a thing,
> Death kept followin', trackin' us down,
>   at least I heard your bluebird sing.
> Now somebody's got to show their hand,
>   time is an enemy,
> I know you're long gone,
>   I guess it must be up to me.[11]

[9]*Fear and Trembling*, 102 (III 149).
[10]*Christian Discourses*, 170 (X 173).
[11]*Bob Dylan: Lyrics 1962–1985* (New York: Knopf, 1985) 371 (fr. "Up to Me,"

For choosing things like slowness and reflection are truly individual and existential matters in any modern time. As Kierkegaard invokes in his *Point of View*, "the world wants to be deceived."[12] Meanwhile, the greatest concession made to human beings, Kierkegaard writes in his journals, is free will, which "at the same time—is eternity's demand upon him."[13] We can choose, and we choose best from a position of reflection and inwardness, which is always where Kierkegaard attempts to place us in his writings.

What is central here for Kierkegaard, according to Kierkegaard scholar Betty Anderson, is that he seemed "to see the greatest hope for mankind as resting in the decision of the individual as he exists each day," and that Kierkegaard "tried repeatedly" to show that individual decisions *do* matter, and that the end result of humanity can be and is altered by the many specific decisions made each day by individuals."[14] Which is why the only question I drill into my students' heads that is at once deeply existential and ethical as much as it is economic and consumer savvy is: "Do I *really need* that gadget because it's supposedly faster than what I currently have? Do I really need that faster iPod or iPhone or iThis or iThat or myThis or myThat?" For it is this kind of question put to the ego about the ego that points to what is truly needful in a life, and it is questions like this that can change worlds one person at a time.

One of the last things Kierkegaard thus claims he would surrender would be his "faith in individual human beings. And this is my faith," Kierkegaard continues in his *Point of View*, "that however much confusion and evil and contemptibleness there can be in human beings as soon as they become the irresponsible and unrepentant 'public,' 'crowd,' etc.—there is just as much truth and goodness and lovableness in them when one can get them as single individuals."[15]

1974, 1976, by Ram's Horn Music).

[12]*Point of View*, 58 (XIII 544, 545).

[13]*Journals and Papers* II, 1261.

[14]"The Melville-Kierkegaard Syndrome," by Betty Anderson, *Rendezvous* III (Pocatello ID, 1968) 47.

[15]*Point of View*, 10-11 (XIII 499).

In a world of FaceBook and virtual individualism that asserts itself cheaply and without the threat of actually needing to practice what it preaches, for it hides amid a collective consumer-driven world and behind collective-data-driven and speed-based digital technologies that dazzle us all — in such a world, fighting *against* time and speed is a central problem of our time. Time and technologies that alter time, however, are not the real enemies. We are our own worst enemies in our sinfully pathetic relationship to time and our time-altering technologies, and Kierkegaard knew it.

There *is* time in our time, and how we bide time in this world determines who we are as human beings and who we become as human beings. We have world enough and time if we use it well, if we discriminate between what is gold from what is trash, if we treat time with the slow and patient respect that it deserves, if we live in time without being a slave to time. If loss of time, as Albert Camus once asserted, is philosophical suicide, then we must constantly remind ourselves that being a slave to time means being a slave to the kind of speed that we wrongly affix to time.

We can do better than this, and Kierkegaard knew that, too. Howard Hong once claimed that the only reason he owned a watch was to turn it backwards from time to time. He was no sentimental nostalgist here; he was simply suggesting that we *can* slow things down to atone for our pathetic impatience in time before time, like us, stops. What do we *really* need instead of speed? *What is truly needful?* Earnest, contrite confession, then penitence — in other words, infinite humility, then a striving borne of gratitude for the greatly abundant, greatly precious time that we have in our own good time.

11

Becoming a Christian in Christendom

Jason A. Mahn

I came to Kierkegaard dishonestly. I imagine many of us do. Amy Laura Hall once remarked that her Duke Divinity School courses on Kierkegaard were enrolled by almost entirely male, mostly white, students—many of whom were searching for a purveyor of an unapologetic, full-bodied faith that could weather the critiques of Enlightenment reason and the disparagement of cultured despisers. Frequent allusions to Kierkegaard in American culture propagate this image of an embattled and self-reliant—and also obscure—Kierkegaard, minus the confessional avowals. (Here's a popular image, allowing a range of variations: A misunderstood male protagonist, waiting for the train out of town, stands leaning, pensive, smoking—reading a book by Kierkegaard.) Many of us who were or are lonely and self-conscious, especially while in school, saw in Kierkegaard a secret confidant—one who would name the turbulences of our souls and, even better, hold them dear. For those of us who went through seminary training, Kierkegaard promised a way of being, or at least looking, fashionably enigmatic with our otherwise all-too-simple faith. I remember first reading *Philosophical Fragments* at Luther Seminary in St. Paul and recognizing in its conceptions both access to robust membership in the Christian community and sure exit from the banality of lighting candles, of reciting creeds, of praying and being conformed. With Kierkegaard and a bed-head hair style, I could be in the church but not of it—a Christian with ironic reserve.

The image of Kierkegaard as a lonely hero of faith among the more benighted is not wholly false. Most images with legs are not. It is only outworn, like Nietzsche's coin that has become effaced from too much circulation and so functions entirely and efficiently as a mere chunk of change. In my view, the best readers and writers of Kierkegaard today seek not so much to get him right as to uncover the artistry that inspires and gets eclipsed by the smooth image.

Moreover, they seek to notice and restore the edges—and the edginess—of the language that Kierkegaard coins or otherwise dispenses. His way with words, like the entire "authorship" itself, always has two sides. It conceals as it illuminates, and illuminates only by withdrawing to the shadows, robbing the reader of the chance to master his writing by translating it into univocal, one-sided concepts. Only with such double-sidedness, and his edginess too, can Kierkegaard's words build up by pressing one down, like a jack—to swap out Nietzsche's trope for that of Kierkegaard.

I prefer to speak of "authors" for those of us who write about Kierkegaard because writing seems more determinative for our professional identities, as for his, than the narrow methodologies of our philosophical or theological disciplines. Any one of us, like he, might be a *kind* of postmodernist, or a *kind* of theologian, or a *kind* of virtue ethicists, etc., but what we directly, unequivocally *do* when circumambulating those positions is to *write*. In Ed Mooney's apt image, we move toward Kierkegaard's words like outfielders responding to the crack of the bat—drawn to the place where we think the words will land, ready to receive them and send them on, newly arcing, with our own linguistic thrusts.[1] Reading and writing, receiving poetized possibilities and sending them on, edges sharpened, was Kierkegaard's primary day job—no, his way of life. At best, secondary commentary will be wary of ending the game by translating his writings into stable concepts that can be mapped among philosophical or doctrinal camps. Too many have attempted to *figure out* Kierkegaard by taking his *figures out* of the text. The tropes that he coins or recasts—the leap of faith, the glance of an eye, Isaac returned, self-consuming sickness, self-emptying divinity, to name just a few—those compact sayings and the capacious possibilities they bear are what first draw us into Kierkegaard's work and promise to nourish us still.

In part, then, Kierkegaard matters because he's a religious writer who authors texts that always mean more than they say. He matters because his writings contain matters still unturned, and—once turned—needing to be turned again. His texts resist conceptual

---

[1]Edward F. Mooney, *On Søren Kierkegaard: Dialogue, Polemics, Lost intimacy, and Time* (Burlington VT: Ashgate, 2007) 67.

transparency and the efficiency of well-worn coins. They are concocted out of potent linguistic materials — parabolic fables, parroting voices, prefaces upon prefaces — that unsettle any distilled proposition, although Kierkegaard gives us propositions as well. The writings are double-sided, like a good poem whose meaning is inseparable from the countermotion it enacts: "one part against another across a silence."[2]

One of Kierkegaard's more controlling metaphors characterizes his corpus as a whole. In his posthumously published report to history, *The Point of View for My Work as an Author*, Kierkegaard "explains" the coherence of his multifaceted authorship — a coherence that he intuits retrospectively and "with the help of providence." He also chastises his Copenhagen contemporaries for receiving his ironic pseudonymous works straightforwardly while virtually ignoring the upbuilding and devotional works that he signed with his own name. Kierkegaard here describes his authorship as a series of "left-handed," pseudonymous works that call into question the presumed knowledge of assistant professors (like myself) and others who presume to more than they do, coupled carefully with a series of "right-handed," works signed with Kierkegaard's name that describe how the life of faith, or what Sylvia Walsh calls the "simplicity of living Christianly,"[3] resembles the spontaneous obedience of birds in the air and lilies in the field. Kierkegaard is ambidextrous — or so his right hand claims. Insofar as we take him at his (retrospective) word, his task was always to lead the reader — with both hands — from an aesthetic "first immediacy" to the "second immediacy" of faith.

The picture of Kierkegaard writing with both hands is only a trope — no closer to resolving the generative tension of his writings than the literary critic solves a poem. If anything the figure of ambidexterity sustains that tension by refusing to set aside critical reason in the avowal of faith, and vice versa. The reason I mention the sides of his corpus, and the edgy two-sidedness of his smaller

---

[2]John Ciardi, *How Does a Poem Mean?* (Boston: Houghton Mifflin, 1959) 995, as cited in Gordon W. Lanthrop, *Holy Things: A Liturgical Theology* (Minneapolis: Fortress, 1993) 82.

[3]Sylvia Walsh, *Living Christianly: Kierkegaard's Dialectic of Christian Existence* (University Park: Pennsylvania State University Press, 2005) 2.

linguistic coins, is because these large and small tensions in his writings set the stage for why Kierkegaard matters—or should matter—to those of us striving to be Christian.

Again by his own account, Kierkegaard sought to reintroduce Christianity into Christendom. His Christendom was not ours, of course. In nineteenth-century Denmark, one officially became Christian by being born on native soil, and subsequently—unless one completed the necessary paperwork to bypass such eventualities—by being baptized as an infant into the Danish Lutheran Church. In another potent image, Kierkegaard likens the state of such nationalistic, cultured Christianity to persons so overly spoon-fed with religion that they can't get it all down. Kierkegaard must induce vomiting before feeding anything that resembles solid spiritual food. This Socratic gadfly of Copenhagen constantly confronts with questions, dislodging deeply seated assumptions by his polemics, however indirect, in order to make room for more thorough Christian formation. His *via remotionis*, this process of giving by taking away, was so important for Kierkegaard that he staked his own religious status on it. He claimed to the end that he, too, was not (yet) a Christian—only trying to become one (TM 340-43). Some of Kierkegaard's most visceral, almost violent, images reflect his wish to "help negatively": inducing nausea in order to feed, jacking up by pushing down, wounding from behind.

And yet, to describe it in this way suggests that Kierkegaard's indirect method, including his authorship of a host of pseudonymous personae that subsequently author "his" writings, comprises but a method that he improvises in light of a peculiar historical occasion, and which might be suspended under better conditions. The predicament becomes this: if Kierkegaard's indirect method is simply a pragmatic tactic in response to the particular ecclesial-cultural-political conglomerate of nineteenth-century Denmark, then we might imagine that method not mattering (or at least not mattering much) for readers now or in the future. There is some truth to this supposition. In her latest book, Walsh reminds us that Kierkegaard always thought of himself as a corrective—one who would chaff his own age "with expert one-sidednesss"—and he warned later generations against making the corrective normative (JP VI:6467). The way around that latter danger, according to Walsh, is for us to become "more balanced" in how we now become

Christian.[4] Such a path forward would resist reifying and canonizing Kierkegaard's corrective — but does it also presume that we can find a kernel in his work (a more balanced Christianity) beneath the layered husk (Kierkegaard's corrective indirection)? And if that is the case, how long will Kierkegaard still matter? Finally, what are we to make of Kierkegaard's assertion that his writing, however corrective, came from one without authority, from one, a bit off-balance, who was still groping his way toward Christianity?

I said there is some truth to the assumption that Kierkegaard adopted his negative method as a pragmatic tactic for disillusioning Christendom from its too-many objective truths. If that assumption implies that Kierkegaard won't always matter, perhaps that is in the cards. Influential authors speak to (and against) particular times and peoples; the flip side of their relevance is the possibility of lying dormant (as did Kierkegaard for a half century after his death) or of being forgotten almost entirely. The latter scenario would actually corroborate Kierkegaard's self-identification as a Socratic teacher. According to *Philosophical Fragments*, Socrates, like any good teacher aside from Christ, disentangles his own identity from the learner and the lesson learned, vanishing once the student comes to truth (PF 10-11). Perhaps any excessive commemoration of the gadfly simply throws doubt on whether one has really learned the truth, at best, and borders on idolatry, at worst.

Still, anyone who insists that Kierkegaard is *only* a corrective whose language is *merely* rhetorical seems also to assume, firstly, that we are beyond or will move beyond the need for his corrective, and secondly, that Kierkegaard's indirect, negative method is ultimately separable from the message it encases.[5] I disagree on both accounts. Regarding the first, it seems to me that the Christendom

---

[4]Sylvia Walsh, *Kierkegaard: Thinking Christianly in an Existential Mode* (Oxford UK: Oxford University Press, 2009), 199.

[5]I should clarify that I have no reason to think that Sylvia Walsh believes this. In fact, those of us who think Kierkegaard matters for theological thinking and Christian identity (a group which is led by Walsh, as well as by David Gouwens, Amy Laura Hall, Lee Barrett, and others) assume that his writing, while always historically situated, also speaks of and to the kind of enduring problems and promises that we can call "theological." For my part, I count the problem of "becoming a Christian in Christendom" among these theological, and not *exclusively* historical, themes.

that Kierkegaard combated exceeded in scope and durability the particular historical arrangements between the Lutheran Church and Danish society. In his writings, "Christendom" becomes a trope among and overlapping with others, including "the crowd," "Speculation," "the present age," "philistines," and most commonly and simply the "spiritless" (*Aandløshed*). Christendom here signals any number of situations in which "spiritless" persons (or better: spiritless "persons") are mistaken for faithful disciples. The task of becoming a Christian, not to mention an authentic human being, entails becoming passionate, committed, and engaged in one's destiny. Infinitely worse off than those who fail at this task, from Kierkegaard's standpoint, are those who never take it up. Worse off still are those who mask their lack of resolve with the presumption of having already won. Kierkegaard's criticism of Christendom, then, indicts not only his own particular Danish-Lutheran state church or the Christian establishment from Constantine's era to his own. He also and more deeply condemns those cultural assumptions and social structures that permit individuals to use the alleged success of the Christian religion to avoid the dangerous task of actually becoming Christian — not to mention fully human. Through self-deception and "willed ignorance," as culturally permitted and sustained, people make Christianity into a refuge and justify their unwillingness to risk failure. Christendom is a problem of redundancy, not of relevance. If one is Christian without the difficult work of becoming that, why go through the trouble? *That* problem seems very much still with us. Mooney claims it always will be.[6]

I want to say a bit more about the kind of Christendom in which twenty-first-century North Americans find themselves. Over the last ten years, there has been an ongoing academic debate about whether or how contemporary Western society is secular. Most have rejected or revised the secularism theory of the 1960s, including Peter Berger, who earlier propounded it.[7] The theory posits that as the modern age advances in enlightened thinking and technological control the need

---

[6]Mooney, *On Søren Kierkegaard*, 32. Mooney describes Christendom in different (and compelling) terms.

[7]Peter Berger, "Secularism in Retreat," *The National Interest* (Winter 1996/1997): 4.

for and presence of religion gradually diminishes. Charles Taylor names this way of thinking a "subtraction story." It takes religious belief to comprise an overleaf of superstition that necessarily drops out as humanity becomes what it essential is: enlightened, self-guided, "secular."[8] While Taylor tells his own, more-complex story about how the lack of religious belief becomes not merely an option, but the default option, of late modern Europeans and North Americans, others with a more functionalist view of religion find it neither waning nor waxing but being disseminated and decentral-ized.[9] For every disestablishment or disappearance of organized religion, new forms emerge in other places (the churches of the Global South, for example) and in other ways (Facebook as commu-nion of saints).[10]

In this view, religion is not being *replaced* by modern secular life, only *re-placed* within it.

Especially as a story revised and rendered complex, "secularism" seems to characterize our age in ways that "Christendom" does not. Is Kierkegaard's problem of Christian redundancy still relevant today? Let's look more closely at Taylor's conception of secularism. For him, Weber's process of disenchantment is best tracked in terms of the emergence of a "detached" or "buffered" self. That new kind of self is "radical reflexivity," to use Taylor's earlier conception.[11] More importantly, the new self becomes essentially protective of powers from without — not only from the influence of other persons but from impersonal powers that, in earlier times, enchanted the world and could very well possess one, for good or ill. Recall that this buffered self is birthed in and by modernity and not simply uncovered once the cloak of religion falls to the floor, as subtraction theories would have it. It follows that with this innovation comes

---

[8]Charles Taylor, *A Secular Age* (Cambridge MA: Harvard University Press, 2007) 22ff.

[9]See Conrad Oswalt, *Secular Steeples: Popular Culture and the Religious Imagination* (Harrisburg PA: Trinity Press, 2003) 1-38.

[10]See Phillip Jenkins, *The Next Christendom: The Coming of Global Christianity* (Oxford UK: Oxford University Press, 2002) and Bruce David Forbes and Jeffrey H. Mahan, eds., *Religion and Popular Culture in America* (Berkley: University of California Press, 2005) esp. part 3: "Popular Culture as Religion."

[11]Charles Taylor, *Sources of the Self* (Harvard University Press, 1987) chap. 7.

novel possibilities, including the option of retreating inwardly in self-protection, of radical disengagement. According to Taylor, a person need not disengage always or frequently for things to change momentously. The very fact that it is possible now to do so — that I can be me apart from you, God, and the rest of the cold, objective world — marks the inception of secularism.[12]

What I find so fascinating in this account of secularism is how it mirrors what Kierkegaard calls Christendom. The problem of Christendom, one recalls, is that apathetic, "spiritless" persons can mask their lack of spiritual resolve by assuming that they are always already Christian — an assumption that churches sometimes spoon-feed people, according to Kierkegaard. The spiritless, like Taylor's buffered selves, become invulnerable, immune from failure. In this light, the difference between the secular citizen and the so-called Christian of Christendom cannot be one of mutual exclusivity — more of one making less of the other. That would simply add up to another subtraction theory. Rather, they name similar sorts of selves — disengaged, protective, uncommitted. When assumptions about Christianity being the cultural norm propitiate and underwrite the capacity of persons to disengage, secularism gets christened as Christendom. The two work rather well in tandem, each bearing and concealing the other.

Someone will be quick to object that, insofar as this is the problem, Kierkegaard is surely part of it. Does this proponent of inwardness and subjectivity do anything but advance the turn toward modern individualism? Much here depends on how we read Kierkegaard's praise of subjectivity and his defense of subjective truth in *Concluding Unscientific Postscript*. Or rather, whether we cease to misread them. In the grip of Cartesian assumptions, not to mention secularism as described by Taylor, we tend to read Kierkegaard's endorsed subjectivity as a sequestered space "in which" I have direct knowledge of a privatized, well-buffered self. That is why suggestions about "subjective truth" scare us so much — they imply truth as not just relative, but atomistic, self-enclosed. As Mooney again reminds us, subjectivity for Kierkegaard is almost the reverse:

---

[12]Taylor, *Secular Age*, 29-41.

> One has more or less subjectivity as one has (or takes) more or less
> responsibility for one's life, or is more or less affectively and
> morally responsive to others and one's ideals, or is more or less
> subject to passions and the heart. Subjectivity for Kierkegaard is an
> openness to be affected by (subject to, responsive to) deeply moral,
> religious, and aesthetic pulls, initiatives, invitations, please, calls,
> demands.[13]

This description seems to me better than right. Subjectivity entails
openness and responsiveness to the call of others. True subjects are
subject to others: available, porous, responsive, vulnerable. I am here
reminded of a line from Kierkegaard that struck me early on: "Most
people are subjective toward themselves and objective toward all
others, frightfully objective sometimes — but the task is precisely to
be objective toward oneself and subjective toward all others" (JP
IV:4542). The idea that one's "own" freedom and subjectivity
necessarily redouble as vulnerable openness to others is a sentiment
that Kierkegaard may have stolen from Luther: "A Christian is
perfectly free lord of all, subject to none. [And yet,] a Christian is a
perfectly dutiful servant of all, subject to all."[14] Then again, both
might be moving, at the crack of the bat, toward the words of the
Christ Hymn in Philippians 2.

Kierkegaard's Christendom is not our own, as I have said. Still,
what he takes to be its most objectionable characteristic — the ability
to remain uncommitted and invulnerable and to seem Christian in
doing so — is still very much with us. Our churches, especially
Protestant ones such as my own, largely imagine Christian salvation
to entail the preservation of "my" self — apart from you and a lifeless
natural world if need be. That's essentially a Gnostic conception[15]
and one on which Christendom turns. In this light, my own first
impression of and attraction to Kierkegaard, as one who would
allow me to hold more engaged Christians at arm's length, was

---

[13]Mooney, *On Søren Kierkegaard*, 63.

[14]Martin Luther, "The Freedom of a Christian," in *Martin Luther's Basic
Theological Writings*, 2nd ed., ed. Timothy F. Lull (Minneapolis: Augsburg Fortress,
2005) 391.

[15]See Philip J. Lee, *Against the Protestant Gnostics* (Oxford UK: Oxford University
Press, 1987). I thank my colleague at Augustana College, Jason Peters, for
suggesting Lee's book to me.

worse than mistaken. It turned Kierkegaard upside down. Or perhaps he was already there turning me, wounding from behind, deceiving me into the truth.

There is a host of other ways that contemporary Western society, especially in the United States, entails new forms of Christendom. Perhaps especially in the Midwest and the Bible belt (the two areas where I have lived and taught), Christianity remains culturally mainstream. For many there, to be Christian means to be normal. In fact, Christianity can become so subsumed within mainstream American culture that often saying, "I'm Christian" becomes indistinguishable from saying that "I'm good or nice or normal or at least not weird." In this case Christianity becomes a cipher or shorthand for any and every value that is considered acceptable: traditional family values, self-reliance, moral innocence, patriotism, good American hard work—the list goes on. The perennial problem of majority consciousness is at work here; becoming a Christian in Christendom is as difficult and as important as the task of a white person learning that she is not without race, or of straight folks understanding themselves to have one of several sexual orientations, or of the upper-middle class coming to realize that they are not classless. Most people like me—white, male, straight, relatively affluent—are rather late in thinking about themselves in these terms at all. We assume that we are colorless, beyond class, and without orientation. So, too, with Christianity in our ostensibly Christian nation. Christians are bound to mistake their own scandalous revelation of God through Jesus of Nazareth with something that is *simply* true and acceptable by anyone who is not eccentric. The Christian faith thereby comes to mean anything and everything but nothing in particular. Certainly nothing strange.

Part of Kierkegaard's difficult gift is to make Christianity strange again. He does so in ways more numerous than I can recount here. Let me name two related examples, both from books authored under pseudonym Anti-Climacus, an imagined "Christian on an extraordinarily high level" (JP VI:6433). In *The Sickness unto Death*, Anti-Climacus writes of how Christians, when understanding sin and redemption, typically "snip a little from both sides" (SUD 100). In the effort to get along more easily, Christendom's Christians liken sin to a momentary drop below the baseline of moral innocence. Redemption then becomes recompense for this lack, a kind of "negation of the negation" that returns a person to where he or she started. When sin becomes the exception to the "norm" of moral innocence, God's response to that exception also becomes contextualized and made understandable according to the same independent framework. Anti-Climacus's response is to restore the peculiarity of Christianity:

> Christianity, which was the first to discover the paradoxes, is as paradoxical on this point as possible; it seems to be working against itself by establishing sin so securely as a position that now it seems to be utterly impossible to eliminate it again—and then it is this very Christianity that by means of the Atonement wants to eliminate sin as completely as if it were drowned in the sea.
>
> (SUD 100)

On this "conception" (which can never be wholly conceptualized), one cannot defend Christianity for its power to do away with sin, seeing as how that problem is first revealed along with its overcoming. Moreover, the problem is much worse than apologetic approaches would have it. It is not that we need some help in returning to innocence; we have no independent framework to decide what innocence is. We can only be (made) open—meaning exposed, susceptible, vulnerable—to powers that rework us from without. If that is what salvation entails, the solution can look more painful than the problem. Christianity "seems to be working against itself" *existentially* (how else to say it?) and not just conceptually.

Anti-Climacus's second book, *Practice in Christianity*, continues to scratch at the wounds that Christianity inflicts while healing:

> When in sickness I go to a physician, he may find it necessary to prescribe a very painful treatment—there is no self-contradiction in my submitting to it. No, but if on the other hand I suddenly find myself in trouble, an object of persecution, because, because I have gone to *that* physician: well, then there is self-contradiction. The physician has perhaps announced that he can help me with regard to the illness from which I suffer, and perhaps he can really do that—but there is an *aber* [but] that I had not thought of at all. The fact that I get involved with this physician, attach myself to him—that is what makes me an object of persecution; here is the possibility of offense. (PC 115)

Anti-Climacus here distinguishes the suffering intrinsic to the Christian cure from all forms of homeopathy. What distinguishes Christian treatment is its lack of an independent framework through which the painful treatment can be understood and endured. The lack of such framework pushes what one means by *salvation* (Latin *salus*, meaning "health") almost to its breaking point.

Anti-Climacus distinguishes the treatments any doctor prescribes from the suffering that ensues from coming to *this particular* Physician. "Getting involved" with or "attaching oneself" to Christ is abhorrent to those outside this faith commitment. Why? The first and primary answer has to do with the incommensurability of Christ, this scandal of particularity. But the other and inextricable factor has to do with the desperate and sinful attempt to make everything commensurable, which Anti-Climacus here calls the "calamity of Christendom" (35). Christian therapy looks so peculiar because it involves the *unconditional* love of a particular Physician. Such excessive love challenges attempts by cultured Christians to mediate all differences, to secure themselves against vulnerability and interruptions *extra nōs*. Kierkegaard makes Christianity strange by emphasizing the intellectual paradox and affective scandal of the Gospel in the face of the many attempts, then and now, to hem in God's unbounded love.

These examples from the works of Anti-Climacus return me to the issue of whether one can divide Kierkegaard's Christian conceptions from his rhetoric. We sense in the examples something of the "countermotion" — one part against another across a silence — that characterizes the work of poets. *The Sickness unto Death* names this countermotion explicitly when it notes that Christianity "seems to be working against itself." *Practice in Christianity* performs it on almost every page by underscoring the ubiquity of the possibility of offense, in order also to reinstate the possibility of *not* being offended, and thereby truly blessed (Matthew 11:6). Such comprise instances of Kierkegaard's *via remotionis*, his nauseating us back to table, breaking us open toward radical healing. To the degree that his peculiar method recapitulates the way of the Christian gospel, we know that it cannot simply drop away under more favorable conditions. Otherwise, we ourselves would be back in control of the homeopathy. Christ would efficiently "function" to get humanity back on its own, exhausting his identity in doing so.

I do not want to suggest that Kierkegaard's writings become something like sacramental bearers of the Christian gospel. Kierkegaard would scribble out that suggestion without having to weigh methodological pragmatics. I *am* claiming that one reason his writings matter to Christians today is because, by inscribing irresolvable tensions and ongoing countermotions, they reenact and perform the very existential countermotions — the attractions and repulsions — characterizing the process of becoming a vulnerable, responsive "subject" before Christ. In this sense, his poetry is not only "about" becoming a Christian in Christendom; it helps make that task difficult — and also possible. Whether Kierkegaard would have regarded himself as an *accomplished* poet of the religious anymore than he regarded himself as a consummate Christian is largely beside the point. For many prospective Christians today, he certainly has become one.

12

Tears of Self-Forgetfulness: Kierkegaard on Self-Denial

Ronald F. Marshall

One of the enduring contributions to Christian theology that Kierke-gaard makes is his understanding of sin and salvation. Nothing he writes about "goes deeper into the mystery of life, or reveals a more profound psychological insight," than what he has to say about these loci in Christian theology.[1] His analysis of them coincides with the historical norms of Christianity and so provides an antidote to the liberal creed that a "God without wrath brought man without sin into a kingdom without judgment through the ministrations of Christ without a cross."[2]

Because this creed still influences large sections of Christianity today,[3] Kierkegaard's words on sin and salvation continue to be of help to those who contend[4] for the truth of the historical Christian teachings. At the heart of his analysis of these concepts is self-denial. This remains true today, even though self-denial has been widely

---

[1]David F. Swenson, *Something about Kierkegaard*, ed. Lillian Marvin Swenson (Macon GA: Mercer University Press, 1983; first published 1945) 178.

[2]H. Richard Niebuhr, *The Kingdom of God in America* (Middletown CT: Wesleyan University Press, 1988; first published 1937) 193.

[3]On the continuing minimization of sin in Christian theology, see Marsha G. Witten, *All Is Forgiven: The Secular Message in American Protestantism* (Princeton NJ: Princeton University Press, 1993) 127: "Conversion is portrayed far less as the need to grapple with sin-nature than as a reorientation of one's psychology toward the creation of a close interpersonal relationship with God."

[4]On this contention see Jude 1:3. Even though Kierkegaard disfavored defending Christianity (CD 162, PV, 80), he did believe in laying out a clear roadmap to the truth (JP 6:6283).

contested as an essential ingredient in key Christian concepts.[5] Nevertheless,

> Kierkegaard has insisted that theology . . . must neither be formed nor receive its content from philosophical positions alien to its own nature. It is not the business of theology to become intellectually respectable to any time; because when properly understood, theology will be a scandal and a stumbling block to the philosophy, the rationalism and the idolatry of any age.[6]

In this essay I want to lay out what Kierkegaard has to say about sin and salvation, and their attending concepts of confession and judgment, in order to show how compelling the rationale is for these historical Christian concepts in a time when they are widely contested.

Sin

Kierkegaard writes that we are all under the scrutinizing eye of eternity — and that we do not stand before God "only during specific hours" of the day (WL 366). This puts us under extreme pressure to measure up to the exalted standards or ideals of eternity that tower over us (UDVS 285). It is "frightful" to be under "eternity's inspection," and this "accounting" by God of what we do and who we are necessarily plunges us "into anxiety and unrest to the point of despair" (TM 29, 278). This is because

> God's thoughts are eternally higher than the thoughts of a human being, and therefore every human conception of happiness and unhappiness, of what is joyful and what is sorrowful, is faulty thinking. By remaining in this circle of conceptions, a person remains continually in the wrong with God. . . . [So the] fundamental relation between God and a human being is that a human being is a sinner and God is the Holy One. Directly before God a human being is not a sinner in this or in that, but is essentially a sinner, is

---

[5]See Harold Bloom, *The American Religion: The Emergence of the Post-Christian Nation* (New York: Simon & Schuster, 1992) 53: "American religion [is based on] the faith of and in the American self." Note also that "American Religion [is a] religion of the self" (265).

[6]Robert L. Perkins, *Søren Kierkegaard*, Makers of Contemporary Theology (Richmond VA: John Knox, 1969) 41.

... unconditionally guilty. But if he is essentially guilty, then he is *always* guilty, because the debt of essential guilt is so extreme as to make every direct accounting impossible.   (UDVS 284-285)

If this guilt is not removed through forgiveness, then God's condemnation of us is "more terrible than any human revenge" (EUD 56) — which is made all the worse since no one can escape it either (CD 207). Imagining that God would never "crush" us in this way (TM 272, 274) is to suppose we can "remodel" him (EUD 331) into someone less terrifying, less demanding, and less exacting.[7] But Kierkegaard opposes such remodeling because Christianity would then be cut off from the norms of the New Testament from which it arises (TM 212, 58, 44, 17). Therefore we "must always be on watch" lest we forget God, because his ways are "so alien" to us (WL 130, 244).[8] His ways are so alien because "the lofty earnestness of the eternal," which neither wants "the recommendation . . . of the majority nor of eloquence,"

> does not dare to promise you earthly advantages if you accept and in appropriation adhere to this conviction. On the contrary, if adhered to, it will make your life strenuous, many a time perhaps burdensome; if adhered to, it will perhaps expose you to ridicule by others, not to mention that adherence might ask even greater sacrifices from you.   (UDVS 136)

When we adhere to God in this way we are led into self-denial — which requires us to "renounce instability and changefulness and caprice and willfulness" (TM 278). This means dying to "every merely earthly hope, to every merely human confidence; . . . to your

---

[7]See also JP 6:6863: "If Christianity is to be proclaimed as it essentially is in the gospels, proclaimed as and being: imitation, sheer suffering, misery and wailing, sharpened by a background of judgment where every word must be accounted for — then it is fearful suffering, anxiety, quaking, and trembling. Quite right. But where in the gospels does it actually say that God intends this earthly life to be anything else? . . . [But still] we want Christianity to leave us in peace. So we turn Christianity around and get an insipid optimism out of the dreadful pessimism which Christianity is in the New Testament. . . . [With] this we shove Christianity out completely and now things are beginning to hum with all the jobs, begetting children, and finite busyness and enjoyment of life, etc., etc."

[8]On this difficulty see JP 4:4038: "I have to concentrate all my earnestness solely on this — that I am a sinner."

selfishness, or to the world" (FSE 77).[9] Enduring ridicule, burdens, sacrifices, and strenuousness, all contribute to this denial of self. These traumas are invaluable because through them alone are we able to discover "that God is" (WL 362).[10] Kierkegaard calls these tears blessed because through them we forget ourselves, deny ourselves, discover God and his salvation, and quit endlessly stewing over our sins.[11]

But because self-denial is so strenuous, we rebel against it. This resistance shows that disobedience or "insubordination" is the "calamity of our age" (BA, 5). Consequently "every sin is disobedience and every disobedience is sin" (WA 35). Kierkegaard links sin to "anxiety" (CA 56-60) and "despair" (SUD 68)[12] as well, which helps him show all the more how defiance (CA 144) and disobedience (SUD 81) are at the heart of sin. Sin, then, cannot be overcome through some life improvement plan.[13] It runs so deeply in us that

---

[9]See also JP 3:2711: "Humanly speaking, Christianity must make a person unhappy if he is earnest about Christianity. It immediately directs his whole mind and effort toward the eternal; he thereby becomes heterogeneous with the whole secular mentality and must collide. . . . [This] doctrine . . . is like a plague to the natural man."

[10]See also JP 6:6262: "I do know how to console. . . . I also know that . . . the sufferer will feel relieved and will take a great liking to me. But the trouble is that I know that this is not Christianity. I take it from another flask. It is poetry with an invigorating addition of the ethical. But Christianity it is not. As a rule Christianity is dismaying rather than consoling." Note as well JP 4:4018: "Only the struggle and distress of the anguished conscience can help one venture to will to have anything to do with Christianity."

[11]See WA 140: "O blessed tears—that in weeping there is also this blessing: forgetting! She has forgotten herself completely, forgotten the setting with all its disturbing elements. A setting like this is impossible to forget unless one forgets oneself. Indeed, it was a setting frightfully and agonizingly designed to remind her of herself—but she weeps, and as she weeps she forgets herself. O blessed tears of self-forgetfulness, when her weeping does not once remind her anymore of what she is weeping over; in this way she has forgotten herself completely."

[12]For an exposition of these linkages, see Sylvia Walsh, *Kierkegaard: Thinking Christianly in an Existential Mode* (Oxford UK: Oxford University Press, 2009) 80-110.

[13]See JP 6:6503: "Christ is not a savior for this life but for eternal life. Yes, what is more, . . . he is the very opposite of a savior for this life." On this point see Alexander Schmemann, *Celebration of Faith*, 3 vols, trans. John A. Jillions (Crestwood NY: St. Vladimir's Seminary Press, 1991-1995) 1:68: "Christianity is a religion of salvation. This means that it is not merely a 'life improvement' plan."

it is beyond sheer ignorance of the right (SUD 95) — being instead "the most dreadful thing" possible (JP 4:4027).[14] As sinners we are dealing with the "one enemy" we cannot conquer by ourselves (EUD 18). If sin were only ignorance, we could chip away at it through education. But because it is rooted in defiance and disobedience, we cannot stop it by simply modifying our behavior.

Confession

Once the intensity and gravity of our sin is fixed in our minds, it can petrify us. In that case the blessings of self-forgetfulness do not mark the tears we shed over our sins (WA 140). Our sins instead leave us "to sit and brood and stare" at them (JP 4:4036). But Kierkegaard wants to move sinners beyond such spiritual stagnation. He thought we could do that simply by asking "about what lasts," for in that question we pass over "from temporality into eternity" (UDVS 77). In inquiring about what lasts, we see that recalcitrance is the last thing we need when facing our sin, for it deprives us of the "medication" that can heal us. Without that medication we are stuck — forever "indisposed" by our sin (JP 4:4048). This questioning about what lasts is the medication we need. It gives us a chance to see that "the object of all faith's work is to get rid of egotism and selfishness in order that God" may "rule in everything." For when we suffer over this questioning about what lasts, the discomfort it brings becomes "the receptive soil in which the eternal can take root" and replace selfishness with obedience (UDVS 259). This brings us to the brink of confession. This makes the tears we shed over our sins a blessing by ushering in self-forgetfulness.

---

[14]See also JP 4:4035: "[It] is part of sin to have only a shallow notion of sin and also because only God, the Holy One, has the truly divine idea." Note further C. Stephen Evans, *Kierkegaard: An Introduction* (Cambridge UK: Cambridge University Press, 2009) 180-81: "It is a consistent theme in Kierkegaard's writings that human sin is not something humans can understand through their own philosophical resources. . . . However, . . . there is still something in the Greek perspective which modern Christendom needs. . . . When Socrates sees someone who does not act in accordance with what he says is true, he concludes that he must not genuinely understand what he claims to know. . . . This echoes the Kierkegaardian distinction between understanding that is purely verbal, and the kind of 'subjective understanding' that links what is understood to a person's existence."

This leads to a confession of our sins which makes us "alone with the Holy One." In this solitude the sinner sees that

> he is the greatest of sinners, because directly before the Holy One he [sees] the essential magnitude of the sin within himself. . . . Anyone who thinks of his sin in this way and wishes in this stillness to learn . . . the art of sorrowing over his sins — will certainly discover that the confession of sin is not merely a counting of all the particular sins but is a comprehending before God that sin has a coherence in itself.   (TDIO 30-32)

This coherence is monumental because it blocks the "perpetual enumerating" of one's sins by "a petty arithmetician in the service of faintheartedness." Counting our sins keeps our repentance from being "before God," and turns it into some corrupt form of "self-love in depression." This "religious debauchery," or debasement of repentance, is "the most dreadful of all" (TDIO 34-35).[15] But this alone does not cure us because we still want to go over our specific sins before God. We fear that gathering our sins together into one general confession will ruin repentance — for we think that it "is nauseated by the empty generality" and its "superficiality" (TDIO 34-35). But this desire for more detail is "fraudulent" and is rather about usurping what rightfully belongs "solely to God" (TDIO 39, 36). God is fully able to keep track of all our many and varied sins. He does not need us to enumerate them before him in our confession. We could compose a long speech about our many and varied sins, but we would never be able to use it in confession. That is

---

[15]On this corruption of repentance, see Martin Luther, "The Smalcald Articles" (1537), *The Book of Concord: The Confessions of the Evangelical Lutheran Church* (1580), ed. T. Tappert (Philadelphia: Fortress, 1959) 309: "Repentance is not partial like repentance for actual sins, nor is it uncertain like that. It does not debate what is sin and what is not sin, but lumps everything together and says, 'We are wholly and altogether sinful.' We need not spend our time weighing, distinguishing, differentiating. On this account there is no uncertainty in such repentance, for nothing is left that we might imagine to be good enough to pay for our sin. One thing is sure: We cannot pin our hope on anything that we are, think, say, or do. And so our repentance cannot be false, uncertain, or partial, for a person who confesses that he is altogether sinful embraces all sins in his confession without omitting or forgetting a single one." Since Kierkegaard thought that Luther was "the master of us all" (JP 3:2465), his attack on weighing, distinguishing and differentiating sin, could well be an illumination of Kierkegaard's attack on enumerating sin.

because going to confession is like being "out to sea . . . in a storm," Kierkegaard writes, where the knowledge we had on land regarding our many sins, fails us once we are at sea — due to the terror, darkness, and powerlessness that disrupts us at sea (TDIO 36). In the storm we are tongue-tied by the terror of it all, and so we are not able to deliver our speech on our many sins. This desire for "much knowledge" deceives us (TDIO 36). It makes us think that we can orchestrate our own confession when we in fact cannot, for the stillness in confession "belongs to God" (TDIO 39). Knowing that we are guilty and that we are sinners is enough — anything else is deceptive, fraudulent, and religious debauchery (TDIO 40).[16]

In this vein, Kierkegaard provides through Anti-Climacus a prayer for confessing our sins which combines generality and specificity — yet without the illegitimate enumeration of personal sins:

> Lord Jesus Christ, our foolish minds are weak; they are more than willing to be drawn — and there is so much that wants to draw us to itself. There is pleasure with its seductive power, the multiplicity with its bewildering distractions, the moment with its infatuating importance and the conceited laboriousness of busyness and the careless time-wasting of light-mindedness and the gloomy brooding of heavy-mindedness — all this will draw us away from ourselves to itself in order to deceive us. . . .   (PC 157)

This prayer cautions us about the temptations we have in pleasure, distractions, busyness, light-mindedness and heavy-mindedness. No specific personal sins are listed in this prayer, but this does not detract from its power to guide any and all repentance.

First, it warns us that pleasure is seductive and not simply a matter of us satisfying our cherished goals. This is based on the conviction that sin has its fleeting pleasures.[17] From this we confess

---

[16]This is what is behind Martin Luther's famous dictum *pecca fortiter* or "sin boldly." Martin Luther, "Letter to Philip Melanchthon" (1 August 1521), *Luther's Works*, 55 vols, ed. Jaroslav Pelikan and Helmut Lehmann (Philadelphia and St. Louis: Fortress and Concordia, 1955–1986) 48:282. To sin boldly does not mean to sin all the more, but to admit that you are a terrible sinner — *fortissimus peccator*. Luther's *pecca fortiter* might well have shaped Kierkegaard's emphasis on the "admission" of one's sinfulness (JFY 102).

[17]See Hebrews 11:25.

how appealing sin is — which is why it is so seductive. As a result we will not be eager to discard it, nor will we be able to get rid of it easily when we try to.

Second, distractions are sinful. They build on the bewildering multiplicity of stimuli that bombards us. This variety is not always the spice of life, but can also drain us. Under the barrage of these many distractions we become diffuse — losing all focus and the ability to get things done.[18]

Third, there is busyness. This rush of tasks makes us feel important — long before we ever are worn out with fatigue. Kierkegaard calls this busyness "conceited laboriousness." This is because this sinful busyness would have us think we are important because of our work. Faith says the opposite — that we are valuable because we glorify and serve the creator and redeemer of us all.[19]

Fourth, there is the superficiality of light-mindedness. Under its sway, the big questions of life are covered over by the trivial concerns of popular culture. The sin of light-mindedness keeps us from pondering and pursuing matters of truth and goodness. It makes us waste our time on the insubstantial.[20]

Fifth, there is heavy-mindedness — the very opposite of light-mindedness. This sin takes seriousness and earnestness and ruins them by turning them into gloom and brooding depression. As a result we despair over our self-control and diligence which leaves us to wallow in self-indulgence and egotism. But if we divert our attention from ourselves and focus on God and our neighbor, then our seriousness is saved from this gloomy, brooding, heavy-mindedness.

Gathering up all five of these considerations into a confession restores the blessedness of self-forgetfulness for the tears that we shed for our many and varied sins (WA 140).

---

[18]On this problem of getting things done, see Galatians 3:3 and Philippians 1:6.

[19]Matthew 22:37-40 calls this the summation of all the law and the prophets.

[20]See Proverbs 9:6: "Leave simpleness, and live, / and walk in the way of insight" (RSV).

Judgment

Even though Kierkegaard was against scaring people to death with the threats and punishments of hell (UDVS 44), he still thought the impending judgment of God could provide "a helping hand" when it came to confessing our sins (UDVS 51).[21] At the beginning of *The Gospel of Sufferings*, Kierkegaard imagines this final judgment day. He offers it as an incentive for following Christ "in the crisscrossing busyness of life," when it seems more than we can handle. In those moments, Kierkegaard warns, we are not to

> forget that it is eternity that will judge how the task was accomplished and that the earnestness of eternity will call for the silence of a sense of shame with regard to everything of the world, about which there was perpetual talk in the world.   (UDVS 223)

If then we have pulled back from following Christ for fear of what the world thinks of us, we must remember that this ploy will only hurt us on judgment day. It is not a good defense then, to say that we did not follow Christ as we should have because we were afraid of being unpopular.[22] Kierkegaard says all such arguments must be silenced at the end, and so we should not depend on them now.

In addition to being stripped of this defense, Kierkegaard argues that the criterion by which we will be judged is especially stringent. This criterion will also be separate from all earthly values and accomplishments.[23] It will be based instead on self-denial. When Christ uses this criterion on judgment day, he will do so with the intensified twist that he

> does not merely know what self-denial is, he does not merely know how to judge in such a way that no malpractice can hide itself — no,

---

[21]On this tension see Jack Mulder, Jr., "On Being Afraid of Hell: Kierkegaard and Catholicism on Imperfect Contrition," *Kierkegaard Studies: Yearbook 2007*, ed. Niels Jørgen Cappelørn, Herman Deuser and K. Brian Söderquist (Berlin: Walter de Gruyter, 2007) 96-122.

[22]This is inspired by Mark 8:38: "For whoever is ashamed of me and of my words in this adulterous and sinful generation, of him will the Son of man also be ashamed, when he comes in the glory of his Father with the holy angels" (RSV).

[23]On this point see Luke 16:15: "[W]hat is exalted among men is an abomination in the sight of God" (RSV).

his presence is the judging that makes everything that looked so good, which was heard and seen with admiration in the world, become silent and turn pale; his presence is the judging, because he was self-denial. He who was equal with God took the form of a lowly servant, he who could command legions of angels, indeed, could command the world's creation and its destruction, he walked about defenseless; . . . he who was the lord of creation constrained nature itself to keep quiet, for it was not until he had given up his spirit that the curtain tore and the graves opened and the powers of nature betrayed who he was: if this is not self-denial, what then is self-denial!   (UDVS 224)

Kierkegaard enhances this criterion in order to terrify us. If Christ, who embodied self-denial, will judge how well we denied ourselves, then we cannot hope somehow to fool him on judgment day.[24] This will be impossible because Christ will judge us in the most penetrating, thorough, and unrelenting way — for he himself will have the most exacting standard, being self-denial himself. On judgment day he will ask

about how often you have conquered your own mind, about what control you have exercised over yourself or whether you have been a slave, about how often you have mastered yourself in self-denial or whether you have never done so, about how often you in self-denial have been willing to make a sacrifice for a good cause or whether you were never willing, about how often you in self-denial have forgiven your enemy, whether seven times or seventy times seven times, about how often you in self-denial endured insults patiently, about what you have suffered, not for your own sake, for your selfish interests' sake, but what you in self-denial have suffered for God's sake.   (UDVS 223-24)

The detail and relentlessness in this examination is terrifying. In self-defense we can imagine ourselves saying, "Well, I know I did not, but wait a minute! Give me a change to explain! This is not fair. You are taking my life in the wrong way!" But such maneuverings

---

[24]Or for that matter, even right now: "Alas, many think that judgment is something reserved for the far side of the grave, and so it is also, but they forget that judgment is much closer than that, that it is taking place at all times, because at every moment you live, existence is judging you, since to live is to judge oneself, to become disclosed" (WL 227-28).

will not finesse Christ — for he embodies self-denial in himself. These divine, rapid-fire interrogations cannot be stopped by any side-stepping on our part. Christ forces us to answer: Did you conquer your mind, control and master yourself, or were you a slave to your own base desires? Did you sacrifice your time and money for a good cause or use it for your own plans and pleasures? Did you forgive your enemies over and over again, or block them, hate them, trip them up and stop them by any means necessary? Did you take the insults hurled at you as if you deserved them, or did you squeal and complain that you deserve more respect? Were you ashamed of God when reasonable, good people pointed out to you how immoral and intellectually disrespectful his ways and will actually are — or did you love and honor him all the more in spite of their arguments?

This description of judgment day is designed to drive us to repent of our sins and to follow Christ all the more diligently. Its point is to keep us from holding back — stressing instead "unconditionally relating oneself to the unconditioned" (JP 4:4906). But it does this without appealing to the fires of hell and the threats of everlasting punishment and condemnation in hell. For Kierkegaard it is enough for us to know what is expected of us — with no need to explore in detail the excruciating punishments awaiting all those who disobey, do not repent, and squander forgiveness. In his day[25] that wretched scenario had already been described:

---

[25]For a contemporary version, see Jack Handey, "My First Day in Hell," *The New Yorker* (30 October 2006) 52: "My first day in Hell is drawing to a close. . . . Most of the demons are asleep now. . . . They look so innocent, it's hard to believe that just a few hours ago they were raping and torturing us. . . . The food here turns out to be surprisingly good. The trouble is, just about all of it is poisoned. So a few minutes after you finish eating you're doubled over in agony. The weird thing is, as soon as you recover you're ready to dig in again. . . . It's odd, but Hell can be a lonely place, even with so many people around. They all seem caught up in their own little worlds, running to and fro, wailing and tearing at their hair. . . . I thought getting a job might help. . . . I became the assistant to a demon who pulls people's teeth out. . . . I decided I had to get away — the endless lines, the senseless whipping, the forced sing-alongs. You get tired of trying to explain that you've already been branded, or that something that big won't fit in your ear, even with a hammer. . . . I had better get some rest. They say the bees will be out soon and that it's hard to sleep with the constant stinging. . . . Tomorrow we're supposed to build a huge monolith, then take picks and shovels and tear it down, then beat each other to death. It sounds pointless to me, but what do I know. I'm new here."

The punishments of Hell . . . are the most exquisite pains of soul and body, . . . arising from the fear and sense of the most just wrath and vengeance of God against sins, the most sad consciousness of which they carry about with them, the baseness of which is manifest, and of which, likewise, no remission, . . . no mitigation or end can be hoped for. Whence, in misery, [the damned] will execrate, with horrible lamentation and waling, their former impiety, by which they carelessly neglected the commandments of the Lord, the admonitions of their brethren, and all means of attaining salvation—but in vain. For in perpetual anguish, with dreadful trembling, in shame, confusion, and ignominy, in inextinguishable fire, in weeping and gnashing of teeth, amidst that which is eternal and terrible, torn away from the grace and favor of God, they must quake among devils, and . . . be tortured without end to eternity.[26]

Kierkegaard assumes this dire end[27]—which may be why he is so emphatic about stressing the great sacrifices we must make now, in order to ward off going to that terrible place of torment at the end, for all of eternity.

Salvation

But all of this confession, condemnation, and judgment can leave our tears without the blessing of self-forgetfulness (WA 140). We can cry over our failures and be "crushed, almost despairing" (JFY 147). We do not live as we should, and our repentance for these sins is all too meager. In fact our very will to follow Christ is contorted by our rebellion—corrupted by the disobedience itself. As a result, our "ability to receive is . . . simply not . . . in order" (PV, 54). Burdened down by this incapacity, Kierkegaard cries out:

---

[26]Matthew Hafenreffer (1561–1619), "Loci Theologici," *The Doctrinal Theology of the Evangelical Lutheran Church*, 3rd ed. (1899), ed. Heinrich Schmid, trans. Charles A. Hay and Henry E. Jacobs (Minneapolis: Augsburg, 1961) 658. "[Hafenreffer's Loci] was especially esteemed in . . . Denmark, where it was generally used as a textbook" (666). Kierkegaard, however, did not have a copy of this book in his personal library. *Auktionsprotokol over Søren Kierkegaards bogsamling*, ed. Herman P. Rohde (Copenhagen: Det Kongelige Bibliotek, 1967).

[27]See UDVS 47, 58; CD 294; TM 121; 211; JP 3:3589.

> From this moment I will no longer believe in myself; I will not let myself be deceived. . . . No, apprehensive about myself, . . . I will seek my refuge with him, the Crucified One. I will beseech him . . . to save me from myself. (CD 280)

These passionate, desperate words push us beyond confession and judgment. For when the judgment in the next world "seeks the place where I, a sinner, stand, . . . it does not find me" (WA 123). So when we recall "the lust of the eye that infatuated, the sweetness of revenge that seduced, the anger that made us unrelenting, [and] the cold heart" that ran away from God, it is our refuge, Christ, who keeps our "minds free," our "courage uncrushed, and heaven open" (EUD 7). Christ does that by being our "high priest" who steps into our place, and suffers "the punishment of sin," that we "might be saved" (WA 123).[28] This sacrifice gives us confidence when before we were almost despairing (JFY 147). It bolsters our efforts to follow Christ — without leaving us to fend for ourselves before God. For this sacrifice in fact draws God closer to us, for "the satisfaction of the Atonement" means that we "step aside" (WA 123). Christ satisfies God's need for justice when he dies in our place. This satisfaction overcomes the wrath of God that separates us from him and would damn to hell for all eternity.[29] By enhancing God's mercy toward us, we are helped along in our life with him. Just enough of the pressure

---

[28]See Sylvia Walsh, *Kierkegaard: Thinking Christianly in an Existential Mode*, 137: "[The] substitutionary perspective is clearly dominant in [Kierkegaard's] soteriology." This soteriological perspective shows the influence of Luther. See his "Sermon on Matthew 2:1-12" (1522), *Luther's Works* 52:253: "Why else did [Christ] die, except to pay for our sins and to purchase grace for us so that we might despair of ourselves and our works, placing no trust in them, so that we might, with courageous defiance, look only to Christ, and firmly believe that he is the man whom God beholds in our stead and for the sake of his sole merits forgives us our sins, deigns to look upon us with favor, and grants us eternal life. That is the Christian faith."

[29]See Matthew 3:12; Mark 9:47-48; Luke 16:19-31; John 3:36, 5:28-29; Romans 5:9; 2 Thessalonians 1:5-10. On Kierkegaard's opposition to universalism, or the view that hell must have no one in it, see Jack Mulder, Jr., "Must All Be Saved? A Kierkegaardian Response to Theological Universalism," *International Journal for Philosophy of Religion* 59 (February 2006): 1-24. Note Mulder's caveat: "[In] much of Kierkegaard's writing, [he] in effect says, 'Stop working on metaphysical questions and start working on yourself!' " (2).

is lifted from our backs so that we can take up our discipleship again—being "kept in the striving" (JFY 147). This is what the "recourse to grace" is for (TM 292).

Striving Born of Gratitude

All these burdens of sin, confession, and judgment are for salvation. They are not meant to end in despair as some may think. Instead they are preparations for salvation. These burdens are to humble us that we will want to reach out to the grace of God. Learning about sin and judgment shows us our need for a salvation which can only be fulfilled from outside of ourselves. It helps us see that we lack the resources from within to heal ourselves. So we have to resist the tendency to attenuate the strictness of Christianity in order that we may be relieved from the burden of sin and judgment. For if we were to do that we would lose the necessary preparation for Christian salvation. But that would be to cut off our nose to spite our face. Kierkegaard resists this temptation and so his authorship is for us a treasure trove of Christian wisdom.

As long as we are plagued by the temptation to cut back on the hard truths of Christianity, what Kierkegaard has to say about sin, confession, judgment, and salvation will be of help. For he is able to show us in a myriad of ways, that "infinite humiliation and grace, and then a striving born of gratitude," is what Christianity truly is (JP 1:993).

13

Hidden Inwardness as Interpersonal[1]

Edward F. Mooney

Climacus reports a scene overheard, seen in a fugitive glance through leaves as he sat on a bench at twilight in "the garden of the dead," a cemetery, most likely Copenhagen's Assistens Kirkegård. The scene is the grief of a grandfather mourning at the grave of his son, and speaking tearfully of the meaning of that death to a ten-year-old boy, his grandson, now fatherless. The "garden of the dead," as it is called, is not at the city's center, but at some remove, not out in the wooded parklands, but nevertheless sufficiently alive with nature's leafy shadows and open skies that Climacus can exalt in a kind of minor ecstasy over the coming of night — as if night were an invitation for a "nocturnal tryst," a beautiful prelude to the more tearful tableau ahead, where a grandfather's grief will spill over as an anguished admonition to his barely understanding grandson. But what can the night tell us of mood, yearning, and heartache? Night beckons with promise of

> a tryst . . . with the infinite, persuaded by the night's breeze as in a monotone it repeats itself, breathing through forest and meadow, and sighing as though in search of something, urged by the distant echo in oneself of the stillness as if intimating something, urged by the sublime calm of the heavens, as if this something had been found, persuaded by the palpable silence of the dew as if this were the explanation and infinitude's refreshment, like the fecundity of a quiet night, only half understood like the night's semidiaphanous mist (197).[2]

---

[1]Twenty-five years ago, Bob Perkins graciously accepted my first Kierkegaard effort. He was putting together a single volume on *Fear and Trembling* that turned out to be a trial run for his extended International Kierkegaard Commentary, a project that was to occupy so much of his boundless spirit through the succeeding years. Now as that series comes to its end, it's appropriate to remember his efforts with another gift for a collection just for him. This is an honor.

[2]Page numbers throughout are keyed to *Kierkegaard: Concluding Unscientific*

Like the coming of night, as Climacus has it, the sublime, for Kant, is only half-understood; but the coming of night would not be Kant's preferred example. For him the sublime is a towering, awesome occasion: the violence of ocean storms, the wonder of starry heavens. In the *Postscript* passage from the garden of the dead, the sublime is a natural but downscaled scene of allure and fear. Death haunts, but the surround is the half-understood breathing, sighing, of a breeze, the "semidiaphanous mist" of the night, the "palpable silence of the dew."

Climacus has us feel an intimate sublime that leaves us in a tremulous, restless repose. "The essence of night", he might say, with Schelling, is "lack, need, and longing?"[3] If an invitation to a nocturnal tryst foretells refreshment, but also anxiety, for this anticipated tryst is not without danger. The coming of dark in the garden of the dead is the coming of death, intimating, at best, "refreshment" half-seen. We yearn for the infinite repose of a beckoning night, as a Christian might yearn for the infinite repose of a savior, seen through a glass darkly. But Climacus is a romantic, not a Christian, and he years for the comfort not of a savior but a comfort sensed in the "silence of the dew", in a "semidiaphanous mist." His evocations of night breeze and dew nevertheless bear comparison with the elegies to the lilies of the fields and the birds of the air (in Kierkegaard's discourses of 1849). Here, as George Pattison notes, nature "signals a kind of transcendence" that evokes "the anxiety of self-relation".[4] The repose of a lily or bird signals the contentment humans yearn for but lack. The anxious dark of the night and the anxious dark of the soul implicate each other in mutual resonance.

Our *mise-en-scène* is barely half-a-dozen pages, a condensed and powerful meditation on death and the inwardness of grief, held by sky above and fresh grave below. Stepping beyond the garden of

---

Postscript, trans. Alastair Hannay (Cambridge UK: Cambridge University Press, 2009).

[3]"The Deities of Samothrace," (*Über die Gottheiten von Samothrake*, 1815), trans. and intro. R. F. Brown (Missoula MT: Scholars Press, 1977) 18.

[4]See "*Poor Paris!" Kierkegaard's Critique of the Spectacular City* (Berlin: de Gruyter, 1999) 128-29.

death and this grief-filled outpouring, we might consider what's meant by "truth is subjectivity", or "true inwardness" but such disquisitions would be at least one step removed from atmospheric settings from which things and persons speak, one step removed from a man broken in grief, a frightened grandson, a fresh grave, an anxious night, a screen of leafy boughs behind which Climacus hides and listens. This tryst with the infinite realizes what *Postscript* figures as an "objective uncertainty" held in "the most passionate inwardness." It intimates restless inwardness:

> the night's breeze . . . repeats itself, breathing through forest and meadow, and sighing as though in search of something, urged by the distant echo in oneself of the stillness as if intimating something. (197)

The sighing of night reflects a sighing soul, and a sighing soul reflects the night breeze, both yearning for a rest signaled by silent dew. It's not as though the physiology of anxiety caused the skies to spin, or the spin of the sky caused the brain to spin. It's a matter of poetic fit, as lightening portends shock to the heart, and shock to the heart portends lightening.

Death disrupts the living, puts the dead under judgment, and warns the living to take heed. Death speaks indirectly through a night breeze and also through words overheard. The grief-wrought old man does not intend his words for the eavesdropping Climacus. But Climacus is taken by them, and takes them up as his own, as they float by more or less anonymously from a graveside. To call his taking up with these words "appropriation" means silencing that term's primary sense of forceful or illicit seizure (as in an illicit appropriation of land or funds). Climacus is overcome by a demand in the grief overheard in the way a love or beauty or truth might overcome him. He does not steal a grief overheard but lets a grief, and its lessons of death and life, steal into his heart, where he makes his own what has captured his soul. Perhaps we should say that the subjective thinker appropriates what first appropriates him.

The old man grieves at the fresh grave of his son, and fears for his soul, for his son was caught up in a cultural illusion, the illusion that philosophical or historical speculation or debate about faith could be a substitute for being of faith. Let grandsons beware!

Erudite scholarly engagement with a religion is not a work of faith but of objectivity. I can lack an analysis of faith yet be of faith; I can have a perfect analysis and be an atheist, or a humorist. Climacus, as humorist, understands the available Christian cure but won't take it. He can upset would-be Christians with a diagnosis of their ills, and know his own ills, and yet be uninterested in the cure of becoming Christian himself. Climacus grieves that the old man is denied a restful old age, so anxious he is that his son faces harsh Judgment. Climacus decides he will do more to unseat the complacency of those who persist in the son's illusion. But that is not to take up with the truth that accosts a Christian and that a Christian must hold.

This scene of inadvertent spying opens disarmingly: "What happened is quite simple. It was four years ago . . . " (197), we are told. The writer simply sat on a bench, becoming inadvertently privy to a conversation. Yet that moment triggers vocation, for Climacus hears a "decisive summons [for him] to come on a definite track" (202). Why? He reflects, "You are after all tired of life's diversions, you are tired of girls that you love only in passing, you must have something that fully occupies your time. Here it is" (202). But this is a farce. A summons is no summons that is welcome only because flirtation has lost its charm.

Graveside weeping awakens Climacus to a need for direction, but his approach is comically inept. A search for vocation, he confides, will be "something like an intricate criminal case in which the very complex circumstances [make] pursuit of the truth difficult" (202). So he confronts a detective's puzzle. But "How should I live?" is an existential question, not a question of fact in a detective "Who done it?" This is not an objective puzzle. Nevertheless, in spite of himself, Climacus stumbles on important truths — for us, if not for him. Pressure from a sharp awareness of death can open the soul to a "summons." Having "a definite track" will partially answer the challenge of death. But the substance of life-and-death urgency eludes him as he frames the anxious "whence-and-whither" of his life as a police matter for gumshoes with flashlights, an answer to boredom as he reflects, you are tired of girls that you love only in passing. And then his flashlight hits on the answer. He'll fill the time of his life by exposing the fraud of abstract philosophy. He has a calling: the summons to do something, is answered by a particular response and resolve (the path is here not there).

Nature, death, and other persons interweave as a concerted open sphere of subjectivity that awakens Climacus to his own self-relations or subjectivity. So we might offer, surprisingly, that subjectivity is a shared natural, embodied, and interpersonal space.

"What happened was quite simple". The author of a 600-page "postscript" is mainly an objective thinker, defending the truth that truth is subjectivity.[5] But ever and again, as in this graveside scene, he slips into a confessional mood that places him within subjective space. He does not just describe it from without. He is subject to intimations of night mist, to sudden earnestness about his life's orientation, taken by effusions from a gravesite that address him. Subjectivity includes capacity to feel from the standpoint of other subjectivities. Climacus is the old man who sees the ruse of philosophy, the child subjected to an insistence that he disavow his father's life, the fearsome corpse, testament to a life squandered (200).

Chalked with age, the old man, anchors a social space linking three generations and an invisible listener. This space is made active by a dead son who prompts inwardness, true or false, in all attending, and by a surrounding night, this concatenation of affect then

---

[5]In the early 1960s Stanley Cavell noted that there was something quixotic in what appears to be Climacus's attempt to *defend* subjectivity. Philosophical defense by definition is an objective project. Yet on second thoughts, that sort of quixotic project is not very foreign to philosophy. Kant, after all, uses reason to limit reason. And, in any case, Climacus is not really *interested* in offering a philosophical defense. He's conducting a kind of thought-experiment, trying out sketches that exemplify features of what must be wrapped up in a way of life, or in a way of living into a life—not trying to *justify* that life. Nevertheless, it can surely *seem* at times that Climacus is doing something academic and philosophical—objective. Later in the 1960s Henry Allison argued that the arguments Climacus delivers are so *patently* flawed that Climacus must be talking tongue-in-cheek. See Alastair Hannay's essay in *Kierkegaard's "Concluding Unscientific Postscript": A Critical Guide*, ed. Rick Anthony Furtak (Cambridge UK: Cambridge University Press, 2010). To *only* laugh, of course would let us off the hook. We are meant to be transformed in a deep way, not just amused by dialectical antics. We can learn something "serious" about death, grief, and earnestness of vocation, about the futility of supposing that historical research can serve as a substitute for faith, and much more, traced in the present essay. We absorb these lessons, even as we appreciate that this "mimic-pathetic-dialectic," this most *unscholarly* antisystematic postscript to some assuming philosophical crumbs, is a dig at pretentious systematic tomes that leave out the would-be engaged writer and reader.

prompting inwardness (or its shadow) in Climacus. This listening and speaking, passive and active ensemble, is at first blush a lonely and solitary affair, but it is ultimately social. If we have true inwardness and subjectivity here, we have what Climacus calls a "natural form of interpersonal association"[6] (203). Inwardness pervades a social space. Only a person well free from the seductions of an indifferent, third-person objectivity could find this place so promising. He waits "womanlike" for the infinite to enter, half-appear, in "the night's semidiaphanous mist."

The night welcomes Climacus to a nocturnal tryst, to be remembered happily on the morrow, yet no such innocent tryst is offered the old man. He lives under an anxious sky, knowing he must die, that his son has just died, that his grandson must live under clouds first of his father's death and then under his grandfather's impending demise. Soon enough he must live alone, only a child. Only faith helps the old man abide the enigmas of farewell.

Evening's leave-taking of the day, and of the one who has lived that day, is a speech in a riddle. Its reminder (of danger) is like the solicitous mother's admonition to the child to be home in good time (197).

Farewells, leave-takings, are exchanged in the confidence that the sun will rise, that the world will return, that our friends will not enter the grave in the night—all this as we know that a final farewell awaits when there will be no tomorrow, when we won't awake, when the beloved will not return. Jonathan Lear remarks that a therapist must have a lively sense of death.[7] In keeping with Climacus's disquieting riddle of a mother fearfully holding yet bravely letting go in bidding her child farewell, the analyst knows that termination, and a respect for it, hangs over developing therapeutic attachments. To "hold" a child's (or analysand's) anxieties is always also to anticipate the day when the child (or analysand) will depart to live in freedom. Good mothering, good mentoring, good therapy thus embodies what Heidegger calls a being toward death, an eye on termination that colors all action and

---

[6]More accurately, proper inwardness corrects an "unnatural form of interpersonal association."

[7]Jonathan Lear, *Therapeutic Action: An Earnest Plea for Irony* (New York: Other Press, 2003) 54-57.

thought prior to it. Climacus offers the unending riddle of foreboding final farewells and irrepressible hopes of return.

Faith brings hope amidst abiding uncertainties, living through the half-innocent riddles of taking leave of the day, bidding adieu, hearing an invitation to a nocturnal tryst. A "tryst with the infinite" brings love and death in tow, a grandfather's graveside love for a grandson unfolding under the infinite night sky, a mother bidding her child to return in good time yet knowing her child will one day not return. She keeps faith through uncertainty (or doesn't).

Climacus has no particular grave to visit. Perhaps he takes himself to be somewhat dead, however, and so does have a grave close by. Can he commune with himself as one communes with the dead?

> There is always in this garden, among the visitors, a beautiful understanding that one does not come out here to see and to be seen. . . . Nor does one need company, here where all is eloquence, where the dead greet one with the brief word placed on his grave, not like a clergyman who gives sermons on that word far and wide, but as a silent man does who says no more than this yet says it with a passion as though the dead would burst open the tomb — or is it not strange to have on his grave "we shall meet again' and to remain down there? (197).

The night speaks without words, now the dead speak yet "remain down there" — and are ready to burst eloquently from the grave. The grave declares, "we shall meet again!" The dead say to the living "we shall meet again!" and the living agree. They will meet in the grave and also with the visitor standing graveside. Visitors speak with their risen dead.

Inwardness permeates our speech with he dead. Of course, inwardness is the wrong English word here, for it concerns, in this case, a manner of speaking with another, a manner of interpersonal address. As Alastair Hannay puts it,

> "Inwardness" is by no means a perfect translation of "Inderlighed". As with Hegel's Innerlichkeit, the sense is not that of inward-directedness [but of] an inner warmth, sincerity, seriousness, and

wholeheartedness in one's concern for what matters, a "heartfeltness" not applied to something but which comes from within.[8]

Letting "inwardness" replace wholeheartedness or heartfeltness
brings psychologists to picture introspection or inner direction, and
philosophers to picture Cartesian divides between private consciousness and public world (with its linguistic and conventional practices). Yet in his graveyard meditations, Climacus sidesteps all this
as he gives human ways we do and do not convey who we are to
each other, expressing ourselves interpersonally and from the heart,
and under the burden of death. Nor does he concede a Cartesian
split as he evokes worlds that intimate unutterable wonder, as in
whisper of night or serenity of dew.

Subjectivity is not cut off from the world. What might seem like
a steel wall is instead porous: Climacus is engaged in the whisper of
night breeze and the muffled tears of a neighbor. Night infiltrates
and he responds. He all but enters souls of a grandfather, a dead son,
an abandoned child — as they enter him. Emotions and passions also
refute purported barriers between inside and outside. But, what,
then can Climacus mean by "hidden inwardness"? He prizes it as a
counterweight to "outward bawling" (as he puts it). Hackneyed
hysterics cover over an absence of heartfelt suffering — wholeheartedness flowing toward others (220).

Earnestness, heartfeltness, courage, or truthfulness are passions
that reach out toward others and things. We are earnest about
something, heartfelt with regard to something. So-called "inwardness" is a passionate reciprocal mode of interpersonal relations: the
heavens offer heartfelt invitation, accepted or refused; a grandfather's grief is a concern for another, who returns a concern. Heavens
invite, an old man pleads, and Climacus responds ears open to
vocation. The world pours into him; he parcels a response that pours
into the world. Taking in and parceling out presuppose "interpersonal association."

There will be false passion and true. "Inwardness [will be]
untrue to the same degree as the outward expression . . . in words
and assurance, is there, ready to hand for instant use" (198).
Whatever is there "ready to hand" gives the mimic ample material.

---

[8]*Postscript*, Hannay note on translation, p. XXXVIII.

But to be true to grief or inwardness will be true to something beyond "outward expression." Good mimes don't express their own subjectivity but only an inherited shadow. "Ready-to-hand" expressions give only "everyday understanding of inwardness" (198).[9]

Commonplace weeping, gesticulations, and words of deep loss can be true. A recoil in disgust can be perfectly true to one's affect and circumstance. (Of course, it might be theater, or a calculated diversion.) Yet a deep grief will be more than a momentary burst of weeping or gesticulating. True grief is preserved, Climacus observes, "not as an instant's excitement, but as the eternal which has been won through death" (198). A passion like grief will veer away from excitement toward the eternal, and this veering is won insofar as one dies to a passion's outward ephemerality. In short, changeable love, changeable grief, are "less true" than their eternal counterparts. We grieve a dead child beyond immediate outbursts. Momentary passion is linked to forgetfulness; deep inwardness is linked to long memory. Some momentary outbursts are fine in their place. "[I]t is not unlovely that a woman gushes over in momentary inwardness nor is it unlovely for her soon to forget it again" (198). The sniff of sexism aside, the point is that lasting grief, eternal grief, is not an outburst from which we move on. Climacus puts it this way: "Praise be to the one living who relates as a dead man to his inwardness." The dead do not burst with public gesticulation. To all the world I might seem as if dead to my grief, never allowing it animation—but buried grief may still live.

A Stoic aim is to diminish or eradicate false emotion, an aim Climacus would endorse. He believes, against the Stoic grain, that love or grief can be true, and so, worth preserving. It's the false fuss and bother around these powerful emotions that must be monitored and erased. We might display grief for a week, or a month, or on an anniversary of a death, but the time for public displays will pass, we suppose. Then we enter a twilight zone where most is at stake. Who would want grief over the loss of a child to cease with the cessation of weeping?

---

[9]This is one of many places where we hear Heidegger, or where Heidegger lifts Kierkegaard's formulations and insights without attribution.

As a refusal, out of deep love, to erase grief for one departed, we can admire the preservation of suffering. A mother's grief extending timelessly after the death of a child might be a pain so entrenched as to have become a very mark of her identity—not to be scorned or eradicated, and not on public display. As Climacus puts it

> It has always stung my shame to witness another person's expression of feeling when he abandons himself to it as one does only in the belief that one is unobserved; for there is an inwardness of emotion which is befittingly hidden and only revealed to God.
>
> (198)

If emotion can be "befittingly hidden and only revealed to God", then reserve in expression of lasting love or grief is only to be expected. It's not treating emotion as an unwanted intruder.

Shunning public demonstration allows inwardness an expression in intimate settings: the old man weeps as he speaks alone to his grandson. He is not utterly mute for the boy and Climacus know the feelings he harbors. And otherwise hidden grief can become unhidden in revelation to God. Daily prayers or meditations can be interpersonal expressions of restful or anxious passion. The limiting case of the truth that inwardness is interpersonal is the occasion when lasting affect arises for God only, bypassing one's neighbor, priest, spouse, or friend.

What is living in Kierkegaard? With sensitive calibration, a dialectical lens gives us a lively interweave of nature and subjectivity and sociality as these are animated by vocation, anxiety, and death. A less dialectical, more lyrical Kierkegaard also sings in the text. Attention to image, setting, and scripts, in the case at hand, gives a poetic narrative of a garden's luminous dark. Midway in his monstrous book of satire and dialectical battle, Climacus sketches a garden of the dead as a lyrical-dialectical miniature of the larger effort. We have the strolling critic of Copenhagen, the false heaven of intellectualistic disputation, the true hells and redemptions of stricken fathers, and the worlds of only briefly innocent sons—the worlds of diaphanous mists and nocturnal trysts, and of the many tensed layers of the heart. Barely half-a-dozen pages, this miniature provides a vivid proof text for all that Climacus tells us elsewhere of truth and subjectivity, double reflection and indirect communication, confession of faith and its revocation, the inward recesses of the heart and their expression, the easy chatter of the classroom and the mystery of inheritance from star-crossed fathers, of farewells from anxious mothers, of receiving word from the risen dead and knowing the costs of a soul's self-betrayal. Here in the span of a hand we have the worlds of the *Postscript* engraved. Or, as in Hamlet's Mousetrap, have a play within a play to catch our conscience by surprise, and return us to the sufferings and smiles that are the wonder of life.

14

Kierkegaard and Murdoch on Knowledge of the Good

M. G. Piety

Philosophers go in and out of fashion. There are a few though, such as Plato and Kant, that remain perennially popular either because of their importance to the history of thought, or because of the captivating nature of their writing, or both. Many people are drawn to Kierkegaard because of the beauty of his prose. It isn't just Kierkegaard's writing style, however, that accounts for the fact that he is one of the few philosophers one can count on finding on the shelves of shopping-mall bookstores. His prose style may attract people to him in the first place, but it is the substance of his thought that accounts for his enduring popularity. It takes a certain sort of personality type to be captivated by Plato's divided line, or Kant's *das Ding an Sich*. We are all preoccupied, however, with the issue of how we ought to live, with what sort of life would be truly fulfilling. That is Kierkegaard's concern, finding the truth that is true for the individual as an individual, the one that will make his or her life fulfilling and whole. That's what makes him perennially popular.

One of the most important aspects of the question of how we ought to live concerns how we ought to relate to other people. This forces us to deal with the issue of what we believe are our moral duties, as well as with the epistemological issue of how much we can know both about those duties and about the people to whom they relate. Few Kierkegaard scholars venture out onto the murky waters of Kierkegaard's epistemology. Robert L. Perkins is one of those few, thus it is fitting that there should be some contribution on Kierkegaard's epistemology in this volume dedicated to Professor Perkins.

Perkins is undoubtedly correct in his claim that Kierkegaard "did not develop a thoroughgoing theory of knowledge";[1] it would be a

---

[1]See "Kierkegaard's Epistemological Preferences," *International Journal for*

mistake to conclude from this, however, that Kierkegaard did not have a thoroughgoing theory of knowledge. Perkins's preoccupation with the issue of Kierkegaard's epistemology reflects the importance of Kierkegaard's views on knowledge relative to the rest of his thought. It is precisely because he viewed knowledge in a particular way that he emphasized the primacy of faith with respect to issues of existential, or more particularly, ethical or religious significance.

Perkins is correct in his claim that Kierkegaard's "views of epistemology are in the direction of empirical realism."[2] He is also correct, however, in his claim that Kierkegaard is a "moral epistemologist."[3] My own interest has been more in Kierkegaard's views on the nature of ethical and religious knowledge than with empirical knowledge, though the latter, of course, forms the background of the former, as we will see in the pages that follow. It would not be possible to give even an outline of Kierkegaard's general theory of knowledge in an essay as brief as those in this collection.[4] What I intend to do here is to elucidate something of Kierkegaard's view of what it means to know the good by contrasting his views with those of Iris Murdoch because while in a superficial sense, the views of these two thinkers appear very similar, understood properly, they are, in fact quite different.

Scholars sympathetic to Kierkegaard tended to find much of the moral theorizing of the twentieth century either unsatisfactory or downright alienating. Many twentieth-century thinkers distinguished between facts and values in a way that meant there really was no such thing as moral knowledge. A book appeared in 1970, however, that heralded a return to what many who are sympathetic to the views of Kierkegaard, consider a more promising approach to moral philosophy. This book was Iris Murdoch's *The Sovereignty of Good*,[5] and it marked a return to a classical, or substantive, under-

---

Philosophy of Religion 4/4 (1973): 214.

[2]"Kierkegaard's Epistemological Preferences," 214.

[3]Robert L. Perkins, "Kierkegaard, A Kind of Epistemologist," *History of European Ideas* 12/1:7.

[4]For a fuller account of Kierkegaard's general theory of knowledge see M. G. Piety, *Ways of Knowing: Kierkegaard's Pluralistic Epistemology* (Waco TX: Baylor University Press, 2010).

[5]Iris Murdoch, *The Sovereignty of Good* (Boston: Routledge & Kegan Paul, 1970).

standing of the individual as a moral agent.[6] Murdoch's ground-breaking approach to moral philosophy was later taken up by thinkers such as Alasdair MacIntyre in his book *After Virtue*[7] and Charles Taylor in his book *Sources of the Self*.[8]

While it is pleasing to see the ranks of professional philosophers becoming more tolerant in terms of the diversity of positions to which they are willing to append the labels "ethics" or "moral philosophy," the Platonic and Aristotelian approaches to moral philosophy bring with them their own difficulties.[9] What I intend to do here is to contrast what one might call an epistemic approach to moral philosophy, exemplified in the works of such figures as Murdoch, MacIntyre and Taylor — using Murdoch as the paradigm example — with the fideistic approach exemplified in the works of Kierkegaard. I have chosen Murdoch's book because it represents the beginning of the trend in moral philosophy that has subsequently been taken up by MacIntyre and Taylor, as well as the beginning of contemporary virtue epistemology.[10]

It is with some reluctance that I embark upon a criticism of *The Sovereignty of Good*. I am hesitant to criticize Murdoch's work on two

---

[6]There are, of course, many diverse approaches to moral philosophy whch may be grouped under the heading "classical." It is not my purpose here to distinguish between these various approaches. What is significant for my purposes is that, with the exception of the ancient skeptics, most classical philosophy could be characterized as exhibiting what Richard Rorty describes "hylomorphic" (i.e., substantive), as opposed to procedural, view of epistemology. Richard Rorty, *Philosophy and the Mirror of Nature* (Princeton NJ: Princeton University Press, 1981) 45. Hence Murdoch's book represents a return to a classical approach to epistemology in that it involves the same substantive view of epistemology.

[7]Alasdair MacIntyre, *After Virtue* (South Bend IN: University of Notre Dame Press, 1981.

[8]Charles Taylor, *Sources of the Self* (Cambridge: Harvard University Press, 1992).

[9]Again, I do not mean to suggest that the views of Plato and Aristotle are essentially the same, but only that they are both substantive.

[10]The historical starting point for contemporary virtue epistemology is generally considered to be Ernst Sosa's paper "The Raft and the Pyramid: Coherence versus Foundations in the Theory of Knowledge," *Midwest Studies in Philosophy* 5:3-25 (repr. in Ernst Sosa, *Knowledge in Perspective* [Cambridge UK: Cambridge University Press, 1991]). Sosa's article is, of course, more explicitly epistemological than is Murdoch's book. Later work in virtue epistemology, such as that of Linda Zagzebski and Robert Roberts and W. Jay Wood, is inconceivable, however, without the precedent of Murdoch's book.

counts. The first is out of a respect for the virtuosity of style it exhibits (emerging as it did in the arid unaesthetic desert of the previous seventy years of moral philosophy, it seemed almost like a miniature oasis). The second is out of a desire to see the type of philosophy associated with the analytic tradition and exemplified in the works of Hampshire, Hare and Ayer, Murdoch's opponents in the book, if not definitively refuted, then at least soundly thrashed.

Many of us who are interested in Kierkegaard's work are similarly dissatisfied with the approach to moral theorizing taken by the analytic tradition. Thus more than a few are sympathetic to the project of Murdoch's book, or, more particularly, to virtue epistemology as it is exemplified in the trend Murdoch started. There is, however, something about virtue epistemology, at least in the form presented in Murdoch's book, that Murdoch herself has failed to notice, something that Kierkegaard, all those years earlier, saw and without which virtue epistemology is ultimately incoherent. Before I attempt to criticize Murdoch's position, however, we must look at the position in some detail.

I

Murdoch's thesis, much like that of G. E. Moore, is that goodness is a "real constituent of the world" (p. 3). Thus she argues that "[v]irtue is *au fond* the same in the artist as in the good man in that it is a selfless attention to nature" (p. 41). From this she goes on to argue that our task as moral agents is to direct our gaze *outward* toward reality — therein to perceive the moral ideal — and not inward, in the hope of finding that ideal within ourselves. Murdoch contends that we can attain *knowledge* of the good, or of that single action that is morally, or ethically, demanded of us, through careful attention to the reality that is before us.

If this conception of "moral seeing," as Murdoch refers to it (p. 35), seems at first unproblematic, we must turn our attention to the following example she uses to illustrate this principle.

> M [a mother] feels hostility to her daughter-in-law. . . . D. M finds D . . . unpolished and lacking in dignity and refinement. D is inclined to be pert and familiar, insufficiently ceremonious, brusque, sometimes positively rude, always tiresomely juvenile. M

does not like D's accent or the way D dresses. M feels that her son
has married beneath him (p. 17).

Murdoch goes on to say, however, that

> M of the example is an intelligent and well-intentioned person,
> capable of self-criticism, capable of giving careful and just *attention*
> to an object that confronts her. M tells herself: "I am old-fashioned
> and conventional. I may be prejudiced and narrow-minded. I may
> be snobbish. I am certainly jealous. Let me look again" (p. 17).

Murdoch contends that M changes her judgment of D as a result
of *renewed attention* to D's behavior or character. Murdoch explains
that when M "looks again," D is discovered to be "not vulgar, but
refreshingly simple, not undignified, but spontaneous, not noisy, but
gay, not tiresomely juvenile, but delightfully youthful, and so on"
(pp. 17-18). But D's behavior, Murdoch contends, has not altered in
any way; it is only M's judgment of that behavior that has altered.

Again, Murdoch contends that goodness is a real constituent of
the world, and that if we are truly or selflessly attentive to the
world — after the fashion of an artist — we will see it. It is as the result
of such attention that, Murdoch argues, M comes to see that D is not
really vulgar or undignified, and so forth. In order to determine if
this is a plausible explanation of what has brought about the change
in M's vision of D, however, we must reexamine the situation as
Murdoch has presented it.

II

We know that initially M believes or, as Murdoch expresses it, sees
D to be "silly and vulgar" (p. 17). Murdoch explains, however, that
M

> is an intelligent and well-intentioned person, capable of self-
> criticism . . . M tells herself: "*I* am old-fashioned and conventional.
> *I* may be prejudiced and narrow-minded. *I* may be snobbish. *I* am
> certainly jealous. Let me look again" (p. 17; emphasis added).

It is clear here that M's moral vision — to stick to Murdoch's
metaphor — has become more acute as the result of her having
focused not upon D or upon the world, in a manner analogous to
that of an artist focusing upon nature, but as a result of her having

directed her gaze inward and having focused upon herself. It would seem, on Murdoch's own account, that our situation as moral "viewers" is precisely disanalogous to the situation of the artist whose engagement with nature is not mediated by the ongoing activity of self-criticism in which we as moral agents or viewers must engage.

Murdoch contends that we can have knowledge of the good, or of how virtue is manifest in the world; and this, she argues, is the result of a "refined and honest perception of what is really the case, a patient and just discernment and exploration of what confronts one" (p. 38). Murdoch's contention is that in order to see the good in the world we must not only be attentive to it in the normal sense of "attentive," but we must endeavor to view the world through the patient eye of Love.

This position certainly has a familiar ring to those of us who are acquainted with what John Elrod has identified as "Kierkegaard's Second Authorship."[11] There is a significant difference, however, between the positions of Murdoch and Kierkegaard. Murdoch contends that we can have knowledge concerning what is really the case, morally, about the world, or more particularly about other people. But it is not clear, on Murdoch's account, how loving attention can result in the perception of what is really the case about the world, rather than simply in an impression of what ideally ought to be the case. Ideally, D's actual character would doubtless correspond to M's second, and more favorable assessment. But Murdoch is not contending that proper attention to the world will reveal that, in fact, everything in the world is good; she is contending rather that if we are properly attentive to the world, we will discern where, in the world, the good is.

Murdoch argues that we can attain knowledge of D's true character if we are properly attentive to D or to her behavior. The question is: How does loving attention serve to deliver up such knowledge? It would seem that M's desire to see D "justly and lovingly" (p. 23) might in fact result in clouding her vision as to D's

---

[11]John Elrod, *Kierkegaard and Christendom* (Princeton NJ: Princeton University Press, 1981).

real character. It is possible, after all, that D really is brusque, rude, and tiresomely juvenile.

Murdoch contends that loving attention results in knowledge of how the good is manifest in the world. It would seem, however, that what has been revealed through M's loving attention is essentially something about M — that is, that she is loving — rather than something about D. M is no closer to knowing something about D's true character, or about the world, as a result of the transformation in the nature of her attention. If she is any closer to knowing anything, it is about herself rather than about the world.

III

I mentioned above that there was something about the sovereignty of good that Kierkegaard had noticed, but that Murdoch had missed. The question is not whether the good is in fact sovereign, but how we are to make sense of this idea. What Murdoch fails to do is to properly distinguish the objects of knowledge from those of belief. It is only through belief, according to Kierkegaard, that good becomes manifest in the world.

Let us ask ourselves, returning to Murdoch's example, what it is in fact that M can be said to know about D. That is, what is there about D that is absolutely indisputable? There is one set of data concerning D that has remained constant throughout both M's original and her revised assessment of the significance of D's actions and that is the actions themselves. D's behavior has not altered in any way. It is only M's judgment of the significance of that behavior that has altered.

Knowledge, asserts Kierkegaard, is "infinitely detached." It places everything in the "infinite indifference [of] equilibrium" (WL 231).[12] What M knows about D is her behavior. She does not attain

---

[12]Kierkegaard's claim that knowledge places everything into an equilibrium of contrasting possibilities makes his position look strikingly like that of the ancient skeptics. The skeptics maintained that whenever one attempted to determine the objective truth of a particular situation (e.g., when one attempted to determine from one's subjective impression of warmth whether it was in fact actually or objectively warm) careful application of the skeptical modes or tropes would reveal that the truth claims of one's subjective impressions are always equally balanced by conflicting impressions on the part of other subjects, or by the simple formal

knowledge of D's character, however, through observing this behavior. She makes judgments in regard to D's character and thus forms beliefs concerning that character, but these beliefs do not constitute knowledge. What M knows about D's behavior might just as well lead her to a negative judgment — as indeed it did initially — as to a positive judgment.

If we cannot attain knowledge of the moral character of others, we are nonetheless inclined to believe that we make judgments concerning people's character on the basis of what we know about them — that is, on the basis of our observation of their actions. This is, however, precisely the view Kierkegaard wants to refute. Is it not true, he argues

> that the one person never completely understands the other? But if he does not understand him completely, then of course it is always possible that the most indisputable thing [that is, what is known about the individual] could still have a completely different explanation that would, note well, be the true explanation. (WL 229)

Knowledge, argues Kierkegaard, "places everything [in the category of] possibility" (WL 230).[13] That is, on the basis of the knowl

---

possibility of such conflict. See Sextus Empiricus, *Outlines of Pyrrhonism*, vol. 1, Loeb Classical Library (Cambridge MA: Harvard University Press, 1933) 21-107. That is, when attempting, e.g., to determine whether it is actually or objectively warm, what one can be said to know is (1) that one has a subjective impression of warmth and (2) that such impressions vary from subject to subject. Thus knowledge leads to an equilibrium of possibilities or what the skeptics called *isostheneia*.

The skeptical arguments are, of course, considerably more sophisticated, and the application of them more complicated, than I have suggested here. This sketch of the skeptical position should be sufficient, however, to show the similarity between the views of the skeptics and those of Kierkegaard. It is interesting to note that Richard Popkin, in his essay "Kierkegaard and Skepticism" (in *Kierkegaard: A Collection of Critical Essays*, ed. Josiah Thompson [New York: Anchor Books, 1972] 342-72) fails to cite *Works of Love* among Kierkegaard's books that exhibit a "powerful and devastating skepticism" (364). This omission is interesting because it is in *Works of Love* that Kierkegaard's skepticism, or more particularly his indebtedness to ancient skepticism, is most clearly exhibited. It would seem Popkin fell prey to the unfortunate and all-too-pervasive tendency to ignore the philosophical significance of Kierkegaard's religious works.

[13]The Hong's first translation of *Works of Love* (New York: Harper Perrenial, 1964) included the material in brackets even though it is not actually in Kierkegaard's original text. This bit of license is, I believe, entirely justified in terms of

edge M has of D's behavior, it is possible to make either a favorable or an unfavorable assessment of D's character. Kierkegaard contends that

> [o]nly half-experienced and very confused people think of judging another person on the basis of knowledge. This is due to their not even knowing what knowledge is, to their never having taken the time and effort to develop the infinite, equal sense for possibilities or with the infinite art of equivocation to grasp the possibilities and bring them into equilibrium or to ponder them in transparency.
> (WL 231)

According to Kierkegaard, we can never determine the truth-values of statements about the moral character of other people, or about the ethical significance of their actions. That's why, as Perkins explains, "Kierkegaard's focus is not upon the objective truth value, but the subjective truth relation."[14] We have beliefs about the moral character of others. We do not have knowledge of their moral character. The moral character of others is not even properly an object of knowledge, according to Kierkegaard. Murdoch's problem would appear to be that she has failed to understand this. That is, it would appear she has confused what is properly an object of belief, or of faith — that is, a person's moral character, as against what are simply his uninterpreted actions — with an object of knowledge.

IV

But if M cannot be said to have attained any knowledge of D's character, what is it that results from her revised judgment concerning the significance of D's behavior? Kierkegaard explains that

> [a]s far as judging another person is concerned, knowledge at best leads to the equilibrium of the opposite possibilities — thereupon the difference becomes apparent in what is now decided. . . . [That is, i]n the very same minute when you judge another person or criticize another person you judge yourself, because when all is said and done, to judge someone else is to judge oneself or to be disclosed yourself.   (WL 233)

---

making the English translation more idiomatic. See M. G. Piety, "Translating Kierkegaard," *Per Contra* (Fall 2007): <http://www.percontra.net/8piety.htm>.
    [14]Perkins, "Kierkegaard, A Kind of Epistemologist," 13.

Thus it becomes clear why it seemed to us earlier that what had been revealed to M, through her loving attention to D was, in fact, essentially something about herself—that is, that she was loving—rather than something about D or about the world. It is here that Kierkegaard possesses a crucial insight into the sphere of the sovereignty of good that Murdoch lacks and it is this lack that makes virtue epistemology—at least in the form articulated by Murdoch—ultimately incoherent and thus entenable.

V

Kierkegaard argues that to the extent knowledge places everything in the category of possibility "it is outside of the actuality of existence" (WL 230). It is for this reason that Kierkegaard considers it is only through belief, or faith, and not through knowledge, that the good comes into existence in the world.

The difficulty with Murdoch's position is clear. If good is merely a constituent of the world and not constitutive of it, then it is unclear how loving attention to the world could result in knowledge of the good. There are two difficulties with such a position. The first difficulty is that of determining when our attention is, in fact, sufficiently loving; and the second difficulty is that of determining that our vision is not excessively loving. That is, M may make an unfavorable assessment of D's character as a result of the fact that her vision is not informed with a sufficient degree of love. But, on the other hand, she may deceive herself into thinking well of D as a result of the fact that her attention is so loving she is unwilling to interpret D's behavior in a manner that is in any respect unfavorable to the girl.

Kierkegaard argues that "Love Believes All Things—and Yet Is Never Deceived" (WL 225-45). What, one may ask, can he possibly mean by this? Let's go back to Kierkegaard's position on the nature of the objects of knowledge. Kierkegaard contends that what we know about a person presents us with two possibilities for interpreting that person's behavior. M is asked to judge D's behavior. She may judge it either favorably or unfavorably. The decision is hers. This decision, Kierkegaard argues, does not essentially reveal anything about D; rather it reveals whether there is love or mistrust in M. D's true character, according to Kierkegaard, is epistemologically inaccessible to M. What is accessible to M, however, is her own character. For M to judge D's actions unfavorably is, according to Kierkegaard, for M to deceive herself in a very significant sense. Kierkegaard contends that

> *in the infinite conception of love . . . to be deceived simply and solely means to refrain from loving, to let oneself be so carried away as to give up love in itself to lose its intrinsic blessedness in that way.* In the infinite sense, only one deception is possible — self-deception.

> (WL 236)

Thus Kierkegaard argues, one "defends himself against illusion precisely by believing all things . . . in . . . love" (WL 236-37).

If our situation as moral viewers is analogous to that of an artist, as Murdoch asserts, then what is presented to our moral view is ourselves. Certainly we can be said to have knowledge of the actions of others, as M has knowledge of D's actions. According to Kierkegaard, however, such knowledge is neither the foundation, nor the culmination of the activity of our moral seeing. We do not judge people, he argues, on the basis of what we know about them. We judge them rather on the basis of how much love or mistrust there is in ourselves. We decide to judge or to interpret another person favorably or unfavorably, and with this decision, Kierkegaard contends, we judge ourselves. We do not have knowledge of how goodness is manifest in the world. When we see good in the world, we see it there because there is good, or love, in ourselves.

What we have in terms of knowledge — for example, the knowledge M has of D's actions — is the possibility of good. That is, our knowledge of a person's actions provides for us the possibility of a decision on our part to bring good into the world, or to make it actual, through a loving interpretation of those actions.

Thus what Kierkegaard has seen and what Murdoch and other virtue epistemologists have missed is that it is not through knowledge, but only through such a decision, and the belief that is consequent upon it, that the good becomes sovereign in the world.

An understanding of this is as important to us now as it was to Kierkegaard's contemporaries. It is perennially important. So, therefore, is Kierkegaard.

15

Kierkegaard's Virtue Epistemology
A Modest Initiative

Robert C. Roberts

Introduction

This paper is about Søren Kierkegaard's treatment of some knowledge concepts. It is a tribute to Bob Perkins, who has done more than anyone else of his generation to promote scholarly and philosophical engagement with the writings of Kierkegaard, and who himself has contributed to the study of Kierkegaard's epistemology.

Kierkegaard matters to many of us because of the unique way in which he combines personal and intellectual quests. It is hard to read Kierkegaard for long without being "built up" both ethicospiritually and intellectually (either that, or offended). Of the many possible angles from which Kierkegaard's writings may be approached, I have found it especially fruitful to follow up this dual import by reading them for what they say about the formation (in both a structural and a developmental sense) of human character—in a word, for what they say about the virtues and vices.[1] But heretofore

---

[1] I have discussed this dimension of Kierkegaard's thought in "Kierkegaard, Wittgenstein, and a Method of 'Virtue Ethics'" in Merold Westphal and Martin Matustik, eds., *Kierkegaard in Post/Modernity* (Bloomington: Indiana University Press, 1995) 142-66; "Existence, Emotion and Character: Classical Themes in Kierkegaard" in Alastair Hannay and Gordon Marino, eds., *Cambridge Companion to Kierkegaard* (Cambridge UK: Cambridge University Press, 1997) 177-206; "Dialectical Emotions and the Virtue of Faith" in Robert L. Perkins, ed., *International Kierkegaard Commentary: Concluding Unscientific Postscript* (Macon GA: Mercer University Press, 1997) 73-93; "The Virtue of Hope in *Eighteen Upbuilding Discourses*" in Robert L. Perkins, ed., *International Kierkegaard Commentary: Eighteen Upbuilding Discourses* (Macon GA: Mercer University Press, 2003) 181-203; "Kierkegaard" in Paul Copan and Chad Meister, eds., *The Routledge Companion to Philosophy of Religion* (Oxford UK: Routledge, 2007) 160-69; and "Kierkegaard and Ethical Theory" in Edward Mooney, ed., *Ethics, Love, and Faith in Kierkegaard: A Philosophical Engagement*

I have not explored the import of the virtues specifically for their *intellectual* fruits, and that is what I propose to make a start on here.

Throughout Kierkegaard's authorship we find remarks that bear on the nature and value of knowledge. These do not amount to what epistemologists in the early twenty-first century would recognize as an epistemology. They are nothing like a definition of knowledge in the manner of recent analytic epistemology, or a theory of epistemic justification. But they do display a characteristic way of thinking about and using knowledge concepts that ties them closely to Kierkegaard's central concerns about the task of becoming a full-fledged human being. Teasing out some of these concepts may help us better understand both Kierkegaard and the knowledge concepts.

My discussion will center on knowledge, know (*Viden, vide*); understand (*forstaa, fatte*); testimony (*Vidnesbyrd*); explanation, explain (*Forklaring, forklare*), and conviction, convince (*Forvisning, forvisse*). As with other concepts in Kierkegaard's thought, these bear heavily on, and are shaped by, his concern for personal development, for character, for the "existence" of the individual—for "strengthening in the inner being [man[2]]," to use the title from the early discourse on which I will concentrate here.[3] Focusing as my paper does on just one small part of Kierkegaard's vast and complicated authorship, it is a modest initiative that I hope will be followed

---

(Bloomington: Indiana University Press, 2008) 72-92. See also David Gouwens, *Kierkegaard as Religious Thinker* (Cambridge UK: Cambridge University Press, 1996) esp. chaps. 3 and 4; John Davenport, "Towards an Existential Virtue Ethics: Kierkegaard and MacIntyre" in John Davenport and Anthony Rudd, editors, *Kierkegaard after MacIntyre* (Peru IL: Open Court, 2001) 265-323; Norman Lillegaard, "Thinking with Kierkegaard and MacIntyre about the Aesthetic, Virtue, and Narrative" in ibid., 211-32; and Anthony Rudd, "Kierkegaard on Patience and Being a Self: The Virtues of a Being in Time," *Journal of Religious Ethics* 36 (2008): 491-509.

[2]The Danish for 'man' here is *Menneske*, which is an almost perfect translation of the Greek νθρωπος of Ephesians 3:16. The Hongs translate *Menneske* as 'being,' which is *not* a very good translation of either *Menneske* or νθρωπος. So I have reverted to the RSV's generic 'man' on the supposition that my readers know enough English not to take this translation as expressing sexism.

[3]"Strengthening in the Inner Being" in *Eighteen Upbuilding Discourses* (EUD), ed. and trans. Howard V. Hong and Edna H. Hong (Princeton NJ: Princeton University Press, 1990) 79-101. Hereafter page numbers of this discourse are in parentheses in the text.

by more comprehensive and ambitious research into Kierkegaard's epistemology.

Greek, Danish, and English all distinguish lexically between understanding and knowledge, but in all three languages knowledge and understanding are strongly associated with one another. They presuppose one another. In the recent renewed interest in understanding, some contemporary epistemologists have tried to keep knowledge and understanding quite separate, even exclusive of one another;[4] I have resisted this tendency, in conformity with ancient Greek thought.[5] Whereas knowledge is a special way of possessing information (typically by believing it, with some kind of warrant or justification, or by some kind of direct contact with it—knowledge by acquaintance), understanding is an appreciation of connections among things, such as to enable its possessor to give explanations, to continue series, to put things together or take them apart, to "see" or "hear" patterns and relevancies and meanings. But it would be very unusual, to say the least, to understand something without having any information at all about it; and even the simplest information could not be possessed by a person who had no understanding of it. Thus if I understand the role of the piston in an internal-combustion engine, I need at least to know what a piston looks like; and I can't very well know *this is a piston* without at least a minimal grasp of the relations between its compression surface and its sliding surface. If my "knowledge" of pistons amounts to nothing more than the ability to say "piston" upon being presented with a piston (as contrasted with saying "spark plug" when presented with a spark plug)—say, in the manner of a parrot or an eighteen-month-old baby—then I don't think we would say that I know what a piston is; I don't understand enough to have knowledge. But even

---

[4]They say such things as that all knowledge is propositional while all understanding is nonpropositional; you can know something without knowing that you know it, but you can't understand something without understanding that you understand it; you can understand *p* without knowing *p*, and you can know *p* without understanding *p*. For discussion, see Robert C. Roberts and W. Jay Wood, *Intellectual Virtues: An Essay in Regulative Epistemology* (Oxford UK: Clarendon Press, 2007) 42-50, 55-57.

[5]See Julius Moravscik, "Understanding and Knowledge in Plato's Philosophy," *Neue Hefte für Philosophie* 15/16 (1979): 53-69.

if we could conceive some cases of understanding without knowledge or knowledge without understanding, it would remain indisputable that these powers are intimately entangled in the vast majority of cases.

Explanations engender and manifest understanding, and thus knowledge, by connecting one proposition (the *explanandum* or explained proposition) with the explanation (the *explanans* or explaining proposition) in such a way that the *explanandum* makes more sense than it would without the explanation. The increase in making sense is an increase in understanding on the part of the person who now sees or grasps the connection between the two propositions. The person who offers the explanation *as an explanation* of the *explanandum* manifests understanding thereby, expressing that he "sees" the connection. If I want to understand why *the temperature in the university swimming pool is 65° F*, and I find out that *the heater is broken*, and connect the two propositions in such a way that the second makes sense of the first, then I have an explanation of the first proposition and the explanation has increased my understanding of it. Of course, such an explanation is shorthand; the "full" explanation is much more elaborate and probably never elaborated. Background suppositions of this explanation are that the water temperature, if correct, depends on a heater; and that there is a heater that can function well or not; and that if the heater were working it would be set at a higher temperature than 65°F. Also, there would have to be propositions about what makes temperature higher than 65°F "correct," as well as ones about molecular motion of the water and the working of the heater, and so forthj.

Testimony is a special kind of information, namely, information actively given by a person (a witness). In Danish a witness is a *Vidnes*, and testimony is a *Vidnesbyrd*.[6] *Byrd* is related to the English "burden," thus testimony is a witness's "payload" so to speak, what the witness supplies or delivers. Thus if I get the information that the pool's heater is broken by way of the maintenance man's telling me

---

[6]In English the noun "witness" can denote either the testimony that a witness gives or the giver of the testimony. The word that Kierkegaard uses 37 times in this discourse is *Vidnesbyrd*. The Hongs translate it 'witness.' The ambiguity of "witness" seems to me to make an already difficult text less clear, so I have substituted 'testimony' wherever Kierkegaard has *Vidnesbyrd*.

so, it is a case of testimony, but if I get it by going into the furnace room and ascertaining for myself that the heater is broken, it is not testimony. Testimony need not be voluntary in the fullest sense; for example, if I get the information by torturing the maintenance man until he tells me, it is still testimony. It may be testimony even if I get it by listening to the maintenance man talk in his sleep, or if he divulges the information by saying something from which I infer that the heater is broken.

As my example suggests, a typical role for a testimony, vis à vis the other four epistemic items, is that it supplies *information* that functions as an *explanation* that makes something *understandable* to someone and thus increases his *knowledge*. So a testimony can be a key to understanding something, and thus to knowledge — not just knowledge of the content of the testimony, but also of the explanation the testimony makes possible. This is the role of the *Vidnesbyrd* to which Kierkegaard refers in "Strengthening in the Inner Man."

Note that the role of testimony that Kierkegaard's discourse makes central differs from the role stressed by Reformed epistemologists like Alvin Plantinga, following Thomas Reid. Plantinga writes of a fourteen-year-old theist who believes God exists because his elders tell him so. Plantinga makes the Reidian point that this child's belief can itself be knowledge, because it is "properly basic"; he needs no further support, in the form of evidence, to turn this belief into knowledge, because he has formed it in an epistemically legitimate way, namely, as a result of being told the truth by reliable witnesses.[7] The reliable testimony of his elders is not *evidence* from which the child *infers*, more or less shakily, that God exists; no, the testimony is itself a basic source of knowledge, more or less on a par with opening one's well-functioning eyes in good lighting and so coming to believe that one is standing in front of a house.

Nothing Kierkegaard says requires that all testimony function as evidence for what the testimony claims (as perhaps it typically does in testimony that is given in court). But the knowledge that interests him in "Strengthening in the Inner Man" is not just bare propositional knowledge of the content of the testimony (say, the testimony

---

[7]*Faith and Rationality: Reason and Belief in God*, ed. Alvin Plantinga and Nicholas Wolterstorff (South Bend IN: University of Notre Dame Press, 1983) 16-93; see 33.

that human beings' place in creation is that of stewards). I do think he supposes that most Christians will just believe such testimonies of scripture as properly basic sources of propositional knowledge. Instead, the discourse focuses on the individual's *understanding* such things as adversity and prosperity, and in this regard testimony functions as a key to reflective success. Here the knowledge that comes from testimony is not the content of the testimony, but something beyond the testimony, that the testimony clarifies. I here propose the hypothesis that this discourse is fairly typical of Kierkegaard's epistemological concerns. In general, he is more interested in understanding than in simple propositional knowledge.

Conviction is the confidence with which one holds a belief. One can believe a proposition with varying degrees of conviction, but if that degree is below a certain threshold, then one does not believe that proposition; and if knowledge requires belief, then one doesn't know it, either. Explanation, by engendering understanding, tends to increase conviction and can raise one's confidence in a proposition above the threshold required for knowledge. Where testimony makes an explanation possible, it can be the source of conviction. The idea basic to virtue epistemology is that some excellent traits (virtues) of a knowing agent may constitute an important part of the explanation of that agent's possession of knowledge and related epistemic goods (understanding, justification, conviction, wisdom, perception). Persons who lack the relevant virtues can be expected to fall short in the possession of such epistemic goods. Some virtue epistemologists think of the virtues as excellences of faculties, such as vision, hearing, rational intuition, and syllogistic competence,[8] while others think of them as excellences of the whole person, such as humility, love, autonomy, and courage — traits which, while they depend on the functioning of the faculties, are not specifically excellences *of* faculties.[9] The virtue epistemology found in Kierkegaard's writings is decidedly of the second kind. Some virtue epistemologists make it a necessary condition of all knowledge

---

[8]See Ernest Sosa, *A Virtue Epistemology: Apt Belief and Reflective Knowledge* (Oxford UK: Clarendon Press, 2007).

[9]See Linda Zagzebski, *Virtues of the Mind* (Cambridge UK: Cambridge University Press, 1996).

whatsoever that the agent's virtue play a role in his acquisition of it,[10] but it is not part of the notion of a virtue epistemology *as such* that virtue *always* plays a role in the acquisition of *all* knowledge, and no such thesis is to be found in, or implied by, Kierkegaard's comments about virtues and knowledge.

Kierkegaard's biblical text

Like most of the *Eighteen Upbuilding Discourses*, "Strengthening in the Inner Man" expounds a biblical text—in this case, Ephesians 3:13-21.[11] In the text, as in the discourse, knowledge concepts are prominent. In verses 14-19 Paul prays that God will strengthen the readers

> through his Spirit in the inner man, and that Christ may dwell in your hearts by faith; that you, being rooted and grounded in love, may have power to comprehend [καταλαβέσθαι] with all the saints what is the breadth and length and height and depth, and to know [γν να] the love of Christ which surpasses knowledge [γνώσεως], that you may be filled with all the fullness of God.
> (Eph. 3:16b-19 RSV)[12]

The object of knowledge here is the extent of the glory, the riches, the greatness, the excellence, the splendor, the magnificence, of God's beneficence to the world in Jesus Christ. It is a "value" (to use a woefully tepid philosophical word) so surpassingly excellent that it cannot be fully grasped, yet it must be known, in at least a partial appreciation, if the readers are to be strengthened by God's Spirit in the inner man.

Paul's is a virtue epistemology[13] because according to him the understanding of the breadth, length, height, and depth of the riches

---

[10]See Sosa, *A Virtue Epistemology*, and John Greco, "Knowledge as Credit for True Belief" in Michael DePaul and Linda Zagzebski, eds., *Intellectual Virtues: Perspectives from Ethics and Epistemology* (Oxford UK: Clarendon Press, 2003) 111-34.

[11]And, like all the discourses, it is saturated with biblical quotations, paraphrases, and allusions—even more than are apparent to a perusal of the many indicated by the endnotes to the Hong translation.

[12]Compare Ephesians 1:18-19.

[13]See my "Emotions in the Epistemology of Paul the Apostle" in I. U. Dalferth, ed., *Claremont Studies in the Philosophy of Religion* (Palgrave Macmillan, forthcoming).

of God's blessing, and the knowledge of Christ's love (which nevertheless surpasses our capacity to appreciate it fully), depend on the faith and love of the knowers. Without the virtues of faith and love, this knowledge is not possible, just as faith and love are not possible without (some beginning of) knowledge. The faith by which Christ dwells in the Ephesians' hearts and the love (presumably for both God and neighbor) in which they are rooted and grounded are causal conditions of the readers' comprehension and knowledge.

The strengthening [κραταιωθ ναι] that Paul prays for is a strengthening of conviction and understanding such that these amount to knowledge. It is, at the same time and by the same token, a strengthening of character. Both conviction and understanding are subject to gradation; one can have more or less conviction, and more or less (profound and extensive) understanding regarding something—in this case, the breadth and length and height and depth of the love of Christ. But to know *this* is to be "filled with the fullness of God," with all the implications such knowledge has for formation of the person. Obviously, such character-integrated knowledge is not mere "justified true belief," but a degree of conviction, integrated with a profundity of understanding, such as to place the knower in intimate contact with the object known.

Kierkegaard's discourse "Strengthening in the Inner Man" begins (80-81) with reflections on the irony of Paul's imprisonment in Rome, the contrast between his triumphal spirit, purpose, and confidence in his message and his utter insignificance from Rome's point of view. It turns then (81-84) to Paul's state of mind in response to his adversity, and in particular to the fact that outwardly his testimony seems to be coming to nothing. What for others might occasion discouragement he turns into an occasion for his strengthening in the inner man. The only complete section break bears the heading "Strengthening in the Inner Man" (84).

On p. 84 to the top of 86 Kierkegaard expounds three deviations from proper human nature as a rational creature in relation to the rational accessibility of the nonhuman creation. Kierkegaard's discussion trades on the biblical testimony that the human being is a steward of God's creation, "the ruler of creation" (84), "God's coworker" (86). We could call these deviations Drifting Thoughtlessness, Rapacious Acquisitiveness, and Craven Irresponsibility. Each of these vices undermines the capacity for knowledge.

Drifting Thoughtlessness is the "unworthy and nauseating" failure to recognize the correspondence between human rationality and the "order in the world" (84). It is a kind of lackadaisical undiscipline in one's intellectual and moral approach to oneself and the world. By contrast, as soon as a person collects himself in a more understanding (*forstandigere*) consideration of life, he seeks to assure himself (*forvisse sig*) of a coherence (*Sammenhaeng*) in everything, and as the ruler of creation he approaches it, as it were, with a question, extorts an explanation (*Forklaring*) from it, demands a testimony (*Vidnesbyrd*) (84). That is, he expresses his natural powers of understanding the world by becoming an active inquirer about it. When he faces a puzzle regarding it, he looks for the clues (*Vidnesbyrdene*) to its coherence that are embedded in it. The clues are testimonies on the assumption that God "offers" them to human beings for their understanding and knowledge.

The exemplar of Rapacious Acquisitiveness has, through discipline, figured out some order in the world and exploits it in service to his "worldly appetites." He "has chosen the glittering bondage of pleasure . . . [and] is satisfied to let the creation bear its testimony (*Vidnesbyrd*) so that he can shrewdly and prudently use it in the service of the moment" (84).

Other words that the context suggests are "clue" and "evidence." We are talking here about clues to the order in nature, clues to how to make crops grow better, evidence that this kind of plough is superior to that, and so forth. This is the clever person who uses his understanding of how the world works to accumulate wealth, comfort, and the wherewithal of pleasure. But despite the "intelligence" (*Forstand*, 85) with which he exploits nature, he is so "thoughtless" (*tankeløs*) about *its relation to himself* that when, his barns filled with the fruits of his cleverness, God comes to him and says "This night I require your soul of you," he doesn't quite "understand" (*forstaae*, 85) what God is about to take from him.

But the person who reflects (*betragter*) on life with any earnestness at all readily perceives that he is not the lord in such a way that he is not also a servant, that it is not his superior intelligence alone that distinguishes man from the animals" (85), but also his awareness of his finitude and mortality and his need for God. The person who uses his knowledge (understanding) of the order in nature merely to dominate it has culpably and self-destructively failed to take his inquiries far enough.

Craven Irresponsibility is a vice that leads to "perpetual deliberations that take [the person] nowhere but only serve as a dissipation in which his soul, his capacity for comprehending (*fatte*) and willing (*ville*), vanishes like mist and is extinguished like a flame" (85). This deficit of understanding is due to his pusillanimous pride, his cowardice and lack of humility. He

> cravenly runs away from every more profound explanation, . . . does not have the courage to assume the responsibility of the master by submitting to the obligation of a servant, . . . does not have the humility to be willing to obey in order to learn how to rule and at all times [to be] willing to rule only insofar as he himself obeys.   (85)

Which explanation, and what needs explaining? A little later in the discourse, we find that what needs "explaining" is prosperity and adversity, and what is puzzling about them is where they come from and why they come as they do. If we are to *understand* (our) prosperity and adversity, we need an *explanation* of them. They do not seem to be reliably correlated with hard work, moral uprightness, high birth, intelligence, and so forth — all the explanations that naturally occur to people. (Each of these phenomena, instantiated, could be considered a putative *Vidnesbyrd*, an evidence, clue, or testimony on which a potential explanation of somebody's prosperity or adversity could be based.) All such explanations, and their correlative understandings, break down. But we are also, as Kierkegaard explained earlier, seekers of coherence. We find absurdity intellectually unsatisfying, at least if we are virtuous people. (If we suffer from Drifting Thoughtlessness, Rapacious Acquisitiveness, or Craven Irresponsibility, we may not notice this about ourselves.)

The correct explanation, the one that leads to real understanding and potentially yields an intellectually and morally satisfactory life, is that we are God's stewards, that we owe obedience to him, that our highest good is a right and loving and obedient relation with him (rather than what unthinking people regard as prosperity; nor is adversity an unambiguously bad thing, for someone who loves God).

Next follow about two pages (86-88) that discuss, in rather general terms, the relation between knowledge of the world and the existence of the inner man. The thesis seems to be this: if it is true that for any important knowledge of the world whatsoever it is necessary to have a *Vidnesbyrd* (evidence) which supplies the wherewithal of an explanation, this will be true also for any knowledge in which the knower grasps the significance of the world for his own personal existence. The different kind of *Vidnesbyrd* that is needed for this kind of knowledge cannot be acquired without a concern for oneself as an eternal creature. This *Vidnesbyrd* is the testimony of the Holy Spirit, which is something both intimate in the consciousness of the subject and a word of revelation that comes from outside the subject. (The evidence that Kierkegaard cites in this regard is biblical: that God assigned man the role and identity of steward over creation, Genesis 1:26-30.)

In this concern, the inner man announces himself and craves an explanation (*Forklaring*), a testimony (*Vidnesbyrd*) that explains the meaning of everything for him and his own meaning by explaining him in the God who holds everything together in his eternal wisdom and who assigned man to be lord of creation by his becoming God's servant and explained himself to him by making him his coworker, and through every explanation that he gives a person, he strengthens and confirms (*bestyrker*) him in the inner man (87).

This knowledge, which is consequent on a person's understanding himself in the light of God's explanations, is accessible only to the person who is *concerned* in the proper way. Paul's words for this concern are 'faith' and 'love,' but for Kierkegaard the concern may also be one that precedes faith and love.

The difference between "mere knowledge (*blot Viden*) about the world and about [a person's] knowledge of himself as a part of it" and "another kind of knowledge, a knowledge that does not remain as knowledge for a single moment but is transformed into an action the moment it is possessed" (86) is not that one requires concern and the other does not. Kierkegaard speaks of a person's "effort to assure himself of the relation of his knowledge to the object [of knowledge]," which is just the effort to assure himself that he has *knowledge*, and behind the effort is plausibly a concern — the concern to know — for one reason or another, or simply for the sake of knowing. Both kinds of knowledge are motivated by some concern; if there is such a thing as completely 'disinterested' knowledge, it is not the kind that people *seek*. The difference lies in the *kind* of concern. The kind of knowledge that chiefly interests Kierkegaard is a kind that people seek because they want to be a coherent person, because they want to be somebody in particular, because they want to have a self that satisfies and passes strong critical self-scrutiny, because they want a life aimed at something worthwhile. Such knowledge is, in its highest development, the kind that Socrates thought incompatible with doing wrong.

In the next ten pages (88-98), Kierkegaard gives a series of examples of occasions on which an increase in understanding or knowledge of the appropriate kind will constitute strengthening in the inner man. The examples are divided into two kinds — prosperity (88-93) and adversity (93-98).

Understanding prosperity. The issue in the first set is to understand one's prosperity, to know why one is prospering or what the purpose of one's prosperity is. Kierkegaard begins by pointing out how popular it is to "complain about the world," time, and other people — finding it puzzling and distressing that all existence appears to be set up to disappoint one's hopes and efforts to prosper. "Seldom is heard a more earnest voice that enjoins everyone to be open to life's schooling [*Underviisning*] and to allow oneself to be brought up in the school of adversity."

Instead, people complain "that all life is nothing but adversity, and that this makes all existence a dark saying that no one can understand [*forstaae*]" (88). Repeatedly, Kierkegaard quotes an imagined interlocutor: "Prosperity [thought of just by itself] is easy to understand" (88, 89, 90, 92, 93). People have a notion of what makes sense, and this notion flows from their own given preferences and personal interests (their concerns): prosperity in its usual forms of wealth (89), "power and sagacity and strength of mind and dauntlessness of heart and perseverance of will" (90), and success (91-93). This they consider "normal" and "rational," and what does not meet such a standard they consider senseless and rationally opaque.

Kierkegaard's prescription is that we listen to a different and deeper concern, one that better fits the way the world is and better fits our own nature as beings with something "eternal" in us. So the fault is to think too small about prosperity, to take it as the purpose of life rather than as an occasion for understanding the purpose of life, as the ideal whole of life rather than an aspect thereof. The fault is that of not seeing (grasping, understanding) prosperity in *context*, in *perspective*. Such seeing, grasping, is one of the ur-forms of understanding. On the ordinary view, prosperity is easy to understand because it is one of the foundations of rationality.

The person who has really understood prosperity is the one who has properly answered questions like "where it all comes from" (89) and *"for what purpose* one has it" (91; Kierkegaard's emphasis). This demand to see one's prosperity in context rather than in isolation from one's larger existence, thus *to understand it*, is a kind of intellectualist demand. It is a demand to *get beyond* a child's "understanding" of life. It is a refusal to rest content with an abstract or "immediate" understanding and to insist on having a reliably *coherent view* of oneself. Some of Kierkegaard's writings seem to celebrate paradox and advocate "the absurd," but here, despite the fact that this discourse "accompanied" the publication of *Fear and Trembling*, we see him in a temper that is, in his own way, rather strongly "rationalistic."[14]

However, this is a rationalism in which emotions play a central role. The honest, courageous, and humble person (that is, the well-functioning person, in contrast to the "light-minded," p. 89) will become aware that he needs to make larger sense of his prosperity, and cannot accept it "at face value." This concern (*Bekymring*) for coherence, in the absence of an adequate explanation (*Forklaring*), will generate anxiety (*Angst, Hjerteangst*, 91).

> [H]is concern and the anxiety in his heart increase—until this concern engenders strengthening in the inner man. Then he knows [*veed*] not only that he has power, but he also knows what that favored one did not know [*ikke vidste*]—to whom the honor is due and to whom it legitimately belongs. Then he rejoices every time his efforts are crowned with success, then he longs to reach the goal

---

[14]These two strands in Kierkegaard's thought combine in the thought that one appreciates the absurd, the paradox, the case that resists understanding, only if one has a fairly rigorous demand for rational coherence, a strong intellectual passion for understanding. A person with a flaccid standard of coherence, the exemplar of drifting thoughtlessness, might come upon a paradox and not notice, or not care enough to get excited.

of his striving, but he rejoices even more in God, longs even more for the moment when he, with his God, will rejoice that they succeeded. Then his soul embraces the whole world, and his plans are far-reaching, but when in the stillness of the night he hears, "Make an accounting of your stewardship," he knows [*veed*] what this summons means, he knows where he has the balance sheet, and even if there are deficiencies in it, he cheerfully leaves the world of thoughts and achievements in which he nevertheless did not have his soul, leaves the elaborately complicated and far-reaching work that from day to day had been the occasion for strengthening in the inner man.   (91-92)

The anxiety is a motivating perception that his mind is not as it should be, while thankfulness (to God) is the state of proper and truthful awareness of God in relation to oneself. This second emotion is apparently also based in part in the (satisfied) concern for comprehensive self-understanding, just as the anxiety betokened in part the same concern, unsatisfied. Anxiety is an awareness of self-impropriety, of disrelation or troubled or inadequate relation with the eternal, while thankfulness is the satisfying awareness of being in right relation with the eternal. And essential to this right relation is understanding. A person whose life's default tone is thankfulness is ready to be called away from his prosperity because he knows its true worth.

On p. 92 Kierkegaard pictures a person who fails to understand his prosperity despite having understood adversity (pretty well). "Adversity he had understood, but prosperity he could not understand" (92). What he understood about adversity was that one can persevere in endeavors without the encouragement of success. This is a deep and courageous insight. He did not, however, understand that adversity is an occasion for persevering *in the hope and present assurance of divine help*. So when finally the light of prosperity began to dawn on his endeavors, he explained the change as due to his perseverance, by the principle that perseverance always pays off in the end: perseverance is a sufficient condition for prosperity. Thus, though he seemed to understand adversity, he did not understand prosperity. He did not understand that, for even the hardest worker and the one who most courageously struggles with adversity, prosperity is a divine gift. By contrast, "the person in whose soul the inner being announces itself" in the concern for an explanation that would comprehend *both* his prosperity *and* his adversity, "won a complete strengthening in the inner man when the day of joy triumphed over darkness" (92) by the strengthening of his conviction about and understanding of God's providential love. When prosperity dawned, he did not suddenly ascribe it to his perseverance and hard work, but continued to love the testimony of God's spirit that enabled him to assimilate both the disasters and the successes of his life with grateful, joyful understanding. "And when in time the Lord called the servant away, he knew [*kjendte*] the way and left everything, and he took along only the testimonies, in which he had had his blessedness" (93).

Understanding adversity. The last major division in the discourse is marked by the italicized sentence at the bottom of p. 93:

> *Then adversity will serve such a person for strengthening in the inner being.*

The previous division was about prosperity as a prompt for virtuous self-understanding, and Kierkegaard claimed that it can so function only if the subject allows the concern that seeks the testimony on which the virtues of faith and love are built to allow him to hear that testimony—the testimony of the Spirit. The present major section (pp. 94-98) is about adversity as the prompt for virtuous self-understanding, for strengthening in the inner man, which is deepening of understanding and strengthening of conviction of God's providential care. But in this case too the concern cannot be just any self-concern, but must be the virtuous one:

> Hardship does indeed make everyone concerned, but does it always make one concerned about God? Has not life more frequently affirmed the truth of those earnest words that are spoken by the same one who warned against prosperity and that therefore have the ring of profound meaning: "that hardships, too, are temptations." (94)

Adversity is discussed in three aspects: in general (93-95), as being wronged by fellow human beings (95-97), and as spiritual trial (97-98). I will comment on the first and third of these.

In the general discussion of adversity Kierkegaard pictures a person who starts out life with a confident hope of success ("a hope that is heaven's fatherly gift to the child," 94), but hardships came into his life and took away his hopefulness.

> Then everything became confused [*forvirrede sig*] for him. No longer was there a sovereign in heaven; the wide world was a playground for the wild pandemonium of life; there was no ear that brought the confusion [*Forvirringen*] together in harmony [*Overensstemmelse*], no guiding hand that intervened.   (94)

In other words, the adversity disabled his feeling that the world made sense. Kierkegaard writes of "the anarchy into which everything seemed to have disintegrated" and says, "He saw what others saw, but his eyes continually read an invisible handwriting in everything, that it was emptiness and illusion" (94). He contrasts the above person with someone who is more insistent about making sense of the world *with* its mixture of prosperity and adversity. This person continues, even in times of prosperity, to be concerned to get the testimony (*Vidnesbyrd*) that will make sense of the mixed character of life. Alluding to Romans 5:3-4, he says that in adversity a person can use his concern for prosperity to deepen his concern to make sense of life, until eventually he discovers the testimony (of God's love). "[H]e gradually threw overboard the worldly weight of earthly desires and rested with the testimony in God, blessed by the hope that he had won" (95).

We see the importance, for Kierkegaard, of testimony and its role in bringing about understanding in the development of spiritually mature hope. But we can also see that such hope just *is* a mature and deep understanding of one's own life in a world of mixed prosperity and adversity. A person who had only a "theoretical" understanding, one responsive only to a concern that we might call intellectual curiosity, would not have the understanding that Kierkegaard is talking about; such understanding, being responsive to a concern for one's own happiness, is an emotionally qualified and integrated understanding.

Spiritual trial (*Anfaegtelse*) is not an "external" adversity such as poverty, public ignominy, disease, disability, imprisonment, betrayal by friends, failure in one's projects, or banishment. It is "spiritual," suffering in one's relationship to God. Kierkegaard describes a person to whom it seemed as if it were God himself who laid his powerful hand on him, as if he were a child of wrath, and yet he could not come any closer to understanding or explaining [*forstaae eller forklare*] how this could be.   (97)

The intellectual opacity, the incomprehensible, inexplicable character of this suffering, makes it especially frustrating. A person may jump from here to a desperate conclusion:

> Then his innermost being [*hans Inderste*] rebelled within him, then he did what is related in an old devotional book: "he boasted that he was lost," and that it was God himself who had plunged him down into damnation. Then the inner man within him froze.
>
> (97-98)

But this is not the only possible response to such suffering. Though clueless as to why he is suffering so, a person can persevere in his concern to find a satisfying explanation — where "satisfying" means that the explanation mediates peaceable relations with God. (After all, the explanation that God is one's enemy is an explanation of *some* sort.)

> Even if he did not find the explanation [*Forklaring* throughout], he nevertheless did find the explanation: that he should wait for the explanation. He nevertheless did find the explanation, that God was testing him. . . . He did not flee the pain of spiritual trial; it became for him a confidant, a friend in disguise, even though he did not comprehend [*fatte*] how, even though he strained his thought in vain to explain [*forklare*] his riddle. But his calmness and humility increased in proportion to his concern, so that, however much he suffered, he always chose to remain with his spiritual trial rather than to be any other place in the world. Then at last the testimony dawned in the full assurance of faith, because he who believes God contrary to the understanding [*mod Forstanden*] is strengthened in the inner man. . . . he learned [*laerte*] the most beautiful thing of all . . . — that God loved him, because the one God tests he loves.   (98)

Mother Teresa of Calcutta provides an apt historical illustration of Kierkegaard's insight.

> In around 1961, Mother Teresa wrote to one of her several spiritual directors,

Now Father—since [19]49 or 50 this terrible sense of loss—this untold darkness—this loneliness this continual longing for God—which gives me that pain deep down in my heart—Darkness is such that I really do not see—neither with my mind nor with my reason—the place of God in my soul is blank—There is no God in me—when the pain of longing is so great—I just long & long for God—and then it is that I feel—He does not want me—He is not there— . . . God does not want me—Sometimes—I just hear my own heart cry out—"My God" and nothing else comes—The torture and pain I can't explain.[15]

Brian Kolodiejchuk tells how Mother Teresa sought an explanation by which to understand her spiritual trial (which lasted for about fifty years, to the end of her life). Since, prior to 1949 she had been blessed with vivid, sweet experiences of Jesus' fellowship and favor, she was at first bewildered by this painful sense of abandonment and loneliness. She sought an explanation, and at first thought she had found it in her sinfulness and weakness. Perhaps the experience was meant to purify and perfect her, she thought.

With the help of her spiritual directors, she progressively came to grasp that her painful inner experience was an essential part of living out her mission. It was a sharing in the Passion of Christ on the Cross—with a particular emphasis on the *thirst* of Jesus as the mystery of His longing for the love and salvation of every human person. Eventually she recognized her mysterious suffering as an imprint of Christ's passion on her soul. She was living the mystery of Calvary—the Calvary of Jesus and the Calvary of the poor.[16]

Though this experience of abandonment never left her, her understanding of it by way of this explanation enabled her to have a relationship with God that was extremely fruitful in ministry.

She was truly a witness to hope, an apostle of love and joy, because she had built the edifice of her life on pure faith. She glowed with a kind of "luminosity" as Malcolm Muggeridge described it, which flowed from her relationship with God.[17]

---

[15]*Mother Teresa: Come Be My Light*, ed. with commentary by Brian Kolodiejchuk, M. C. (New York: Doubleday, 2007) quoted on 1-2.

[16]*Mother Teresa: Come Be My Light*, 3-4.

[17]*Mother Teresa: Come Be My Light*, 4.

Because of her love for God, the experience of abandonment was not only interpersonally painful, but also puzzling. Her struggle was in part a struggle to *understand*. She needed, and eventually found, an explanation that enabled her life in God to continue and deepen. The explanation of Mother Teresa's spiritual trial is also naturally conceived as a case of testimony. The story of Jesus' ministry of which it partakes is testimony, both of the apostles and of the Holy Spirit who inspired them. The particular use of that testimony as the key to the explanation that Mother Teresa needed was mediated to her by way of her spiritual directors, who were spiritually formed men who could also speak for the Spirit, on the basis of Church tradition. It is clear, moreover, that Mother Teresa's depth of understanding and knowledge of God were due in significant part to her virtues of faith, love and hope.

A very long paragraph (spanning three pages in the Hongs' translation, 98-101) follows Kierkegaard's comments on spiritual trial, and the discourse ends with a brief paragraph (separated by a space) on the blessedness of the person who, surveying his life, can say, "God in heaven was my first love" (101).

16

Yes, Kierkegaard Still Matters

Edmon L. Rowell. Jr.

Marry, and you will regret it. Do not marry, and you will also regret it. Marry or do not marry, and *you will regret it either way....* Laugh at the stupidities of the world, and you will regret it; weep over them, and you will also regret it. Laugh at the stupidities of the world or weep over them, *you will regret it either way....* Hang yourself, and you will regret it. Do not hang yourself, and you will also regret it. Hang yourself or do not hang yourself, *you will regret it either way....* This, ... is the quintessence of all the wisdom of life [or, the sum of all practical wisdom].[1]

[A]lthough external matter may act as a cause for our experience of pain and pleasure, *the principal cause that determines whether we experience happiness or suffering lies within.* This is the reason why, when Buddha identified the origin of suffering, he pointed within and not outside, because he knew that *the principal causes of our suffering are our own negative emotions and the actions they drive us to do.*[2]

Our own Marc Jolley, the well-put-upon and long-suffering compiler/coeditor of this present Festschrift, does not like autobiographical introductions or additions to works that are supposed to be about someone other than "the present author."

---

[1]Søren Kierkegaard,"An Ecstatic Discourse," in *Either/Or* Part I, KW III, ed. Edna H. Hong and Howard V. Hong (Princeton NJ: Princeton University Press, 1987) 38-39; emphasis added. As he was wont to do, Kierkegaard followed Socrates—and of course against Hegel, as he also was wont to be. (It intrigues me that Kierkegaard was as much against his near-contemporary Hans Christian Andersen, the storyteller, as he was against the German philosopher Hegel.) Alastair Hannay's 1992 Penguin Classic abridgement of *Either/Or* offers the better translation, as illustrated by his rendering of the last phrase, here in brackets. (But, then, the Hongs tended to be as pedantic as Kierkegaard himself.)

[2]The (Fourteenth) Dali Lama, *Dzogchen. Heart Essence of the Great Perfection* (Ithaca NY: Snow Lion Publications, 2000) 103-104; emphases added.

Our just-as-long-suffering senior editor agrees.

However, a publisher's foreword—which many years ago I forced upon our then-editor in chief, Dom Don Haymes—the best editor and one of the smartest, and (really) pious persons I know—began: "Editors, as a rule, should neither be seen nor heard. If we do our work well, no one should be able to see us doing it; if we do not perform well, everyone will know." Don went on to say: "This book is an exception to the rule."[3] Indeed.

This essay also is an exception to the rule.

I cannot speak—I cannot *think*—of our International Kierkegaard Commentary (IKC) and its compiler/editor Robert L. Perkins without including something about myself. Because I have been intimately involved with this more-than-a-quarter-century project *almost as much* as Perkins himself. (Bob would want to write a scathing disputatious dissertation regarding that "almost as much.")

So, if my autobiographical introduction offends you—Johannes Climacus, or more probably Silentio, might say—So be it.

I came to Søren Aabye Kierkegaard rather late in life. It was after my eighteen months in Korea and while I was an older student at Howard College (the mother college of Samford University), in the late 1950s, when I stumbled on SK. No, "stumbled" is not correct: Arthur L. Walker, Jr.—my favorite teacher, mentor, and best friend at Howard (May his memory be a blessing!)—*insisted* I read "The Gospel of Suffering" (elsewhere, and probably more correct, "Sufferings," plural). I tried. And I've been trying ever since to read The Gospel according to Kierkegaard.

I still remember being almost stunned by the simple and utterly obvious truth—a keynote in chapter 2:

> [W]hen human wisdom cannot see a hand's breadth [sic] before it in the dark night of suffering, then faith can see God, *for faith sees best in the dark*.[4]

---

[3]Don Haymes, foreword to Clayton Sullivan, *Called to Preach, Condemned to Survive. The Education of Clayton Sullivan* (Macon GA: Mercer University Press, 1985; paperback repr. 2003) vii.

[4]Kierkegaard, "How the Burden Can Be Light though the Suffering Is Heavy," in *The Gospel of Suffering and the Lilies of the Field*, trans. David F. Swenson and Lillian Marvin Swenson (Minneapolis: Augsburg, 1948) 32. Typically, Hong and Hong up

It was not until several years later—I wrote in the gutter "1 March 1962"—that I acquired my first very own Kierkegaard volume—from Dick Stevens's Book Shop across the street from Southeastern Baptist Theological Seminary. (Back when, as some wiseacres are wont to say, we had a real seminary at Southeastern.) That first volume—of course—was Lillian Marvin Swenson and David F. Swenson's English version of *The Gospel of Suffering and The Lilies of the Field*. It cost $1.95. I like to think I had to skip lunch to pay for it. I've been skipping lunches ever since and my library is running over with books by and about Søren Aabye Kierkegaard. (Marc Jolley's collection of Kierkegaard is much broader than mine—I could hope he caught the SK bug from me—or maybe from Bob Perkins.)

As for me, I'm *still* trying to "read" Kierkegaard.

One of my problems with reading Kierkegaard, I think, may be because at the same time I discovered Kierkegaard I also discovered Lord—I want to add *Have mercy!*—Bertrand Arthur William Russell (18 May 1872–2 February 1970), a twentieth-century gadfly—at least for me. About the same time I got my first Kierkegaard I bought two of Russell's books—*Why I Am Not a Christian* (1927) and *Marriage and Morals* (1929). Trying to read Russell *and* Kierkegaard became an extracurricular challenge for me, a challenge that almost caused me to drop out of seminary and get a real and productive job—say, ditch digger or garbage engineer.

I thought then—and still do—that Kierkegaard and Russell were kindred spirits, and that both of them were out to accomplish the same thing: to make the rest of us as miserable as they were. I vowed then to one day write a dissertation (still to come of course) setting forth proofs that Russell and Kierkegaard were cut from at least some of the same cloth. Both of them did live a miserable existence. Both seemed determined to infect the rest of us with that selfsame misery. For countless "students" of the Dour Dane and the Righteous (his characterization, not mine) Russell, they succeeded.

---

the ante on vocabulary: "[W]hen in the dark night of suffering sagacity cannot see a handbreadth ahead of it, then faith can see God, *since faith sees best in the dark*" (UDVS 238). Emphasis added in both versions.

Every Cinco de Mayo Mexicans and Mexican-Americans grandly celebrate Mexico's 1862 victory over invading French forces. But every Fifth Day of May we at Mercer University Press pause to pay homage to Kierkegaard on his birthday.

Routinely, our director—whose SUV sports a bumper sticker boldly proclaiming "Kierkegaard Is My Co-Pilot [*sic*]"—reminds the rest of us that it is Søren's birthday, and waxes eloquent with SK quotes, at least until he tears up and can't stand to think any more about the Grand Dane. (Of course, Jolley's bumper sticker is reminiscent of Flying Tiger General Robert L. Scott, Jr.'s *God Is My Co-Pilot* [*sic*] [1943], an unfortunate phrase that insults both God and Scott. Why not *I'm Trying to Be God's Copilot*? Or maybe *I'm Trying to Be SK's Copilot*?)

Countless Kierkegaardians could wear Jolley's bumper sticker. Kierkegaard's influence—"The Father of Existentialism" (?)—has been phenomenal, especially since he was rediscovered in English translation (in Texas of all places) during the early twentieth century. Kierkegaard has been and still is required reading in many college philosophy courses, especially as required by professors who grew up as themselves required-reading Kierkegaard students in the late 1950s and early 1960s. Editor Bob Perkins and his minions could wear that bumper sticker on their foreheads.

Sometime in 1981 or 1982—I don't recall the exact scenario—we began discussions with Robert L. Perkins (then chair of Philosophy at the University of South Alabama—which department he founded!) about a commentary series on the works of Søren Kierkegaard. At the time, Hong and Hong and Princeton University Press were in progress on their projected twenty-six-volume, newly translated, edited, introduced, and annotated, definitive series of Kierkegaard's Writings (KW). The idea of an International Kierkegaard Commentary (IKC) series based on this new definitive edition of Kierkegaard's writings was fascinating if also mind-boggling for this toddler (b. 1 July 1979), small, underfunded, struggling university press.

I don't know why Robert L. Perkins came to us. Perhaps it was for the very reason that we were a new, small, underfunded, struggling university press. But also—I think—it was because we had in-house several persons who at least knew a little more about Kierkegaard than just how to pronounce his name. (And, I should add, who were as fascinated with the prospect of a new and definitive edition of Kierkegaard as was Perkins.)

At any rate we drew up a tentative agreement—tentative in that if the first few volumes worked we would go right on; if not, we would back off. Over the years I have had occasion to recall especially one of the provisions of that agreement—that Mercer University Press (namely, the present senior editor) would have final say regarding whether or not to include a certain essay. Several times I have almost exercised that provision to pull what I at least thought to be an especially anemic, turgid, or obtuse essay. I have never done so, primarily out of respect for the judgment of Bob Perkins.

Any multiauthor work is bound to be uneven, in research, scholarship, and presentation. That's true of the IKC. But the last IKC volume is due out this fall, and in my humble opinion the series as a whole is excellent and will serve well a new generation of Kierkegaard students and scholars. It has been "lang a-growing" but well worth the trip.

Twenty-eight years, Bob, and we not only have survived but have thrived!

Princeton's first in their Kierkegaard's Writings series was volume 14, *Two Ages* (1978). So the first in our IKC series was volme 14, *Two Ages* (1984). (N.B.: Neither Princeton's KW nor our IKC was published by volume number seriatim, for us, perhaps, primarily for having to depend on our many authors' writing schedules.) The first volume in IKC was 14; the last volume (November 2010) is volume 22, *The Point of View*.

(Then, of course, I suppose I will start back at the beginning working on a revised and newly edited version to be reprinted and also digitized on the web. . . . *That* is the first and last joke in this essay!)

The perceptive reader will notice some changes in page makeup and style from the beginning volume to the last, several changes in fact, and at various times. (We have, for example, of necessity changed the text font at least two times.) The times do change; so do the ways we (are sometimes forced to) do things.

At the beginning, Bob would send us a package of essays by the several authors of the volume in progress. (I could say that the quality of, not just the content, but the writing itself was very uneven—some neatly typed, some appearing to be typed by

Shakespeare's monkey . . . but I won't say that. And, apparently, some authors still do not comprehand the meaning of "plain text . . . just plain text.")

At the beginning, with a lot of help from, for example, Don Haymes, I would mark up the manuscripts and hand them to our best clerk-typist who would key them in on a slave computer terminal to be recorded on our Burroughs B-1860 (later a B-1900).

Then I would give the keyed and dot-matrix-printed version another look-see and send the approved files to our Data General page-designer computer, thence to our Merganthaler photodigital typesetter from which we would punch out the pages on long strips of photographic paper. We would cut these photo strips into page units — adding the footnotes from separate photo-paper strips — and make photocopies to send to Bob and his authors for a final proof-reading. Bob would return these copies to us, ofttimes full of red marks, and either I or one of our keyboard persons would make the changes or corrections as marked. Then back to the DG page designer and output at the photodigital typesetter.

Finally, our page designer would cut up the page units, hot-wax them (the wax was adhesive but gently so and moveable on the "boards," similar to thin poster paper), and lay them out on single-page, folio, or signature boards to be sent to the press where the pages (now a real "book") would be printed, cut, trimmed and folded, and smyth sewn. Then on to the binder where the trimmed, folded, and sewn pages would be gathered between cloth-covered and stamped boards, pasted in, rounded and backed, and, finally, jacketed, packed in boxes, stacked and strapped on flats, and shipped to our warehouse.

(For a brief time, we did the printing and binding ourselves on used equipment we purchased at a "yard sale." But we simply did not have the volume of work to keep the expensive presses and bindery going. Besides, it is so much more efficient, and economical, to let the experts do it.)

Between times of course — that is, between the time when we did everything by hand, including especially keying manuscripts and making pages on photographic paper — until now when much of the work of making pages is accomplished with the aid of increasingly complex computer programs — there have been mind-numbing changes in the way we make books, including the IKC. At the very beginning — before IKC was dreamed — we did not make pages; we made *lines* of type on an old Addressograph-Multilith (A/M) using "font wheels" we had to change every time we changed fonts, and recorded the results on eight-inch floppy disks to be printed out, cut, waxed, and pasted on boards — all by hand.

(To the practiced eye, the lines in our earliest books are not perfectly straight and the "leading" between lines routinely varies. . . . Don't look. Just take my word for it.)

(Lest the reader be confused, the computer most certainly does *not* do the work for us in these modern times. In fact, I sometimes wish for the good old days when we made up the pages by hand. Besides having better control over the appearance of the text, we had a much more intimate relationship with the content. In the beginning, I read *every* word of *every* article that Bob Perkins sent to me. Nowadays I have to spend so much time managing computers and texts that I have time left to only scan the text. I still read as much as possible, especially the quotations and notations, but there just isn't opportunity to give as much attention as I would like to the text because I have to give attention to the computer at the same time. Let me have any computer salesman at my terminal for five minutes and I will disabuse him/her of the patently false claim that now — with our glorious computer software and hardware — *anyone* can make a book. No. Not a book good enough to be part of the IKC!)

We moved quickly from the slow, clanging A/M to our "top-of-the-line" Burroughs (for text input), Data General (for font output and page design), and Merganthaler photodigital typesetter, ending of course with one or more of our keen-eyed page-makeup artists with a hot-wax machine and a supply of X-acto knives.

But of course Bill Gates (and his former hallmate Steve Ballmer) at Microsoft and Steve Jobs at Apple would not — still — leave well enough alone. Computer software was "upgraded," it still seems, almost every week. And of course rapidation in software required just-as-rapid changes in hardware to manage the software. We went from a computer system that filled a climate-controlled 12x16 room with its massive processor, a dot-matrix printer bigger than a large kitchen stove (and as loud as a pile driver), and a recording unit (the size of *two* large kitchen ranges) with its sealed stack of five twelve-inch recording platters which I had to change over and fire up every evening to record the days work. (It took most of the night for this very fast machine to do that archiving. I always took the previously recorded platter unit home with me, just in case disaster struck in the computer room.)

That 12x16 room full of our Burroughs B-1860, then B-1900, however, was only the tip of the iceberg. Scattered around the house were about twelve slave terminals serviced by the Burroughs. Our Data General page-maker hardware, to which the Burroughs transmitted raw data, was the size of a refrigerator and its sophisticated printer (it printed dot-matrix facsimile pages on that now-obsolete green-striped computer paper for preliminary proofreading) was as large as a clothes dryer. But that was not the end of the system. The DG page maker transmitted page-ready text to the Merganthaler photodigital typesetter in its darkroom where text was photographed and processed in our photo processor. (Which, by the way, was the first time we could see what the text would actually look like on the page.) The Merganthaler typesetter with its photo-processing unit was housed in an 8x12 darkroom.

In time, Bob Perkins sent articles for the IKC, first on 5.25-inch diskettes, then on 3.25-inch diskettes. (Sometimes both kinds of diskettes would be in the same batch.) Then of course we graduated to CDs and/or DVDs. We still get text on CDs and DVDs, but more and more on "zip drives" or (Lord, help us!) via e-mail attachments. I no longer take home a large five-platter recording of the day's work. But I do take home an archive recording of the jobs in process on my own computer. I carry that archive in my pocket (!), a zip drive about the size of my fingernail clippers and much lighter in weight. I have recorded on that zip drive almost every job I am working on and many jobs of the past year and even some jobs I will later be working on. And there is still room on the zip drive for more—pictures of our grandchildren and our yarden (roses, tomatoes, so forth), for example. That little zip drive, hardly noticeable in my pocket, will hold more data than our ancient Burroughs B-1900 would hold in a 12x16 room! (At present, there are at least four IKC volumes recorded on my pocket zip drive, in addition to a host of other "jobs.") Kierkegaard—even Hegel himself—would be astounded!

Finis. I have spent so much time telling about IKC production mechanics because, frankly, I probably am the only one left here who could do so, and because I think we need an archive account of those mechanics. But the mechanics of production by Mercer University Press is only a part, even the smaller part, of the IKC production story. The greater part belongs to Compiler/Editor Robert L. Perkins.

That Bob managed — over a quarter century! — to decide a great host of subjects for commentary, then find and recruit authors to address those subjects with understanding and present them with clarity, is an accomplishment of first magnitude. Not to mention also finding and recruiting referees. Yes, every article was read and criticized not alone by Bob himself but by others who added their own understanding of Kierkegaard.

Yet there was much more. Editor Perkins copyedited each article himself and, with his and the referee's remarks, criticisms, suggestions, would return the article to the author for any necessary changes, corrections, rewrites. Only then would Bob collect the various articles of the volume in progress and send the whole to me to make a book of it. Just that he survived working with a host of disciples of the Dour Dane is a herculean achievement in itself. That he did so always with patience and grace, yet firmly in control of his "child," was yeoman's labor of the first order. This generation and those following owe to Robert L. Perkins a debt far beyond adequate recompense.

Now, lest we wax too eloquent, let me conclude by admitting that Editor Robert and Senior Editor Edd did not always agree. We had our moments. Bob was always very gracious and grateful when, for example, I would discover that an author had misquoted a source, whether SK or some other. But he was sometimes somewhat less grateful when I would, for example, insist on *Webster's* as against *Oxford's* spellings. Or I could mention the times (more than once) when a package would arrive containing a motley collection of manuscripts and an as-motley collection of diskettes and/or CDs on which the text of those manuscripts was recorded. Sometimes, before I could get the package open, I would check my e-mailbox and there would be a message from Bob wanting to know where were the galleys. (Of course he had been suffering for months waiting on his authors to get their offerings written and in his hands, and I became the happy, but not too happy, reason for subsequent delays in production — not that I didn't have a dozen or more other projects staring across my desk.) Those, however, are really insignificant examples.

Yes, over the years we sometimes did "have words." I am happy to say those words were few and far between, always edible, and never one whit damaged the relationship between us — speaking of course for myself.

It needs to be said: "The conception of two people living together for twenty-five years without having a cross word suggests a lack of spirit only to be admired in sheep" (Alan Patrick Herbert, 1890–1971).

We made the Silver; I suspect we would go for the Gold if this race were still on. But the race is run, the battle's done, and, Bob, not only have we survived, we have overcome!

One more word. I have learned a lot over the past quarter century working with Bob Perkins and his comrades. Regarding which I am reminded of one of my favorite — Marc Jolley can quote it — vignettes from college days.

Fifty-one years ago, W. T. (Dub) Edwards was fresh out of seminary and teaching at Howard College. I signed up for his course "Re 221: New Testament: Epistles." For my term paper I decided to do an exegesis/exposition of 1 Timothy 1:15. I entitled it "According to the Chief: On Paul and Sin." When Professor Edwards returned my paper he had given me an "A" but had added a note: "Learned a lot about Rowell, and a little about Paul." (We became fast and now lifelong friends after that, but Dub never has told me whether I earned the "A" or he took pity and gave it to me.)

I feel much the same way about some, perhaps even much, of the IKC; I suspect Bob Perkins does also. We learned a *lot* about a whole corps of Kierkegaard "scholars" and a *little* about the Dour Dane himself. But that little is more than enough. Besides, to learn about the student is to learn also about the teacher. Learning from and about this grand host of Kierkegaard students who have shared with us something about Kierkegaard has taught me not only something about Kierkegaard (and myself); it has made stronger my appreciation of Kierkegaard himself.

Robert Perkins is semiretired now, still senior research professor of Philosophy at Stetson University. But while giving full time to his professorial work over the years he has given some of the best parts of his "spare" time and energy and talents to the IKC for, lo, these twenty-eight years. I don't know what he will do with himself after November when volume 22 hits the shelf. Over these many years I have learned that Robert L. Perkins is one of the most knowledge-able Kierkegaard scholars it has been my privilege to know and work with. Not only does he know the broad field of SK's work, he also knows those—from Copenhagen to California, from Texas to Tasmania, and sundry points in between—who are as knowledge-able as he regarding SK, and has managed to recruit this host of Kierkegaard scholars to contribute to IKC. That in itself is an achievement of remarkable proportion.

One of the primary marks of a genuine scholar is humility. Almost from the beginnings of IKC, Bob has ended his editor's introduction with these words:

> Thus far the authors can lead us. We invite the readers of this volume of the International Kierkegaard Commentary to learn what they can here and then become the authors' best teachers.

Also, from almost the beginning, he has ended *every* acknowledg-ment page with

> Finally, I wish to thank my wife, Sylvia Walsh, for assistance at every stage of this project and for making our life together an unutterable joy.

That Robert says such about his readers and about his best compan-ion and helper (more than just "helper," I think) says a lot about the man, a lot of very good things.

I doubt I'll ever understand Søren Kierkegaard. That's OK. That doesn't diminish my appreciation of SK at all.

I don't think I will ever understand Robert L. Perkins. That's OK too. Because my appreciation of him is, indeed, "unutterable."

17

Two Friends: Robert and Søren

Merold Westphal

It was, I suppose, by means of what Kierkegaard would call Governance and I would call Providence that I came to Kierkegaard. It was very early in my teaching career. I had been scheduled to teach the Kant seminar to undergraduates, and I was excited about the possibility of spending a whole semester on the *Critique of Pure Reason*. It would be my third, having already spent a semester on that text first with Wilfrid Sellars and then with John Smith. The former restricted itself to the Analytic, while the latter focused primarily on the Dialectic. I have sometimes jokingly claimed to be the only graduate student who, while not writing a dissertation on Kant, read the entire book.

But the department chair called me in and explained that while anyone in the department could give the Kant seminar only I could give the needed Kierkegaard seminar. This surprised me, since I was hardly equipped for such a task. My undergraduate classes had included no Kierkegaard, and my graduate classes only a very brief excursion into the first volume of *Either/Or* as a running start toward the textual *Sache selbst*, *Being and Time*. I was, quite frankly, disappointed. But the seminar proved to be an exhilarating experience and gave rise to one of the first papers I published, and I have been reading, teaching, and writing about Kierkegaard ever since (about four decades). In spite of Kierkegaard's warnings about giving thanks (CUP 1:177-79; CD 167-68), I am grateful to God. It would not be the last time that disappointment proved to be providential.

So it was that very early on I purchased the two-volume Harper paperback version of Walter Lowrie's biography (or maybe, hagiography) of Kierkegaard. The frontispiece of the first volume is a portrait by Chr. Kierkegaard entitled "Kierkegaard as a Youth." A friend and neighbor of ours was gifted as an artist, and my wife would sneak this volume over to her every morning after I left for school and make sure it was back on the shelf by the time I returned.

So I received as a genuine surprise Christmas present a very skillful charcoal version of this portrait in an oval frame. For forty years it has been hanging on my wall.

Staring at me. For the dominant feature of the portrait is the piercing eyes, the kind that look right through you, asking that, yes, existentialist question: "What about you? I gather that you are that single individual for whom I have written and that you have, indeed, been reading me. So what have you been doing about it?" I have known better than to say, "I have been teaching courses, giving lectures, and writing essays, even books about your work." In fact I have known better than to give him any answer, for we both have understood that the matter is not between him and me but between me and myself and between me and God.

It may sound as if I have experienced Kierkegaard primarily as a judge, but that would be misleading. I have experienced him, through the portrait to be sure but primarily through his writings, as a Socratic teacher. By calling him a Socratic teacher I mean primarily two things. First, that the point of every conversation is to call me into question. Every lesson ends with that same question, "What about you?" Second, that he teaches "without authority," that his role is a maieutic one, that he can only remind me of what in some sense I already know.

Of course, this is not a purely Platonic recollection, for part of what I already know in some sense comes not from unaided human reason but from divine revelation, from what Karl Barth has called the threefold word of God: Jesus Christ as the living Word, the Bible as the written Word that bears witness to the living Word, and preaching as the spoken Word that bears witness to the living Word on the basis of the written Word. Of course, teaching, whether in person or through writings can be understood as a first cousin of preaching, especially if it is written with the intent to be upbuilding. In other words Kierkegaard has been able to teach me only what I have other grounds for believing. I am enough of a Lutheran to share with Kierkegaard the view that revelation means not only that God gives me essential truth I could not otherwise discover but also gives me the condition for recognizing it as the truth. The Lutheran formula for this is Word and Spirit. Unlike Hegel, Kierkegaard does not think that this Spirit is the human spirit raised to the level of Absolute Knowing.

When trying to explain this notion of revelation to my students I ask them the name of the little girl on whom I had a crush in second grade. They can't. I write on the board Laura, Linda, and Lucy. I tell them the truth is staring them in the face and point out that they are unable to recognize it. I might have had a Platonic recollection of this truth. I remember that there was such a girl and that her name began with L, but I can't remember what it was. So I Google "girls names beginning with L" and look through the very long list. When I get to Linda, I have an Aha experience. I recollect what I could not remember. It was Linda. The list was the occasion.

But this won't work for my students. They can learn the right answer only when I tell it to them and when they accept it on my authority. Since this is not divine revelation the Holy Spirit is not needed. So the analogy is imperfect, but nevertheless very useful for illustrating an important Kierkegaardian idea, namely, that even when the truth is staring us in the face we may not be able to recognize it as such.

So Kierkegaard has been my teacher, and I have often been challenged not only by his account of the Socratic teacher but of the god as teacher and servant: "Teaching is his labor, and caring for the learner is his rest from labor."[1] This has always been in the back of my mind when I think about the pastoral role of the teacher, the privilege of working in this way as a teacher, and the very limited way in which I have followed this example.

So what have I learned from Kierkegaard? What has he helped me to recollect on the basis of my human experience and Christian faith? He has "taught" me

• That faith is not reducible to doctrinal belief. The example of Abraham has helped me to recollect that faith is primarily trust in the promises of God and obedience to the commands of God. We read that Abraham believed God, but this is belief-in and not merely belief-that. It is not merely an act of intellect. Of course, faith, faith in the God of the Bible, includes beliefs, and they are important. They tell me who God is and what promises and

---

[1]This is from the earlier Swenson/Hong translation (Princeton NJ: Princeton University Press, 1962) 71. The version in PF 57 is hopelessly wooden.

commands God has given. Such beliefs presuppose the belief that God is personal, sufficiently personal to perform speech acts such as making promises and issuing commands. In Lutheran language this means that faith is a personal relation to the God of Gospel and Law.

• That faith is essentially relational. It may seem redundant to say that a personal relation is a relation, but Kierkegaard reminds me that it is more complex than that. I myself by myself am already a relation, or rather a set of relations, since I am the dialectical tension between the temporal and eternal, the possible and the necessary, the finite and the infinite, and so forth. What is more, as this set of relations I am related to myself in both reflective and prereflective self-consciousness and in the freedom by which I decided what to do with the self I have been given. But I cannot be myself by myself. However narcissistic I may be psychologically and morally, I am essentially related to alterities that are physical, social, and, above all, divine. So faith is at one and the same time my relation to myself and my relation to God. God is the middle term between me and myself.

• That faith is also a relation to my neighbor, who turns out to be every other human being, including my enemy. Neither my relation to myself nor my relation to God is reducible to my relation of obligation and responsibility to and for my neighbor. But this latter relation is an essential dimension of my related-ness to self and to God. Since God commands me to love my neighbor as I love myself, God becomes the middle term between me and my neighbor, and the neighbor joins God as the middle term between me and myself. This is not as strange as it seems. The point is simply that I cannot rightly be related to myself if I am not rightly related to God and my neighbor. Put a bit differently, these relations are essential ingredients in my identity, in who I am. They are essential formally, indicating what it is to be a self, and they are essentially substantially, indicating what particular self I have (so far) become.

• That the right relation to my neighbor is an infinite debt of love grounded in the command of God and the love of God. The loves celebrated by poets, erotic love and friendship, are grounded in natural inclination. They are spontaneous and therefore need not be commanded, and they are preferential in the sense that erotic love and friendship always select one or more among the many others because they are in some way attractive to me. This is why they can be described as self-love even if we wouldn't necessarily describe the parties to such relations as selfish. Since spontaneity does not take us beyond preference in this sense, a neighbor love that will recognize every other as my neighbor will have to be commanded. The divine command to love my neighbor as I love myself is grounded in God's love in three ways: it is a participation or imitation of God's love for every neighbor, it makes sense because every other, like myself, has been created by an act of God's love, and it makes sense because every other, like myself, has been redeemed by Christ. God has already loved both me and my neighbor in our unloveliness.

• That faith, including love as an essential component, is a passion. Passions are feelings, but this can be misleading. We might think of feelings as fleeting episodes, like an itch or an ache. Philosophers sometimes call these "raw feels." In addition to being fleeting they are also noncognitive, nonintentional. They are not about anything, not construals of anything as something. But the feelings associated with faith as a passion are not fleeting but recurring, so we might say that faith as a passion is (among other things) a disposition to have feelings of a certain kind. Moreover, these feelings are cognitive in the sense of being evaluative construals.

The reason is makes sense to speak here both of passion and feelings and not just the latter is that our passions are what we care about deeply. I can be passionate about fly fishing or about the (hapless) Chicago Cubs. My passion for the Cubs makes me happy when they win, sad when they lose, and angry when they make a stupid trade. These affects are intentional, they are about something, and they are tied to certain beliefs. They are rational in the sense that they can be modified when the beliefs with which they are associated are undermined. I didn't learn all this from Kierkegaard, but it helps me understand what he does say. Faith is the passion that cares deeply about my relation to myself as mediated by my relation to God and neighbor; it gives rise to feelings or emotions that are at once affective and cognitive. That religious life has an emotional dimension is not, as such, a reason to disparage it, for a careless life, a lift without passion, would hardly be human.

• That faith goes beyond reason by resting on divine revelation. I have just suggested that faith is reasonable in its affective dimension by virtue of being, not arbitrary, but amenable to my beliefs. But my beliefs, at least the ones most important to my faith, are not reasonable if by reason is meant the powers of human thought unaided by the gift of divine revelation. As briefly described above, they go beyond what I can figure out for myself, even with the help of human genius. I need an apostle (or a prophet or a God in time) whose divine authority is backed up by the Holy Spirit who helps me to see that the message comes from God and what that message is.

• That faith goes against reason when the reason it goes beyond takes itself to be absolute. Unaided human cognitive powers can recognize their finitude and accept divine revelation, playing an ancillary role. Kierkegaard's name for this mode of reason, interestingly, is faith. But unaided human reason all too often takes itself to be ultimate, the highest norm of understanding and truth. Especially in the modern world, this means that God is neither a variable nor a constant in reason's equations. God is left out of the picture entirely, sometimes quietly, sometimes vociferously. Kierkegaard sometimes refers to human reason that purports to be autonomous as "worldly understanding" or "humanly understood" as opposed to "Christianly understood"; and in relation to reason in this sense he insists, following Paul in the opening chapters of 1 Corinthians, that faith is foolishness: paradoxical, absurd, madness. In Kierkegaard's day this "reason" was primarily speculative philosophy. In our day it is more likely to be the natural or even the social sciences.

• That faith goes against reason when reason has become ideology. Kierkegaard doubts that this self-congratulatory self-absolutizing of human understanding is ever a matter of purely disinterested theory. He sees it rather as the attempt, not necessarily fully conscious, of a given social order to legitimize itself by making its practices, theoretical and behavioral, the very definition of reason. Thus, to call faith paradoxical, absurd, and madness relative to the prevailing definition(s) of reason is to say that faith is inherently countercultural, a prophetic critique of the tendency of every society to absolutize itself. Karl Marx and Kierkegaard came on the literary scene together in 1843. While the latter is usually seen as the father of ideology critique, Kierkegaard shows that ideology critique need not be either materialistic nor atheistic. Its origin is to be found is the prophetic stands of the Bible, which means that Marx is a plagiarist who should have given at least some footnotes to Isaiah, Amos, Hosea, Jesus, Paul, and James.

• That the self-sufficient, self-absolutizing society that effectively puts God as creator, revealer, and redeemer out of play can be called paganism, and that paganism can be found flourishing in Christendom. In other words, neither religion in general nor the Christian church in particular renders a society or culture immune from the desire for autonomy, not the weak autonomy of genuine human agency but the strong autonomy of being normatively and cognitively self-sufficient. Secular societies are quite candid about this. Religious societies can be more subtle, making pious profession the disguise under which they render themselves, including their religious beliefs and practices, absolute and thereby immune to prophetic critique. Whereas secular societies say there is no God, paganism in Christendom occurs when a religious society says, in effect, we are God. Our ways are the divine ways, and our truths are the eternal truth.

So, then, what sort of a friend is this Kierkegaard? I have a simple formula for answering this question: he is the kind of friend who will tell you what your best friend won't tell you. Perhaps what our best friend won't tell us is what we most need to hear, and perhaps we all need the kind of friend Kierkegaard can be.

Throughout most of my long tutelage under the eye and through the texts of Kierkegaard I've been privileged to enjoy another friendship. It involves an indebtedness of a quite different sort, but it is nevertheless an indebtedness I am happy to acknowledge without in the least pretending or even wanting to repay. The three loves that Kierkegaard discusses, erotic love, friendship, and neighbor love all involve indebtedness, and I think that in each case we understand love better when we discover the joy of being indebted. No doubt that seems easier in the case of the celebrated loves, but that may be misleading. Finding the true indebtedness in erotic love and friendship and the true joy it contains may be harder than it seems. No doubt it seems harder in the case of neighbor love, and this is doubtless true. Finding joy in an infinite, commanded obligation is indeed the task of a lifetime, a school in which we are always in kindergarten.

But I digress. I was referring to another friend, Bob Perkins. He has been a fellow learner and from time to time a teacher in my friendship with Kierkegaard. Certain moments in any friendship stand out for one reason or another. One of the most memorable moments for me, probably because it was so unexpected and even bizarre, was when we ran into each other in Antwerp, having somehow wandered into the Marxist Hegel Society meeting. Listening to dreary papers from Moscow, Prague, and East Berlin in German even worse than my own, it was good to find myself not entirely alone.

Our friendship has not been restricted to involvement with the International Kierkegaard Commentary, but since these essays are a celebration of the completion of that gargantuan task, I am pleased to express my gratitude for the privilege of contributing from time to time and for the ways in which the essays of others have helped me. But I am not grateful simply on my own account. All of us who love Kierkegaard and struggle with him are deeply indebted to Bob for devoting so much of his life and indefatigable energy to this major contribution to Kierkegaard scholarship. As we know, Kierkegaard feared falling into the hands of assistant professors, and probably he would find things in IKC that would disturb him. But I am convinced both that there is much that he would find expressing a spirit akin to his own and that it is the spirit of Bob Perkins that is to "blame" for this happy fact. So for myself and for so many others, heartiest thanks for the work and for the selfless spirit in which it has been carried out.

Based on experience, I have developed the following mantra: to write a book is hard; to edit a book is impossible. The latter makes herding cats look like falling off a log. But the impossible happens, and in Bob's case it has happened again and again and again. What patience! What devotion! What self-sacrifice! What a debt of gratitude we all owe him! I suspect that some day our Lord will greet Bob with a "Well done, good and faithful servant." And if, from somewhere in the balcony we hear a loud "Amen", it just might turn out to have come from our mutual friend, Søren Kierkegaard.

Contributors

WANDA WARREN BERRY (emerita) is professor of Philosophy at Colgate University. She is a contributor to the International Kierkegaard Commentary.

ANDREW J. BURGESS is professor of Philosophy emeritus at the University of New Mexico and cochair of the "Kierkegaard, Religion, and Culture Group" of the American Academy of Religion. He is a former member of the advisory board of the International Kierkegaard Commentary series and volume consultant for the volume on *Practice in Christianity*.

DAVID CAIN is Distinguished Professor of Religion, University of Mary Washington, Fredericksburg, Virginia, and long-time contributor to International Kierkegaard Commentary. He is author-photographer of *An Evocation of Kierkegaard / En Fremkaldelse af Kierkegaard* and editor of *Sermons of Arthur C. McGill: Theological Fascinations*, volume 1. *Theological Fascinations*; volume 2 is forthcoming.

GEORGE CONNELL is professor of Philosophy and division chair for Arts and Humanities at Concordia College, Moorhead MN. He received his BA from Mercer Unviersity and his PhD from Vanderbilt University. At present, he is working in particular on the issue of Kierkegaard and religious pluralism.

JOHN DAVENPORT is associate professor of Philosophy at Fordham University and president of the Kierkegaard Society of North America (2010–2011). He has published widely on Kierkegaard and topics in moral psychology, including *Kierkegaard After MacIntyre* (coedited with Anthony Rudd), *Will as Commitment and Resolve* (Fordham, 2007), and articles on existential faith in a collection by Edward Mooney and another collection by David Wood and Aaron Simmons.

STEPHEN DUNNING recently retired after thirty years in Religious Studies at the University of Pennsylvania. He is the author of *The Tongues of Men: Hegel and Hamann on Religious Language and History* (Scholars Press, 1979); *Kierkegaard's Dialectic of Inwardness: A Structural Study of the Theory of Stages* (Princeton University Press, 1985); and *Dialectical Readings: Three Types of Interpretation*

(Pennsylvania State University Press, 1997). His current project is to research and write on the thought of Oswald Chambers, a British Baptist (1874–1917) who has been called "an evangelical mystic."

C. STEPHEN EVANS (Ph.D. Yale) is currently University Professor of Philosophy and Humanities at Baylor University. His prior positions include serving as Curator of the Hong Kierkegaard Library at St. Olaf College. His recent publications include *Kierkegaard: An Introduction* and *Natural Signs and Knowledge of God.*

M. JAMIE FERREIRA is the Carolyn M. Barbour Professor of Religious Studies at the University of Virginia. Among her books are *Kierkegaard: An Introduction* (2008); *Love's Grateful Striving: A Commentary on Kierkegaard's Works of Love* (Oxford University Press, May 2001); and *Transforming Vision: Imagination and Will in Kierkegaardian Faith* (Oxford University Press, 1991).

SHERIDAN HOUGH is professor of Philosophy at the College of Charleston in Charleston, South Carolina. She has contributed articles to three volumes of the International Kierkegaard Commentary; she is also the author of *Nietzsche's Noontide Friend: the Self as Metaphoric Double* (Penn State Press, 1997).

MARC A. JOLLEY is director of Mercer University Press. He is the author of *Safe at Home: A Memoir of God, Baseball, and Family* published by Mercer University Press. He is a senior lecturer at Mercer University.

JAMIE LORENTZEN teaches high school English in Red Wing Minnesota and chairs the Friends of the Howard V. and Edna H. Hong Kierkegaard Library at St. Olaf College, Northfield, Minnesota. He is the author of *Kierkegaard's Metaphors* (Mercer, 2001); *Sober Cannibals, Drunken Christians: Melville, Kierkegaard and Tragic Optimism in Polarized Worlds* (Mercer, 2010); and editor of *Toward the Final Crossroads: A Festschrift for Howard and Edna Hong* (Mercer, 2009).

JASON MAHN teaches Theology and Contemporary Religion at Augustana College, Rock Island IL. His first book, *Fortunate Fallibility: Kierkegaard and the Power of Sin* (Oxford University Press, 2011) investigates Kierkegaard's curiously positive descriptions of anxiety, temptation, and the possibility of offense from a theological perspective

RONALD MARSHALL is pastor of First Lutheran Church of West Seattle.

EDWARD F. MOONEY is professor of Religion and Philosophy at Syracuse University. He is author of many Kierkegard books, most recently *On Soren Kierkegaard: Dialogue, Polemics, Lost Intimacy, and Time*. He has been a frequent contributor to the International Kierkegaard Commentary. His most recent book is, *Lost Intimacy in American Thought: Recovering Personal Philosophy from Thoreau to Cavell*.

M. G. PIETY is an associate professor of Philosophy at Drexel University. She has published many articles on Kierkegaard and other philosophical subjects in both scholarly books and journals and online. Her translations of Kierkegaard's *Repetition* and *Philosophical Crumbs* were published by Oxford University Press (2009) and her book *Ways of Knowing: Kierkegaard's Pluralistic Epistemology* was published by Baylor University Press (2010). She is currently working on a book entitled *Fear and Dissembling: The Copenhagen Kierkegaard Controversy* for Gegensatz Press.

ROBERT C. ROBERTS is Distinguished Professor of Ethics at Baylor University. He works on the moral psychology of the virtues, ancient moral psychology and epistemology, and the writings of Søren Kierkegaard. He is the author of *Faith, Reason, and History: Rethinking Kierkegaard's Philosophical Fragments* (Mercer, 1986); *Emotions: An Essay in Aid of Moral Psychology* (2003, Cambridge); and, with W. Jay Wood, *Intellectual Virtues: An Essay in Regulative Epistemology* (Clarendon Press, 2007).

EDMON L. (EDD) ROWELL, JR., was senior editor of Mercer University Press from 1 August 1980 until 31 August 2010, and was the Press's editor for all twenty-four volumes of the International Kierkegaard Commentary.

MEROLD WESTPHAL is Distinguished Professor at Fordham University. In addition to essays on Kierkegaard in various reference works, he has written *Kierkegaard's Critique of Reason and Society, Becoming a Self: A Reading of Kierkegaard's Concluding Unscientific Postscript*, and *Levinas and Kierkegaard in Dialogue*. He is a past president of the Kierkegaard Society.